C000147284

The Essentia

AMHARIC

The National Language of Ethiopia

Andrew Tadross   **Abraham Teklu**

አንድሩ ታድሮስ   አብርሃም ተኽሉ

Edited by
Haimanot Shewandagne

2016

THE ESSENTIAL GUIDE TO AMHARIC:
The National Language of Ethiopia
Copyright © 2015

Andrew Tadross / Abraham Teklu

All Rights Reserved

For more information, contact peacecorpsworldwide@gmail.com.
Peace Corps Writers and the Peace Corps Writers colophon are
trademarks of PeaceCorpsWorldwide.org

ISBN-13: ISBN 978-1-935925-65-1

Library of Congress Control 2015950558
First Peace Corps Writers Edition, September 2015

A PEACE CORPS WRITERS BOOK

AKNOWLEDGEMENTS

Special thanks to Hiriti, Almaz/Hagos, Nigisti/Girmay, Genet/Markos, Atsede/Daniel, Elizabeth/Daniel, Nebiat/Justin, Eyeru/Angaw, Lucia/Omar and Andrew for his continuous motivation and encouragement.

My sincere appreciation also goes to Dr. Weini Teklu, Neway, Afrina, Sara and Aaron Mulugeta for their inborn wishes to my success and their desire to see me become successful.

Abraham Teklu

I would like to thank and appreciate for helping me learn Amharic and develop this book: Sewareg Binayew, Zetseat Bekele, Muluemabet Alula, Samuel Abebe, Tsegaye Gebre, Alex Gezahagn, and friends from Endodo (Ngasi, Tsehayo, Kiros, Erkihune, Yeshi, Asmeru, Ngusti, and many others).

To my wife, Haimanot Shewandagne, you are the best. እወድሻለሁ.

Andrew Tadross

Art work by:
Meron Bekele
Brittany Franck (RPCV-Ethiopia 2011-2014)
Eldon Katter (RPCV-1962-1964)
Solomon Kassahun (thank you Alan Smith RPCV for providing)
Andrew Tadross (RPCV-2012-2013)

By the same authors:

The Essential Guide to Tigrinya: The Language of Eritrea and Tigray Ethiopia. (A.Tadross / A.Teklu) 2015.

Afan Oromo: A Guide to Speaking the Language of Oromo People in Ethiopia (A. Bulto / A.Tadross) 2016.

CONTENTS

TOP 25 BASIC PHRASES NEEDED

ENGLISH	PHONETIC	AMHARIC
Excuse me. / Pardon me.	yqrta.	ይቅርታ
Good bye	dehna hun	ደህና ሁን
Hi. / Hello.	selam / tadiyas	ሰላም / ታዲያስ
How are you? (m/f)	ïndemn neh? / nesh?	እንደምን ነህ? / ነሽ ?
How much?	snt new?	ስንት ነው?
I am ___. / I am not _	_____ neñ. / aydelehum,	____ነኝ። / አይደለሁም.
I am from _____.	ke ___ neñ	ከ __ ነኝ።
I don't know.	alawqm.	አላውቅም።
I don't understand.	algebañ'm.	አልገባኝም
I don't speak Amharic.	amarña alnagerm.	አማርኛ አልናገርም።
I don't want.	alfelgm.	አልፈልግም።
I have ____. / I don't have	____ / aleñ / ___yeleñm	___ አለኝ። / __የለኝም
I like ____		
I want ____ / I need	___ ïfelgalehu.	___እፈልጋለሁ።
Do you have ___? (m/f)	___ ale? / ___ alesh?	___አለ? / ____አለሽ?
My name is _____.	____ ïbalalehu .	____ እባላለሁ።
No problem.	chg'r yelem.	ችግር የለም።
Please (m/f)	ïbakh / ïbak'sh	እባክህ / እባክሽ
Ok	ïshi	እሺ
Thank you.	amesegnalehu	አመሰግናለሁ
There is none.	m'nm yelem.	ምንም የለም።
What is your name (m/f)?	s'mh (smsh) manew?	ስምህ (ስምሽ) ማነው?
When?	mechie?	መቼ?
Where is the toilet?	shnt biet **yet new**?	ሽንት ቤት የት ነው ?
Yes / No	awo / aydel'm	አዎ / አይደለም

ETHIOPIAN CULTURAL ITEMS

1   ሰፌድ / sefied - woven device for sepating wheat from chaf. Also decorative.

2   ሚዶ / mido Traditional Ethiopian hair comb

3   ማጭድ / machʹd - a sickle, used for harvesting wheat, barley, teff etc.

4   ማሲንቆ / masinqo - traditional stringed instrument played somewhat like a violin

5   ከዘራ / kezera - walking stick typically used be rural men, for fashion and defense against hyenas. Also called, ዱላ / dula

6   ሹሩባ / shuruba - braided Ethiopian hair style

7   መሶብ / mesob - used to store injera for 3-4 days at a time

8   ጉርሻ / gurʹsha - feeding by hand, a show of affection

9   ድስት / dʹst - used to cook and contain ʹwetʹ like chiro, that is eaten with injera

10 ብርሌ / brlie - the glass container used to drink tej (honey wine). Held with 2 fingers only.

11 ስኒ / sʹni - coffee / tea cups

12 በርጩማ / berchuma - traditional Ethiopian wooden sitting stool. Also called, ዱካ / duka

13 መቀጫ ና ዘነዘና / muqecha na zenezena - mortar and pestal (often a piece of re-bar) used for hand grinding coffee

14 ፈንዲሻ / fendisha - popcorn, a common Ethiopian snack

15 ጀበና / jebena - typical Ethiopian clay coffee pot

16 ከሰል ማንደጃ / kesel mandeja - traditional coal cooker for coffee or food

17 ቀጠማ / qetiema - fresh cut grass, placed in home or around coffee ceremony for celebrations

18 ጎጆ / gojo - Traditional Ethiopian hut with grass/thatched roof

8

Regional Map
Horn of Africa

Amharic is the national language of Ethiopia. It is the first language for the Amhara people as well as for people from many parts of the Ethiopia. It is a second language for many people who live in regions such as Tigray, Oromia, Gambella, etc. Amharic is used in the Federal Government and is taught in public schools across the country.

INTRODUCTION TO AMHARIC

Amharic is the primary language of the Amara people and official language of the Federal Government of Ethiopia. Amharic and its sister language Tigrinya, share the ancient Ge'ez script that dates back thousands of years and is considered part of the Semitic body of languages, which also includes Arabic and Hebrew. Amharic has adopted many words from English (hotel, internet, motor etc.). It also uses many English cognates, has borrowed some Italian words, and shares many words in common with Tigrinya and Arabic.

9

When it comes to reading and writing the language, the spelling of words tends to be more loosely defined than in English partly due to regional differences in pronunciation. Any attempts by foreigners to communicate in Amharic are very much appreciated and one is likely to make friends quickly. Even if your attempt to speak Amharic is full of errors and mispronunciations, your new friends are likely to exclaim, *"You are speaking Amharic perfectly!"*

While perfection is elusive, the goal of this book is to provide the student of Amharic the necessary basics to be able to live and function amongst native speakers. While the language might have thousands of words and innumerable grammatical variations, by absorbing this content and practicing regularly, one can expect to soon be communicating and sharing culture with the people of Ethiopia. A native speaker (Abraham) and a foreigner who learned the language (Andrew) wrote this book, so the goal is that it is both accurate and user friendly.

HOW TO USE THIS BOOK

Learning a language can be compared to a four-legged stool. One must *speak, listen, read,* and *write.* The phonetic parts of this book are useful for a beginner to read the language and memorize words and phrases quickly. However, because the phonetic is useless if used independently, it is very important that one quickly adapt to reading Amharic script and sounding out words alongside their phonetic translations.

This book provides an overview of Amharic grammar. While it is not an exhaustive resource on grammar, it provides more than enough information to get you quickly communicating with people in Amharic using basic grammar 'rules.' The word 'rules' is in quotation marks, because there are many irregularities, as in each language. The authors have tried to capture these rules but be aware there are many exceptions.

Following the grammar section is essential vocabulary, arranged by topics such as greetings, food, jobs, etc. There is also a section of non-categorized words at the end of the vocabulary section, as well as an extensive list of antonyms for vocabulary development. Learning these is an excellent way to improve your ability to describe people, places, and conditions. Finally, there is a list of more than 400 common verbs.

One of the simplest ways to use this book is to place a checkmark or dot by each word or phrase that you memorize. If you make it a goal to remember the words you use regularly, you will quickly amass a strong vocabulary. Also, try to use the grammar rules to express yourself using appropriate conjugations, pluralization, and sentence structure. Writing down key phrases and words reinforces memorization. If you are trying to use the book like a dictionary and search for a specific word, first try looking by category from the table of contents. If you do not find it there, look in the list of non-categorized words that start on page 151, or the list of antonyms. If you can still not find the word, there are some online Amharic dictionaries and apps that will be helpful.

Be aware that as in any language, there are regional differences and multiple ways to say the same thing. Amharic is not an easy language to learn, but you can be speaking basic phrases in a matter of weeks, holding conversations after a few months, and talking almost fluently after a year. Do not be shy; practice Amharic whenever you can with native speakers.

HOW TO USE THE PRONUNCIATION GUIDE

The Amharic alphabet is called **Fidel.** In this guide, each Fidel sound is translated into English letter(s) **using a coding system** under phonetic chart, based on how that character would sound phonetically. In Fidel, as well as the phonetic system, each syllable is pronounced. Typically, there are not *silent* letters as in English. Some of the sounds do not perfectly translate using this code, but this is the closest approximation and easiest to adapt. To know exactly how a word is pronounced, it is best to read it using this phonetic translation and then ask a native speaker to pronounce it clearly.

There is no official phonetic pronunciation code for Amharic. Every Amharic language reference uses different phonetic pronunciation guidelines. However, this book has been coded to make the pronunciation guide very easy for beginners to understand. It can be completely different from what you are used to in your daily use of the English language. For example, pronouncing the English *bay* would be written as **bey** in Amharic phonetic use. That is the combination of sounds **be** (1st order) and **y** (6th order).

The Amharic alphabet typically has **seven main orders** or family of symbols, called *Fidel* each with unique characteristics of shape and sound. For example, the 'l' letter in English has the following seven representative *Fidel* characters. Written in the following table is their English phonetic equivalent. Historically, Amharic language is derived from Ge'ez and other Ethiopian languages. Each symbol not only represents a unique shape, but also might represent unique historical definition.

Representing a general pattern, the seven representative sounds (the main orders) and symbols for the English letter 'l' are as follows:

Order	1st	2nd	3rd	4th	5th	6th	7th
Phonetic - *Fidel*	le - ለ	lu - ሉ	li - ሊ	la - ላ	lie - ሌ	l - ል	lo - ሎ

This is described as a *general* pattern because there are a couple odd exceptions. For example, the first order **h** letter (ሀ) is pronounced **ha**, similar to the first order, rather than **he**. Also, the first order vowel is **a** (አ) is like the 4th order **a**, rather than the **e** sound in most first order letters. It can be confusing, but one must accept that languages are weird and irregular at times. As a learner, the student can ignore why there are similar phonetic sounds for two different Ge'ez symbols.

Following are examples of words in English that demonstrate the pronunciation of the seven main orders of *Fidel*. In parenthesis, the phonetic spelling is shown – how that word would sound per the phonetic code developed for this book. For example, *feet* in English, would be spelled **fit** because the letter **i** is coded to be pronounced like the 'i' in spaghetti. The table below also attempts to explain how one should sound out these letters using examples from English.

1st *	2nd	3rd	4th	5th bake (biek)	6th	7th
men(men)	toot (tut)	heat (hit)	fat (fat)		lime (m)	pope (pop)
net (net)	lube (lub)	feet (fit)	dad (dad)	make (miek)	blind (bl)	boat (bot)

*Remember there are a few exceptions for first order pronunciation such as the first order ᐁ which is **ha** rather **he**. In addition, the first order አ sounds like **a** rather than **e**.

Note that the sixth order can be any consonant but without a vowel phonation associated; such as the *m* sound in lime, or the *b* sound in *blind*. There are 6th order vowels, which sound like the *i* in *lick* or *illness*.

As you might notice, some of these vowel sounds are similar, like the 1st and 5th order. There are variations in spelling, but using this guide will help you communicate easily. Some of the letters have additional sounds after the normal seven orders, but these are rarely used.

It is important that in using the phonetic guide you remember the phonetic equivalents and **do not pronounce them as you would in English**. For example, based on this guide **hi** would sound like *hee*. Remember that the phonetic spelling is only to help with pronunciation until you can learn to read *Fidel*.

PHONETIC CHART OF FIDEL

1st	2nd	3rd	4th	5th	6th	7th
ሀ	ሁ	ሂ	ሃ	ሄ	ህ	ሆ
ha	hu	hi	ha	hie	h	ho
ለ	ሉ	ሊ	ላ	ሌ	ል	ሎ
le	lu	li	la	lie	l	lo
ሐ	ሑ	ሒ	ሓ	ሔ	ሕ	ሖ
he	hu	hi	ha	hie	h	ho
መ	ሙ	ሚ	ማ	ሜ	ም	ሞ

me	mu	mi	ma	mie	m	mo
ሠ	ሡ	ሢ	ሣ	ሤ	ሥ	ሦ
se	su	si	sa	sie	s	so
ረ	ሩ	ሪ	ራ	ሬ	ር	ሮ
re	ru	ri	ra	rie	r	ro
ሰ	ሱ	ሲ	ሳ	ሴ	ስ	ሶ
se	su	si	sa	sie	s	so
ሸ	ሹ	ሺ	ሻ	ሼ	ሽ	ሾ
she	shu	shi	sha	shie	sh	sho
ቀ	ቁ	ቂ	ቃ	ቄ	ቅ	ቆ
qe	qu	qi	qa	qie	q	qo	explosive
በ	ቡ	ቢ	ባ	ቤ	ብ	ቦ
be	bu	bi	ba	bie	b	bo
ቨ	ቩ	ቪ	ቫ	ቬ	ቭ	ቮ
ve	vu	vi	va	vie	v	vo
ተ	ቱ	ቲ	ታ	ቴ	ት	ቶ
te	tu	ti	ta	tie	t	to
ቸ	ቹ	ቺ	ቻ	ቼ	ች	ቾ
che	chu	chi	cha	chie	ch	cho
ኀ	ኁ	ኂ	ኃ	ኄ	ኅ	ኆ
ha	hu	hi	ha	hie	h	ho
ነ	ኑ	ኒ	ና	ኔ	ን	ኖ
ne	nu	ni	na	nie	n	no
ኘ	ኙ	ኚ	ኛ	ኜ	ኝ	ኞ
ñe	ñu	ñi	ña	ñie	ñ	ño
አ	ኡ	ኢ	ኣ	ኤ	እ	ኦ
a	u	i	a	ie	ï	o
ከ	ኩ	ኪ	ካ	ኬ	ክ	ኮ
ke	ku	ki	ka	kie	k	ko
ኸ	ኹ	ኺ	ኻ	ኼ	ኽ	ኾ
khe	khu	khi	kha	khie	kh	kho
ወ	ዉ	ዊ	ዋ	ዌ	ው	ዎ
we	wu	wi	wa	wie	w	wo
ዐ	ዑ	ዒ	ዓ	ዔ	ዕ	ዖ
a	u	i	a	ie	ï	o

13

ዘ	ዙ	ዚ	ዛ	ዜ	ዝ	ዞ
ze	zu	zi	za	zie	z	zo
ዠ	ዡ	ዢ	ዣ	ዤ	ዥ	ዦ
zhe	zhu	zhi	zha	zhie	zh	zho
የ	ዩ	ዪ	ያ	ዬ	ይ	ዮ
ye	yu	yi	ya	yie	y	yo
ደ	ዱ	ዲ	ዳ	ዴ	ድ	ዶ
de	du	di	da	die	d	do
ጀ	ጁ	ጂ	ጃ	ጄ	ጅ	ጆ
je	ju	ji	ja	jie	j	jo
ገ	ጉ	ጊ	ጋ	ጌ	ግ	ጎ
ge	gu	gi	ga	gie	g	go
ጠ	ጡ	ጢ	ጣ	ጤ	ጥ	ጦ
te	*tu*	*ti*	*ta*	*tie*	*t*	*to*
ጨ	ጩ	ጪ	ጫ	ጬ	ጭ	ጮ
che	*chu*	*chi*	*cha*	*chie*	*ch*	*cho*
ጰ	ጱ	ጲ	ጳ	ጴ	ጵ	ጶ
pe	*pu*	*pi*	*pa*	*pie*	*p*	*po*
ጸ	ጹ	ጺ	ጻ	ጼ	ጽ	ጾ
tse	*tsu*	*tsi*	*tsa*	*tsie*	*ts*	*tso*
ፀ	ፁ	ፂ	ፃ	ፄ	ፅ	ፆ
tse	*tsu*	*tsi*	*tsa*	*tsie*	*ts*	*tso*
ፈ	ፉ	ፊ	ፋ	ፌ	ፍ	ፎ
fe	fu	fi	fa	fie	f	fo
ፐ	ፑ	ፒ	ፓ	ፔ	ፕ	ፖ
pe	pu	pi	pa	pie	p	po

The table rows marked **explosive**: *te/to* row, *pe/po* row, and *tse/tso* row (the ፀ series).

Explanation of the 6ᵗʰ Order

The 6th order (pronunciation without vowel) is such as the consonant at the end of a word. For example, *camel* in Amharic is ግመል or **gmel**. The (ግ) (**g**) and the (ል) (**l**) are 6th order and are written phonetically as **g** and **l**. The sound is similar to the g-sound you make when you say green. The 6th order is sometimes confusing for people because it can represent a consonant with no vowel.

In this book you will notice that the apostrophe (') is sometimes used to express reading a consonant without vowel. Particularly, if not used it might give a

14

different meaning. An example is the word for *polite*. Using *Fidel,* it is spelled as follows: ትሁት. It has a two syllabi pronunciation format like this: **t'hut** (sounds like: t'hoot). The apostrophe shows that there is a brief pause after the t-sound, so it will be pronounced as **t'hut** rather than…**thut**.

The apostrophe is not used in all 6th order consonants, just when it is needed to indicate a brief pause before the next letter. For example, the word for *diamond* is **almaz** (አልማዝ). It is pronounced as **'al'+maz**. The l is 6th order but only an l sound is pronounced without any vowel attached to it.

As you can see in the following table, the **ï** is used to represent the 6th order vowel sound **እ**. Example: the word for *God* is እግዚአብሄር. Phonetically, it is spelled as **ïgziabhier**. When broken down phonetically it looks like: **ïእ gግ ziዚ aአ bብ hieሄ rር**. The **ï** is similar to how one would pronounce the **i** in *silk*.

እ	ኡ	ኢ	አ	ኤ	እ	ኦ
a	u	i	a	ie	ï	o

The Explosive Consonants

Note on the pronunciation guide that some letters are labeled *explosive*, or they are sometimes called *glottalized*. Some consonants of the English language are spelled alike in Amharic, but have different sounds. For example, the Amharic sound and symbol for **che** is written as ቸ and the Amharic sound and symbol for *che* (italic) is written as ጨ. However, the ጨ has an *explosive* sound, meaning it is a quicker and sharper phonation. In order to understand the difference, it is best to practice with a native speaker. The explosive p-sound (ጳ), t-sound (ጠ), and ch-sound (ጨ) are itialized to differentiate them from their non-explosive equivalents.

There are also different *Fidel* sounds and symbols of the English letter *k*. In this guide, **ke** has the symbol ከ. The more explosive sound of **ke** is symbolized as **qe**, which is written as ቀ. The explosive ቀ sound is similar to **ke** but uses more force to produce the sound farther back in the roof of the mouth. These letters are similar, except the latter has a breathier, more guttural sound (which vibrates the back/top of the palette) and is associated with Semitic dialects. The *ts*-sound (ፀ) sounds like an s but has more pressure at the front of the mouth when spoken.

Vowel Pronunciation

The Amharic alphabet has two sets of vowels that follow the seven orders of pronunciation. The vowels እ ኡ ኢ አ ኤ እ ኦ are like the English vowels (see below) with a soft pronunciation and some symbolic changes. Note the 1st a sound and the 4th a sound below. Also, note the difference on the corresponding Amharic symbols. Therefore, both have similar phonations, but different symbolic representations.

አ	ኡ	ኢ	አ	ኤ	እ	ኦ
a	u	i	a	ie	ï	o
lab	tube	spaghetti	bath	fade	lick	mocha

The ñ

The phonetic sound **gn** is symbolized by (**ñ**), and expresses the sound that is similar to the Spanish word *niño* or the French word *champagne*. An example of this sound is the word for *judge* / ዳኛ, which is pronounced as **daña**.

Additional Fidel

As mentioned, some Fidel characters are outside the main seven orders. You are unlikely to use these often but they are listed here for your general knowledge. Occasionally, they are found in the language, but it is not as necessary to memorize them as the main orders.

ሏ	ሯ	ሷ	ሗ	ቋ	ዧ	ጧ	ቷ
lua	rua	chua	*chua*	qua	zhua	tua	tua
ሗ	ሷ	ቯ	ኗ	ቿ	ሟ	ጷ	ፗ
hua	sua	vua	nua	qhua	mua	pua	pua
ሿ	ቧ	ኟ	ጇ	ፗ	ዟ	ዷ	ጯ
shua	bua	ñua	jua	fua	zua	dua	chua
ቈ	ቍ	ቊ	ቋ	ቌ	ቐ	ቑ	ቌ
que	quu	qui	quie	qhue	qhuu	qhui	qhuie
ኰ	ኵ	ኲ	ኳ	ኴ	ዀ	ዅ	ዂ
kue	kuu	kui	kua	kuie	khue	khuu	khuui

by Eldon Katter

A Few Pronunciation Outliers

There are a few outliers to be aware of, where even the phonetic version is somewhat different from how the syllables are actually pronounced. Be aware of the following:

ነው (new) *He is / She is / It is.* The word ነው in this book is spelled **new**. Technically, that is correct because ነ sounds like **ne** and ው is like **w**. However, as most people speak it sounds like **no** rather than **new** (nu). Example: Selam new? = (selam no) – *How are you? Is everything peaceful?* Selam = Peace.

አለሁ (alehu) *I am here!.* This is a stand-alone word as well as a typical first person present-tense suffix. Phonetically, we spell this **alehu**, and it is generally spoken like that. However, when **alehu** (a-le-hu) is used as part of a longer word it kind of gets shortened to **alo**, almost like a conjunction. For example, *I go* is spelled phonetically as **ï'hiedalehu** – pronounced more like **ï'hiedalo'**.

መጣሁ (me*ta*hu) *I came* / ገዛሁ (gezahu) *I bought.* Phrases ending with **ahu** often sound more like **aw** they are pronounced as if smashed together. Instead **of me-*ta*-hu**, it sounds more like **me*ta*w** or **gezaw** when spoken at a normal speed.

ናችሁ (nachihu) *You are (plural).* At regular conversational speed, it will sound more like **nacho** or **nachew** than **na-chi-hu**.

አዎ (awo) *Yes.* Though its phonetic translations is **awo**, when spoken quickly, it sounds somewhile like **ow**…or like *ouch* without the *ch*.

There may be other situations where you encounter words that sound somewhat differently than spelled in the phonetic in this book. Do not forget, the phonetic is artificial – even more reason to practice speaking with a local and reading Fidel.

The goal of this book is to teach beginners enough vocabulary and grammar to communicate effectively in Amharic. Imperfect accents and grammatical errors are inevitable but by using the book along with classes and interacting with locals, you will learn quickly.

Take some time to study this guide, as it will improve your pronunciation, listening and comprehension.

AMHARIC GRAMMAR

Vocabulary is an extremely important building block of a language. However, grammar is what ties nouns and verbs together to make coherent and meaningful phrases. By combining the basic grammar rules and a broad vocabulary, you can begin to speak Amharic effectively.

Like every language, there are general grammatical rules that provide a way to speak most phrases coherently. However, there are also many irregularities and many variations by region in spelling and pronunciation. When learning Amharic, the spelling, pronunciation and vocabulary might slightly vary depending on the geographic location. However, generally Amharic is understandable and learnable. By memorizing the general rules, and adapting to the occasional irregularities, one can manage to learn the language. This section outlines the basic rules of Amharic grammar, including the following:

- Punctuation
- Pronouns
- Demonstrative Adjectives
- Key verbs (to be, to have, to be present, to become)
- Reflexive pronouns / Object Pronouns
- Possessive
- Questions
- Present tense / Present continuous
- Past tense / Past continuous
- Future tense
- Negatives
- Imperatives
- Pluralizing nouns and adjectives
- Gender specific nouns and adjectives
- Expressing 'when/while'
- Expressing preference…and more

PUNCTUATION

Amharic uses its own symbols for punctuation. It is not mandatory to use most of them since punctuation is less used in Amharic than English, but it is helpful to be familiar with the symbols and their names.

English			Amharic		
apostrophe	'	'	chiret	ጪረት	'
colon	;		hulet netb	ሁለት ነጥብ	:
comma	,		netela serez	ነጠላ ሰረዝ	፣
exclamation mark	!		qale agano	ቃል አጋኖ	!
paranthesis	( )		qn'f	ቅንፍ	( )
period	.		arat netb	አራት ነጥብ	።
question mark	?		tyaqie m'l'kt	ጥያቄ ምልክት	?
quotation mark	"		tmhr'te t'qs	ትምህርት - ጥቅስ	" "

ASKING QUESTIONS

Amharic has question words like *who, what, where*, etc. Here are some of the most important questions to memorize.

ow much is it?	snt new?	ስንት ነው?
How much? / How many?	snt?	ስንት?
How?	ïndiet?	እንዴት?
What time is it?	snt se'at new?	ስንት ሰዓት ነው?
What?	mn?	ምን?
What happened?	mn hone?	ምን ሆነ?
When?	mechie?	መቼ?
Where?	yet?	የት?
To where?	wediet?	ወዴት?
Which one?	yetñaw?	የትኛው?
Who?	man?	ማን?
Whose?	yeman?	የማን?
Why?	lemn?	ለምን?
Is it?	new ïndie?	ነው እንዴ?
Yes / No	awo / aydel'm	አዎ / አይደለም

Within the sentence structure, it is simple to make a *YES/NO* question. One can change a statement into a question. For example:

Do you like it? (f)	wededshw?	ወደድሽው?
Is there coffee?	buna ale?	ቡና አለ?

If you want to express a question using the verb *to be* / **mehon** (መሆን), one simply adds **ïndie** (እንዴ) to the end of the conjugated verb *to be*. So that *Is it hot?* becomes **muqet new ïndie?** Examples follow.

Are you sad? (m)	azenk ïndie?	አዘንክ እንዴ?
Are you sick? (m)	amemeh ïndie?	አመመህ እንዴ?
Are you sleeping? (f)	teñteshal ïndie?	ተኝተሻል እንዴ?
Is it good?	t'ru new ïndie?	ጥሩ ነው እንዴ?
Is she fat?	wefram nat ïndie?	ወፍራም ናት እንዴ?
Is he fat?	wefram new ïndie?	ወፍራም ነው እንዴ?
Is he American? (m)	amerikawi new ïndie?	አሜሪካዊ ነው እንዴ?
Is she Ethiopian? (f)	ityopiyawit nat ïndie?	ኢትዮጵያዊት ናት እንዴ?
Is he in Addis Ababa?	addis abeba new indie yalew?	አዲስ አበባ ነው እንዴ ያለው?

When the verb is a *to be* question in the past tense, one uses the past tense of the verb **menor**.

Were you a bad girl? (f)	merfo siet nebersh ïndie?	መጥፎ ሴት ነበርሽ እንዴ?
Was it good?	t'ru neber ïndie?	ጥሩ ነበር እንዴ?
Were we in Addis?	addis neber ïndie?	አዲስ ነበር እንዴ?

As in other languages, you can also make a question by raising the tone of your voice at the end of a statement; for example, *You like it? You are coming.* Using this type of tone, it is not necessary to say **ïndie?**

PRONOUNS

Subject pronouns are words that take the place of a subject in a sentence. For example, *he* replaces *Samuel* in the *sentence Samuel (He) is the best football player in town.* The following table shows Amharic subject pronouns. Like English, these are used to describe the subject of the sentence (i.e. *He went to the park*). When speaking Amharic, it is not always necessary to say the pronoun since the conjugated verb has prefixes and suffixes that indicate the subject verb agreement.

When translating *it*, one uses the pronoun and verb agreement that is equivalent to him/her. The gender of specific objects is customarily determined by what fits the situation. There is no known rule why an object is considered feminine or masculine. Make a guess!

In Amharic, there are several ways to say *you* because there are male and female forms of the pronoun depending on whom you address. As well, there are *respect* forms that you reserve for speaking politely to elderly or persons of stature. When speaking Amharic, a beginner might not use the correct form between the informal/polite, the female/male forms, but attempts to use the correct pronoun form are always appreciated.

Note the following abbreviations:
(m) = male, singular   (f) = female, singular
(m/f) = both male and female
(m. pl) = male, plural (f. pl) = female, plural

Pronoun	Phonetic	Amharic
I	ïnie	እኔ
you (m)	ante	አንተ
you (f)	anchi	አንቺ
you (m/f. pl /respect)	ïnante	እናንተ
he / it (m)	ïsu	እሱ
he (respect)	ïr'sachew	እርሳቸው
she (f)	ïr'suawa	እርሷ
she (respect)	ïr'sachew	እርሳቸው
we / us	ïña	እኛ
they (f. pl)	ïnesu	እነሱ
they (m. pl)	ïnesu	እነሱ
it	yachi / ya (f/m)	ያቺ/ያ

For the sake of simplicity, not all forms are shown for each grammar example. Various examples are provided throughout this book.

Demonstrative adjectives

Demonstrative adjectives replace nouns. They place emphasis on specific things or people. They can also indicate whether they are replacing singular or plural words and give the location of the object.

Example: *this* book, *that* cow, *those* people, *these* days; etc.

Demonstrative Adjectives	Phonetic	Amharic
this (m)	y'h	ይህ
this (f)	yhchi	ይሀቺ
that (m)	ya	ያ
that (f)	yachi	ያቺ
those (m/f.pl)	ïneziya	እነዚያ
these (f. pl)	ïnezih	እነዚሁ
none	m'nm	ምንም
neither	and'm	አንደም
either	andun	አንዱን

Example	Phonetic	Amharic
This is my house.	**y'h** yenie biet new	ይህ የኔ ቤት ነው።
Those are nice.	**ïneziya** tru nachew	እነዚያ ጥሩ ናቸው።
That is the problem.	ch'gru **ya** new.	ችግሩ ያ ነው።
These are big.	**ïnezih** t'lq nachew	እነዚሁ ትልቅ ናቸው።
Either one.	kehulet **andun**	ከሁለት አንዱን።
None are available.	**m'nm** altegeñem	ምንም አልተገኘም።

by Eldon Katter

REFLEXIVE PRONOUNS

Reflexive pronouns are used to refer the action back to itself. For example, *I did it myself. She ate it by herself. Let us congratulate ourselves,* etc. Following are Amharic reflexive pronouns. The suffixes in **bold** are not for phonetic emphasis, it simply shows the suffix that is added to indicate the pronoun.

Reflexive Pronoun	Phonetic	Amharic
myself	ïra**sie**	እራሴ
yourself (m)	ïras**'h**	እራስህ
yourself (f)	ïras**'sh**	እራስሽ
himself	ïra**su**	እራሱ
herself	ïra**sua**	እራሷ
ourselves	ïrasa**ch'n**	እራሳችን
yourselves (m/f.pl)	ïrasa**ch'hu**	እራሳችሁ
themselves	ïrasa**chew**	እራሳቸው

Examples	Phonetic	Amharic
I did the work **myself**.	srawn **ïrasie** serahu.	ስራውን እራሴ ሰራሁ።
Get it **yourself**.	**ïras'h** agñew.	እራስህ አግኘው።
He hurt **himself**.	**ïrasun** goda.	እራሱን ጎዳ።
We love **ourselves**.	**ïrasach'n'n** ïnwedalen.	እራሳችንን እንወዳለን።
They pay for **themselves**.	le'**ïrasachew** y'keflalu.	ለእራሳቸው ይከፍላሉ።

POSSESSIVE

Possessive grammart is used to express ownership of something. One way to show possession is using the possessive pronoun, shown in the following table. As you can see from the sample sentences, the possessive pronoun is spoken before the verb, so literally translated, you are saying *Yours it is. Mine it is*, etc. Any of these possessive pronouns can preceed a noun to indicate possession. For example, *my job* could be translated as **yenie s'ra** (የኔ ስራ).

Possessive Pronoun	Phonetic	Amharic
my / mine	yenie	የኔ
yours (m)	yante	ያንተ
yours (f)	yanchi	ያንቺ
yours (m/f. pl.)	yenante	የናንተ
yours (respect, m/f)	yeirswo	የእርስዎ
his (m)	yeirsu	የእርሱ
hers (f)	ye'ïrsua	የእርሷ
theirs (m/f. pl)	ye'ïnersu	የእነርሱ
ours	yeña	የኛ

Examples		
Is this **his / hers**?	**yersu** new? **yersua** new?	የእርሱ ነው? የእርሷ ነው?
Is this yours? (m)	**yante** new?	ያንተ ነው?
It is **mine**.	**yenie** new.	የኔ ነው።
This is yours (m).	yh **yante** new.	ይህ ያንተ ነው።
This is yours (f).	yh **yanchi** new.	ይህ ያንቺ ነው።

Note: The Amharic **new** (ነው) is pronounced more like *no*, rather than new/nu.

Another way to express possession is to add a suffix to the end of a noun that refers to the owner. As you can see in the following table the noun *s'ra* (meaning *work* or *job*) is amended with the typical suffix unique to that pronoun. In the following table, the bold text highlights the suffix that is added to the noun to indicate possession.

my job	s'ra**yie**	ስራዬ
your job (m)	s'ra**h**	ስራህ
your job (f)	s'ra**sh**	ስራሽ
your job (m/f. pl)	s'ra**ch'hu**	ስራችሁ
their job (m/f.pl)	s'ra**chew**	ስራቸው
our job	s'ra**ch'n**	ስራችን

I love **my** wife.	mis'tien afeqralehu.	ሚስቴን አፈቅራለሁ::
My shoes are white	*cha*mawoch*ie* ne*ch* nachew.	ጫማዎቼ ነጭ ናቸው::
Your dog is big.(m)	wshah t'lq new.	ውሻህ ትልቅ ነው::
His house is beautiful.	bietu qonjo new.	ቤቱ ቆንጆ ነው::
Her name is Haimanot.	s'mua haymanot new.	ስሟ ሀይማኖት ነው::
Their cat is white.	dmet**achew** ne*ch* new.	ድመታቸው ነጭ ነው::
Our baby is a girl.	ljach'n siet nat.	ልጃችን ሴት ናት::
Our country is big.	agerach'n t'lq nat.	አገራችን ትልቅ ናት::

An **n** is added to the noun when receiving the action of a verb. For instance, as in the example *I love my wife* (**mis'tien afeqralehu**)...or *I want his house* (**bietun ïfelgalehu.**) You will still be understood, without this, but its grammatically correct.

One can also use the word **ye** (የ), meaning *of.* For example:

That is Aster's dog. **ya ye astier wsha new.** (*ያ የአስቴር ውሻ ነው::*). In this example, the **ya** indicates *that* or *that one over there.*

by Meron Bekele

TO BE

The following set of tables introduce the most important verbs, which also happen to be irregular. Verbs provide the action attached to a noun. Conjugations of the verbs *to be* (**mehon** / መሆን) and *to have* (**menor** / መኖር) must be memorized immediately to become expressive in Amharic. Don't forget the pronouns that attach to these verb conjugations. (ïnie, ante, anchi, etc.)

to be - (mehon) (መሆን)

PRESENT				PAST			
I am	neñ	ነኝ		I was	neberku	ነበርኩ
You are (m)	neh	ነህ		You were (m)	neberk	ነበርክ
You are (f)	nesh	ነሽ		You were (f)	nebersh	ነበርሽ
You are (m/f. pl)	nach'hu	ናችሁ		You were (m/f. pl)	neberach'hu	ነበራችሁ
He is / It is	new	ነው		He was / It was	neber	ነበር
She is	nat	ናት		She was	neberech	ነበረች
They are (m/f pl)	nachew	ናቸው		They were (m/f pl)	neberu	ነበሩ
We are	nen	ነን		We were	neber'n	ነበርን

NEGATIVE PRESENT				NEGATIVE PAST			
I am not	aydelehum	አይደለሁም		I was not	alneberkum	አልነበርኩም
You are not (m)	aydelehm	አይደለህም		You were not (m)	alneberkm	አልነበርክም
You are not (f)	aydeleshm	አይደለሽም		You were not (f)	alnebershm	አልነበርሽም
You are not (m/f. pl)	aydelach'hum	አይደላችሁም		You were not(m/f. pl)	alneberach'hum	አልነበራችሁም
He is not	aydelem	አይደለም		He was not	alneberem	አልነበረም
She is not	aydelechm	አይደለችም		She was not	alneberechm	አልነበረችም
They are not	aydelum	አይደሉም		They were not	alneberum	አልነበሩም
We are not	aydelenm	አይደለንም		We were not	alneber'nm	አልነበርንም

In verb **mehon**, you see the most basic sounds that you'll hear over and over in Amharic. For example, **neh** = *you are* (m). **nesh** = *you are* (f). **new/nat/nachew/nen**, etc. Become familiar with these quickly because this is the most basic verb – when you internalize these you will know whom one is talking about quickly.

26

Examples (Present)	Phonetic	Amharic
I am Ethiopian.	ityo*pi*yawi neñ.	ኢትዮጵያዊ ነኝ፡፡
You are short (m/f)	a*ch*r neh (nesh).	አጭር ነህ (ነሽ)፡፡
He is **not** a doctor.	dokter aydelem.	ዶክተር አይደለም፡፡
She is beautiful.	qonjo nat.	ቆንጆ ናት፡፡
Are you all Americans?	hulach'hum amierikawiyan nach'hu?	ሁላችሁም አሜሪካዊያን ናችሁ?
We are Americans.	amierikawiyan nen.	አሜሪካዊያን ነን፡፡
They were **not** safe.	selamawi alneberum.	ሰላማዊ አልነበሩም፡፡
Examples (Past)		
I was a doctor.	hakim neberku.	ሃኪም ነበርኩ፡፡
You were sick.	tameh neber.	ታመሁ ነበር፡፡
Were you sick?	tameh neber?	ታመሁ ነበር?
She was wrong.	tk'kl alneberech'm	ትክከል አልነበረችም፡፡
He was happy.	desteña neber.	ደስተኛ ነበር፡፡
We were brave.	jegnoch neber'n.	ጀግኖች ነበርን፡፡
They were **not** red.	qeyoch alneberum.	ቀዮች አልነበሩም፡፡

Note: The subject pronoun of each sentence can be unspoken because the verb indicates the pronoun.

TO BECOME

In English, we use the word *become* to describe a change that has happened or is in the process of happening or is developing into something. In Amharic, phrases that describe *become* in past or present are derived from the infinitive **mehon** – *to be.*

Past	Phonetic	Amharic
I became	honku	ሆንኩ
You became (m)	honk	ሆንክ
You became (f)	hon'sh	ሆንሽ
He became	hone	ሆነ
She became	honech	ሆነች
We became	hon'n	ሆንን
They became	honu	ሆኑ
Present Continous		
I am becoming ...	...ïyehonku new	...እየሆንኩ ነው
You are becoming... (m)	...ïyehonk new	...እየሆንክ ነው
You are becoming ... (f)	...ïyehon'sh new	...እየሆንሽ ነው
He is becoming...	...ïyehone new	...እየሆነ ነው
She is becoming...	...ïyehonech new	...እየሆነች ነው
We are becoming...	...ïyehon'n new	...እየሆንን ነው
They are becoming...	...ïyehonu new	...እየሆኑ ነው
Examples		
I became a runner.	rua*ch* honku.	ሯጭ ሆንኩ።
You became a teacher (m).	astemari honk.	አስተማሪ ሆንክ።
They became rich.	hab'tm honu.	ሃብታም ሆኑ።
You are becoming smart (f).	gobez ïyehonsh new.	ጎበዝ እየሆንሽ ነው።
He is becoming lazy.	senef ïyehone new.	ስነፍ እየሆነ ነው።
She is becoming beautiful.	qonjo ïyehonech new.	ቆንጆ እየሆነች ነው።
What happened?	mn hone?	ምን ሆነ?
What happened to you? (m)	mn honk?	ምን ሆንክ?

Notice with the use sentences that in a typical sentence the noun is spoken first and the verb list. For example, *I became a runner* is directly translated as *A runner I became* (**rua*ch* honku**).

28

TO HAVE

The verb *to have* / **menor** (መኖር) is important to the Amharic language. The table on the next page shows examples of the verb **menor** (መኖር) to express possession.

to have - (menor) (መኖር)

PRESENT			PAST		
I have	aleñ	አለኝ	I had	nebereñ	ነበረኝ
You have (m)	aleh	አለህ	You had (m)	nebereh	ነበረህ
You have (f)	alesh	አለሽ	You had (f)	neberesh	ነበረሽ
You have (m/f. pl)	alach'hu	አላችሁ	You had (m/f. pl)	neberach'hu	ነበራችሁ
He has	alew	አለው	He had	neberew	ነበረው
She has	alat	አላት	She had	neberat	ነበራት
They have	alachew	አላቸው	They had	neberachew	ነበራቸው
We have	alen	አለን	We had	neberen	ነበረን
NEGATIVE PRESENT			**NEGATIVE PAST**		
I don't have	yeleñm	የለኝም	I didn't have	alnebereñm	አልነበረኝም
You don't have (m)	yelehm	የለህም	You didn't have (m)	alneberehm	አልነበረህም
You don't have (f)	yeleshm	የለሽም	You didn't have (f)	alnebereshm	አልነበረሽም
You don't have (m/f. pl)	yelach'hum	የላችሁም	You didn't have (m/f. pl)	alneberach'hum	አልነበራችሁም
He does not have	yelewm	የለውም	He didn't have	alneberewm	አልነበረውም
She does not have	yelatm	የላትም	She didn't have	alneberatm	አልነበራትም
They do not have	yelachewm	የላቸውም	They didn't have	alneberachewm	አልነበራቸውም
We do not have	yelenm	የለንም	We didn't have	alneberenm	አልነበረንም

Examples	Phonetic	Amharic
I have a cat.	dmet aleñ.	ድመት አለኝ፨
He does not have a cat.	dmet yelewm.	ድመት የለውም፨
We had clothes.	lbsoch neberen.	ልብሶች ነበረን፨
You didn't have a dog.(m)	wsha alneberehm.	ውሻ አልነበረህም፨
Ethiopia has riches.	ityopiya habtoch alat.	ኢትዮጵያ ሃብቶች አላት፨

TO BE PRESENT

The verb **menor** has several different ways it can be conjugated. This table represents the English verb *to be present*. It also indicates the presence of something tangible or intangible, such as *There is beer in the refrigerator* or *We don't have peace.*

to be present - (menor) (መኖር)

PRESENT			PAST		
I am present	alehu	አለሁ	I was present	neberku	ነበርኩ
You are present (m)	aleh	አለህ	You were present (m)	neberk	ነበርህ
You are present (f)	alesh	አለሽ	You were present (f)	nebersh	ነበርሽ
You are present (m. pl)	alach'hu	አላችሁ	You were present (m. pl)	neberach'hu	ነበራችሁ
You are present (f. pl)	alach'hu	አላችሁ	You were present (f. pl)	neberach'hu	ነበራችሁ
He is present	ale	አለ	He was present	neber	ነበር
She is present	alech	አለች	She was present	neberech	ነበረች
They are present	alu	አሉ	They were present	neberu	ነበሩ
We are present	alen	አለን	We were present	neber'n	ነበርን
NEGATIVE PRESENT			**NEGATIVE PAST**		
I am not present	yelehum	የለሁም	I was not present	alneberkum	አልነበርኩም
You are not present (m)	yelehm	የለህም	You were not present (m)	alneberkm	አልነበርህም
You are not present (f)	yeleshm	የለሽም	You weren't present (f)	alnebershm	አልነበርሽም
You are not present (m/f pl)	yelach'hum	የላችሁም	You weren't present (m/f. pl)	alneberach'hum	አልነበራችሁም
You are not present (f. pl)	yelach'hum	የላችሁም	You weren't present (f. pl)	alneberach'hum	አልነበራችሁም
He is not present	yelem	የለም	He was not present	alneberem	አልነበረም
She is not present	yelechm	የለችም	She was not present	alneberechm	አልነበረችም
They are not present	yelum	የሉም	They were not present	alneberum	አልነበሩም
We are not present	yelenm	የለንም	We were not present	alneber'nm	አልነበርንም

When someone asks *How are you?*, a common informal response is **alehu**, literally translating as *I am here* but meaning *I'm fine*. One might also say **alen**; meaning *We are still here / We are alive.* If someone asks *Where are you?* a response could be **posta biet alehuñ**, meaning *I am at the post office.*

30

Examples:	Phonetic	Amharic
There is food.	mgb ale.	ምግብ አለ።
Abraham is not here.	abraham ïzih yelem.	አብርሃም እዚህ የለም።
She is not at school.	ïswa tmhrt biet aydelechim.	እርሷ ትምህርት ቤት አይደለችም።
They had bananas.	muzwoch neberachew.	ሙዞች ነበራቸው።
There are dogs.	wushoch alu.	ውሾች አሉ።

by Eldon Katter

OBJECT PRONOUNS

An object pronoun is a personal pronoun that receives the action of the verb indirectly. Object pronouns include *Me/Him/Her/Us/Them* rather than subject pronouns such as *I/He/She/We/They*.

In the sentence, *She gave it to him*; <u>she</u> is the subject pronoun and <u>him</u> is the object pronoun. If you say *The story is about me*, the object pronoun is <u>me</u>, while the subject is *story*. In Amharic, objects are expressed as a suffix following a command, verb, or preposition. Following are object pronouns expressed as suffixes.

There are generally two types of suffixes for the object. One is more direct. These are used for *Give me, Tell him, Help her, Pay us,* and *Take them*.

The other form is somewhat indirect. In English, it would be the equivalent of asking or telling someone to do something *for* him/her. For example, *Bring for me, Call for him, Pray for her. Do it for us. Give for them* (meaning, give on their behalf).

The main difference between these forms is that the example with *for* me/him/her etc.) uses an 'l' sound. Notice in the examples the difference between *take me* and *take it for me*. Also notice whether phrase indicates <u>to</u> me/him/her, etc...or <u>for</u> me/him/her, etc.

Do it for me.	adrgl**ñ**.	አድርግልኝ
Do it for us.	adrgl**n**.	አድርግልን

31

| Write it for me. | *ts*'aflñ. | ፃፍልኝ |
| Write it for us. | *ts*'afln. | ፃፍልን |

Object	Suffix	Amharic	Example	Meaning
me	...ñ	...ኝ	s'*te*ñ	Give (to) me.
him	...w	... ው	s'*te*w	Give (to) him.
her	...*a*t	... ጣት	s'*ta*t	Give (to) her.
us	...n	... ን	s'*te*n	Give (to) us.
them	...*ta*chew	... ጣቸው	s'*ta*chew	Give (to) them.
me	... lñ	... ፕልኝ	s'*tl*ñ	Give **for** me.
him	...let	... ፕለት	s'*t*let	Give **for** him.
her	...lat	... ፕላት	s'*t*lat	Give **for** her.
us	...ln	... ፕልን	s'*t*ln	Give **for** us.
them	...lachew	...ፕላቸው	s'*t*lachew	Give **on their behalf.**

Examples (order to...)	Phonetic	Amharic
Call **me.** (m)	dewl'*l*ñ.	ደውልልኝ::
Call **me.** (f)	dewy'lñ.	ደውይልኝ::
Call **them.** (m)	dewl'lachew.	ደውልላቸው::
Bring it **for me.** (m)	am*ta*lñ.	አምጣልኝ::
Bring it **for us.**	am*ta*ln.	አምጣልን::
Take **me.** (m)	wsedeñ.	ውሰደኝ::
Take it **for me.** (m)	wsed'lñ.	ውሰድልኝ::
Take it **for him.** (f)	wsej'let.	ውሰጅለት::
Give **me** the book.* (m)	me*ts'ha*fun s'*te*ñ.	መፅሓፉን ስጠኝ::
Give **her** the book.* (m)	me*ts'ha*fun s'*ta*t.	መፅሓፉን ስጣት::
Give **us** the book.* (m)	me*ts'ha*fun s'*te*n.	መፅሓፉን ስጠን::
Tell him. (m)	n'gerew.	ንገረው::
Show them. (m)	asay**achew.**	አሳያቸው::
Help us. (m)	ïrdan.	እርዳን::

*Note that *book* is translated as **metshaf**. The book (a definite article) is **mets'hafu**. There is information provided on page 60 about using definite articles (the...).

I told you.	ïnie negerkuh.	እኔ ነገርኩህ::
She **asked** him.	ïsua *te*yeqechw.	እሷ ጠየቀቸው::
We forgot **them.**	ïña resana**chew.**	እኛ ረሳናቸው::

Following are examples of object pronouns when used with common prepositions.

about me	s'le'ïnie / s'lenie	ስለ እኔ (ስለኔ)
about you (m)	s'le'ante	ስለ አንተ (ስላንተ)
about you (f)	s'le'anchi	ስለ አንቺ (ስላንቺ)
about you (pl)	s'le'ïnante	ስለ እናንተ (ስለናንተ)
about him	s'le'ïrsu (s'lesu)	ስለ እርሱ (ስለሱ)
about her	s'le'ïrsua	ስለ እርሷ
about us	s'le'ña	ስለኛ
about them (m./f. pl)	s'le'nesu	ስለነሱ
It is about her.	s'le'ïrsua new.	ስለ እርሷ ነው።

Note that the word **s'le** (ስለ) is translated as *about*. It also is used as in the phrase **s'lezih** (ስለዚህ) meaning *therefore*.

for / to me	le' ïnie (lenie)	ለ እኔ (ለኔ)
for / to you (m)	lante	ላንተ
for / to you (f)	lanchi	ላንቺ
for / to you (pl)	lenante	ለናንተ
for / to him	lesu	ለሱ
for / to her	lesua	ለሷ
for / to us	leña	ለኛ
for / to them (m. f. pl)	lenesu	ለነሱ
Give it to them. (m/f. pl)	lenesu s'*ta*chew.	ለነሱ ስጣቸው።
with me	kenie gar	ከኔ ጋር
with you (m)	kante gar	ካንተ ጋር
with you (f)	kanchi gar	ካንቺ ጋር
with you (m. pl)	kenante gar	ከናንተ ጋር
with you (f. pl)	kenante gar	ከናንተ ጋር
with him	kesu gar	ከሱ ጋር
with her	kesua gar	ከሷ ጋር
with us	keña gar	ከኛ ጋር
with them	kenesu gar	ከነሱ ጋር
I came with you. (m)	kante gar me*ta*hu.	ካንተ ጋር መጣሁ።
without you (m)	kale ante	ካለ አንተ
without you (f)	kale anchi (kalanchi)	ካለ አንቺ
without him	kale ïrsu (kalersu)	ካለ እርሱ
without her	kale ïrsua	ካለ እርሷ
without us	kale ïña	ካለ እኛ

THE INFINITIVE VERB AND THE PRESENT TENSE

Amharic verbs have an infinitive form, the basic form of each verb. In English, the infinitive is preceded by *to*. For example, *to eat, to go,* etc. In Amharic, the infinitive usually starts with the 1ˢᵗ order **መ** as the me sound in cement. It would be used to say something like *He wants to speak* – **menager yfelgal** (መናገር ይፈልጋል). See following examples of infinitive for of verbs:

to eat	meblat	መብላት
to go	mehied	መሄድ
to speak	menager	መናገር

Prefixes and suffixes are added to indicate the pronoun when converting the infinitive form of the verb to the present tense *I, you, he, she, we, they* form. As you can see, the bold letters in the following table are generally consistent for all regular verbs. Once memorized, they can be used each time when speaking in the present tense. Be aware there are some irregular verbs, like *to be* - **mehon** / (መሆን) that do not follow regular patterns of conjugation.

In Amharic, unlike English, it is not always necessary to say the pronoun when making a phrase because the verb itself indicates the pronoun. For example, to say *We ate*, it is only necessary to say **belan** (በላን). It is not necessary to precede the verb with *we* / **ïña** / እኛ because that is made somewhat redundant since the verb conjugation indicates already that it is speaking of *We*. Saying **ïña** before the verb places an emphasis on the pronoun, so it can be omitted, unless the intention is to emphasize the subject or pronoun. For instance, *WE are the champions*!

by Eldon Katter

Verb: (to eat)	Pronoun	meblat	መብላት
I eat	ïnie / እኔ	ïbelalehu	እበላለሁ
You eat (m)	ante / አንተ	t'belaleh	ትበላለህ
You eat (f)	anchi / አንቺ	t'beyalesh	ትበያለሽ
You eat (m/f. pl)	ïnante / እናንተ	t'belalach'hu	ትበላላችሁ
He eats	ïsu / እሱ	ybelal	ይበላል
She eats	ïsua / እሷ	t'belalech	ትበላለች
We eat	ïña / እኛ	ïnbelalen	እንበላለን
They eat (m/f. pl)	ïnesu / እነሱ	y'belalu	ይበላሉ

Verb: (to go)	Pronoun	mehied	መሄድ
I go	ïnie / እኔ	ï'hiedalehu	እሄዳለሁ
You go (m)	ante / አንተ	t'hiedaleh	ትሄዳለህ
You go (f)	anchi / አንቺ	t'hiejalesh	ትሄጃለሽ
You go (m./f. pl)	ïnante / እናንተ	t'hiedalach'hu	ትሄዳላችሁ
He goes	ïsu / እሱ	yhiedal	ይሄዳል
She goes	ïsua / እሷ	t'hiedalech	ትሄዳለች
We go	ïña/ እኛ	ïnhiedalen	እንሄዳለን
They go (f. pl)	ïnesu / እነሱ	yhiedalu	ይሄዳሉ

Verb: (to speak)	Pronoun	menager	መናገር
I speak	ïnie/ እኔ	ïnageralehu	እናገራለሁ
You speak (m)	ante / አንተ	tnageraleh	ትናገራለህ
You speak (f)	anchi / አንቺ	tnageriyalesh	ትናገሪያለሽ
You speak (m/f. pl)	ïnante / እናንተ	tnageralach'hu	ትናገራላችሁ
He speaks	ïsu / እሱ	ynageral	ይናገራል
She speaks	ïsua / እሷ	t'nageralech	ትናገራለች
We speak	ïña / እኛ	ïn'nageralen	እንናገራለን
They speak (m/f. pl)	ïnesu / እነሱ	ynageralu	ይናገራሉ

While there are a few irregularly conjugated verbs, most verbs follow this basic pattern in the present tense. As you can see, each infinitive verb is broken down into a <u>root</u> form; the most basic form without prefix or suffix.

meblat/<u>bela</u> -- mehied/<u>hiede</u> -- menager/<u>tenagere</u>.

35

The roots (**bela, hiede, tenagere,** etc) do not have meanings by themselves, but they are the basis for which the verbs are constructed with the appropriate prefixes and suffixes. At a minimum, learn the difference between the second person male and female suffixes (**eh / esh**).

It may take some time to learn the basic present tense form (without prefix/suffix) of each infinitive. Generally, they resemble the infinitive, with the 'm' dropped. Here are some examples, with the root underlined.

	Infinitive	(1ˢᵗ person singular)
believe	ma<u>men</u>	a<u>mn</u>alehu
	ማ<u>መን</u>	አ<u>ምን</u> አለሁ
call (phone)	me<u>dewel</u>	ï<u>dewl</u>alehu
	መ<u>ደወል</u>	እ<u>ደው</u>ላለሁ
gain/increase	me<u>chem</u>er	ï<u>chem</u>ralehu
	መ<u>ጨም</u>ር	እ<u>ጨም</u>ራለሁ
finish	me<u>cher</u>es	ï<u>cher</u>salehu
	መ<u>ጨረ</u>ስ	እ<u>ጨር</u>ሳለሁ
see	ma<u>yet</u>	a<u>y</u>alehu
	ማ<u>የት</u>	አ<u>ያ</u>ለሁ
sell	me<u>she</u>t	ï<u>she</u>talehu
	መ<u>ሸጥ</u>	እ<u>ሸጣ</u>ለሁ

It can be challenging to conjugate Amharic verbs. The prefix and suffixes are consistent but changing the infinitive form to the root conjugated form varies somewhat. In lieu of memorizing these irregular patterns, it might be easier to memorize the actual conjugation using the extensive list of verbs provided on 169. If you study this list, you will notice that verbs that start with ma / (ማ) have 1ˢᵗ person conjugations that start with **a** / (አ). See *believe* in the table above. The majority of verbs start with **me** / (መ), and are conjugated in first person starting with **ï** / (እ). See *finish* in the table above.

USING TWO VERBS

In English, many sentences use two verbs (*He wants to play*). The simplest way to combine verbs is to use the **infinitive followed by the conjugated version of a verb**. This pattern is the same for present, past, continuous, or future tenses. See the following examples. In the middle column, a literal translation is shown to help understand typical sentence structure. The pronoun is shown in parenthesis.

I enjoy running.	(anie) mero*t* des yleñal.	(እኔ) መሮጥ ደስ ይለኛል፡፡
	Lit: I to run enjoy.	
You need to eat.	(ante) meblat yasfelghal.	(አንተ) መብላት ያስፈልግሃል፡፡
	Lit: You to eat need.	
She doesn't want to drink.	(ïswa) me*teta*t atfelgm.	(እሷ) መጠጣት አትፈልግም፡፡
	Lit: She to drink doesn't want.	
She hates to drive.	(ïswa) mendat t'*r*elalech.	(እሷ) መንዳት ትጠላለች፡፡
	Lit: She to drive hates.	
He didn't learn to read.	(ïsu) manbeb altemarem.	(እሱ) ማንበብ አልተማረም፡፡
	Lit: He to read didn't learn.	
We learn to pray.	(ïña) metseley ïnmaralen.	(እኛ) መፀለይ እንማራለን፡፡
	Lit: We to pray learn.	

THE PRESENT CONTINUOUS TENSE

The present continuous form of a verb describes something that is currently happening. For example, *I am eating. They are drinking*, etc. To make a present continuous statement in Amharic, use a combination as follows:

- (ïye + present tense conjugated verb) + (new / ነው)
- ïye replaces the typical verb prefix.

In the example, the verb *to go* (mehied) is expressed in the present continuous. The first word is the continuous tense conjugation of **mehied**; the second word is *new*/ነው meaning *is*. When combined, they express the present continuous. Notice the prefix is always ïye (እየ). Study the suffixes and commit them to memory to speak in the present continuous. This can also be used as a question by the tone of voice, for example... *I am going? / Am I going?*

Example	Phonetic	Amharic
I am going.	**ïye**hiedku new.	እየሄድኩ ነው፡፡
You are going. (m)	**ïye**hied'k new.	እየሄድክ ነው፡፡
You are going. (f)	**ïye**hiedsh new.	እየሄድሽ ነው፡፡
You are going. (m/f pl.)	**ïye**hiedachuh new.	እየሄዳችሁ ነው፡፡
He is going.	**ïye**hiede new.	እየሄደ ነው፡፡
She is going.	**ïye**hiedech new.	እየሄደች ነው፡፡
We are going.	**ïye**hiedn new.	እየሄድን ነው፡፡
They are going (m/f pl.).	**ïye**hiedu new.	እየሄዱ ነው፡፡

Other examples of present continuous:

I am waiting.	**ïye***te*beqku new.	እየጠበቅኩ ነው።
You are writing. (m)	**ïye***tsa*fk new.	እየፃፍክ ነው።
She is talking.	**ïye**tenagerech new.	እየተናገረች ነው።
We are learning.	**ïye**temarn new.	እየተማርን ነው።
They are eating.	**ïye**belu new.	እየበሉ ነው።
Are you going? (m)	**ïye**hiedk new?	እየሄድክ ነው?

GERUNDS

In English, a gerund is the _ing_ form of a verb, and is often used like a noun. For example, _learning, playing, thinking_ are activities. In Amharic, the verb in its infinitive form can be used the same as a noun. Expressing _to play_ and _playing_ would both be expressed as **mec***h*a**wet** (መጫወት). One could say _To play is fun –_ _or – Playing is fun._ Of course, if expressing _He is playing_ then it would be conjugated as typical for the male third-person present continous tense.

English	Phonetic	Amharic
to dance	medenes	መደነስ
I am dancing.	ïyedenesku **new**.	እየደነስኩ ነው።
Dancing is fun.	**medenes** yasdestal.	መደነስ ያስደስታል።
to steal	mesreq	መስረቅ
She is stealing.	ïyesereqech new.	እየሰረቀች ነው።
Stealing milk is easy.	wetet **mesreq** qelal new.	ወተት መስረቅ ቀላል ነው።
to speak	menager	መናገር
She is **speaking**.	**ïye**tenagerech new.	እየተናገረች ነው።
Speaking is hard.	**menager** kebad new.	መናገር ከባድ ነው።
My favorite activities are **running**, **singing**, and **reading**.	**merot, mezfen,** ïna **manbeb** temerach ïnqsqasiewochie nachew.	መሮጥ፣መዝፈን እና ማንበብ ተመራጭ እንቅስቃሴዎቼ ናቸው።

PAST TENSE

The past tense form of a verb is used to describe something that has already happened. For example, _I took the car. He told the truth. We climbed the mountain,_ etc. There are two forms of the past tense in Amharic. If you are a beginner, and only commit one form of the past tense to memory, it is likely you

38

will still be understood, however, the two forms, are used for particular situations. In general, one form is used for the recent past, and one form is used for more distance past.

For both forms, start by eliminating the present tense verb prefix. You'll need to figure out the stem form of the verb. Here are some examples of the stem for the recent past and distant past. It may take a little time to figure these out, but just observe the verb list at the end of this book, and you'll see 400+ examples.

Verb	Infinitive	Recent Past Stem	Distant Past Stem
buy	megzat	geza	gez
	መግዛት	ገዛ	ገዝ
pay	mekfel	kefel	kef
	መክፈል	ከፈል	ከፍ
take	mew'sed	wesed	wes'
	መውሰድ	ወሰድ	ወስ
work	mesrat	serah	ser
	መስራት	ሰራ	ሰር

After you have removed the prefix and established the stem, add the appropriate suffix to make the verb complete. The following table shows typical past-tense suffixes for each pronoun, depending on whether it's a recent or distant past tense sentence.

Pronoun	Recent Past Suffix	Distant Past Suffix
I	hu / ku	alehu
You (m)	k	ehal
You (f)	sh	eshal
You (pl)	ch'hu	ach'hual
He	e	ual
She	ch	alech
They	u	ewal
We	n	enal

Study the following tables to understand the pattern.

To buy መግዛት megzat	Present Tense		Past Tense (recent / distant)
I buy	ïgezalehu እገዛለሁ	I bought	gezahu / gez'chalehu ገዛሁ / ገዝቻለሁ
You buy (m)	tgezaleh ትገዛለህ	You bought	gezah / geztehal ገዛህ / ገዝተሃል
You buy (f)	tgezhialesh ትገርአለሽ	You bought	gezash / gezteshal ገዛሽ / ገዝተሻል
You buy (pl)	tgezalach'hu ትገዛላችሁ	You bought	gezach'hu / geztach'hual ገዛችሁ / ገዝታችኋል
He buys	ygezal ይገዛል	He bought	geza / geztual ገዛ / ገዝቷል
She buys	tgezalech ትገዛለች	She bought	gezach / geztalech ገዛች / ገዝታለች
They buy	ygezalu ይገዛሉ	They bought	gezu / geztewal ገዙ / ገዝተዋል
We buy	ïngezalen እንገዛለን	We bought	gezan / geztenal ገዛን / ገዝተናል

To Pay መክፈል mekfel	Present Tense		Past Tense (recent / distant)
I pay	ïkef'lalehu እከፍላለሁ	I paid	kefelku / kef'yalehu ከፈልኩ / ከፍያለሁ
You pay (m)	tkef'laleh ትከፍላለህ	You paid	kefelk / kef'lehal ከፈልህ / ከፍለሃል
You pay (f)	tkefyalesh ትከፍያለሽ	You paid	kefel'sh / kef'leshal ከፈልሽ / ከፍለሻል
You pay (pl)	tkef'lalach'hu ትከፍላላችሁ	You paid	kefelach'hu / keflach'hual ከፈላችሁ / ከፈላችኋል
He pays	ykef'lal ይከፍላል	He paid	kefele / kef'lual ከፈለ / ከፍሏል
She pays	tkef'lalech ትከፍላለች	She paid	kefelech / kef'lalech ከፈለች / ከፈለች
They pay	ykef'lalu ይከፍላሉ	They paid	kefelu / kef'lewal ከፈሉ / ከፍለዋል
We pay	ïnkef'lalen እንከፍላለን	We paid	kefeln / kef'lenal ከፈልን / ከፍለናል

To take መውሰድ / mew'sed	Present Tense		Past Tense (recent / distant)
I take	ïwesdalehu እወስዳለሁ	I took	wesed**ku** / **wes'jalehu** ወሰድኩ / **ወሰጃለሁ**
You take (m)	t'wesdaleh ትወስዳለህ	You took	wesed**k** / **wes'dehal** ወሰድክ / **ወሰደሃል**
You take (f)	t'wesji'alesh ትወስጇአለሽ	You took	wesed'**sh** / **wes'deshal** ወሰድሽ / **ወሰደሻል**
You take (pl)	t'wesdalach'hu ትወስዳላችሁ	You took	wesed**ach'hu** / **wes'dach'hual** ወሰዳችሁ /**ወሰዳችኋል**
He takes	ywesdal ይወስዳል	He took	wesede / **wes'dual** ወሰደ / **ወሰዲ**ል
She takes	t'wesdalech ትወስዳለች	She took	wesed**ech** / **wes'dalech** ወሰደች / **ወሰዳለች**
They take	ywesdalu ይወስዳሉ	They took	wesedu / **wes'dewal** ወሰዱ / **ወሰደዋል**
We take	ïnwesdalen እንወስዳለን	We took	wesed'**n** / **wes'denal** ወሰድን / **ወሰደናል**

To work መስራት me'srat	Present Tense		Past Tense (recent / distant)
I work	ïseralehu እሰራለሁ	I worked	serahu / **serchalehu** ሰራሁ / ሰርቻለሁ
You work (m)	t'seraleh ትሰራለህ	You worked	serah / **ser'tehal** ሰራህ / ሰርተሃል
You work (f)	t'serialesh ትሰራአለሽ	You worked	serash / **ser'teshal** ሰራሽ / ሰርተሻል
You work (pl)	t'seralach'hu ትሰራላችሁ	You worked	serach'hu / **ser'tach'hual** ሰራችሁ / ሰርታችኋል
He works	yseral ይሰራል	He worked	sera / **ser'tual** ሰራ / ሰርቷል
She works	t'seralech ትሰራለች	She worked	serach / **ser'talech** ሰራች / ሰርታለች
They work	yseralu ይሰራሉ	They worked	seru / **sertewal** ሰሩ / ሰርተዋል
We work	ïnseralen እንሰራለን	We worked	seran / **sertenal** ሰራን / ሰርተናል

Past Tense Examples (r-recent past / d- distant past)

(r)	Did you add sugar? (f)	s'kuar *che*mersh?	ስኳር ጨመርሽ?
(r)	Yes, I added sugar.	awo s'kuar *che*merku.	አዎ ስኳር ጨመርኩ።
(d)	Did you attend college? (f)	koliej gebteshal?	ኮሌጅ ገብተሻል?
(d)	I studied in Hawassa.	hewasa w'st temrie'alehu.	ሀዋሳ ውስጥ ተምሬአለሁ።
(r)	I just woke up.	ahun neqahu.	አሁን ነቃሁ።
(d)	You worked on the farm. (m)	ante ïreshaw lay sertehal.	አንተ እርሻው ላይ ሰርተሃል።
(r)	You forgot the key.(f)	qulfun resash.	ቁልፉን ረሳሽ።
(d)	He studied engineering.	mhnd'sna a*t* 'ntual.	ምህንድስና አጥንቷል።
(r)	He locked the door.	berun qolefe.	በሩን ቆለፈ።
(d)	She died 20 years ago.	kehaya amet befit motalech.	ከሀያ ዓመት በፊት ሞታለች።
(r)	She arrived 2 minutes ago.	kehulet deqiqa befit deresech.	ከሁለት ደቂቃ በፊት ደረሰች።
(d)	They came last year.	yalefew amet me*t* 'tewal.	ያለፈው ዓመት መጥተዋል።
(r)	They just came.	ahun me*tu*.	አሁን መጡ።
(d)	We lived in Korem.	korem norenal.	ኮረም ኖረናል።
(r)	We missed the bus.	aw'tobisu amele*t*en.	አውቶቢሱ አመለጠን።

To see the first person male singular past tense conjugations for 400+ verbs, see the fourth column of the VERB LIST. If you learn the appropriate suffixes, it is very easy to speak in the past tense.

PAST CONTINUOUS

When describing actions that were happening, one uses the past continuous tense. For example, *They were running. They were following. What were you thinking?*, etc. Speaking in past continuous is similar to present continuous. The word **neber** is from the verb **menor** and means *was happening*. Do the following to make a past tense verb into present continuous.

- Remove the prefix from the verb; replace it with **ïye** (or **ïya**), and follow the verb with **neber (ነበር)**.

	Past tense	Past continuous
English	I said ____.	I was saying ____.
Amharic	____አልኩ::	____ እያልኩ ነበር::
Phonetic	____alku.	____ ïyalku neber.
English	You ate (m/f)	You were eating.
Amharic	በላህ / በላሽ::	እየበላህ ነበር / እየበላሽ ነበር::
Phonetic	belah / belash	ïyebelah neber / ïyebelash neber.
English	You ran. (m/f)	You were running.
Amharic	ሮጥክ / ሮጥሽ::	እየሮጥክ ነበር / እየሮጥሽ ነበር::
Phonetic	rot'k / rot'sh.	ïyerot'k neber / ïyerot'sh neber.
English	He threw.	He was throwing.
Amharic	ወረወረ::	እየወረወረ ነበር::
Phonetic	werewere.	ïyewerewere neber.
English	She laughed.	She was laughing.
Amharic	ሳቀች::	እየሳቀች ነበር::
Phonetic	saqech.	ïyesaqech neber.
English	They read.	They were reading.
Amharic	አነበቡ::	እያነበቡ ነበር::
Phonetic	anebebu.	ïyanebebu neber.
English	We cried.	We were crying.
Amharic	አለቀስን::	እያለቀስን ነበር::
Phonetic	aleqesn.	ïyaleqesn neber.

Question: *Was she drinking?* – ïyetetach neber? አየጠጣች ነበር?

FUTURE TENSE

The future tense form of a verb describes something that *will* happen or is *going to* happen. For example, *I will take the test. She is going to sell the car. We will find the key,* etc. In Amharic, the present-tense conjugation can be used for the future actions, simply by clarifying with phrases such as *tomorrow, next week, on my birthday,* etc.

NEGATIVE TENSE

Speaking in the negative is simply the opposite of a positive statement, for example, *I am <u>not</u> going. They are <u>not</u> there. We do <u>not</u> like it,* etc. A negative can be spoken in the past tense, present, future, or continuous.

43

To speak in the negative present tense, one of the prefixes **al/at/ay** is added before the root form of the verb and the suffix **m** is added after the verb. This rule is generally very easy to follow, with the exception of a few irregular verb patterns such the verb *to be*.

If you are making the phrase a command, the suffix **m** is omitted. For example, *Do not think* can be translated as **ataseb** / (አታስብ), which is rather an advice to imply *not to worry*, rather than **atasbm** / (አታስብም) which means *You do not think'*, i.e. *You don't use your mind.*

The Negative Prefix and Suffix

Speaking in the negative in Amharic is only somewhat regular. There are common prefixes and suffixes attached to verbs to indicate the pronoun, but in some cases these are not present – so it is inconsistent. The prefixes *generally* stay consistent among verbs, however, the suffix can vary depending on the infinitive form of the verb. However, by following the general patterns shown below you can learn to express the negatve.

Pronoun	Prefix	Suffix (varies)
I	al	m
you (m)	at	m
you (f)	at	im
he	ay	m
she	at	m
we	an	m
you (pl)	at	um
they	ay	um

Following examples show the verb *to know* / **maweq** / (ማወቅ) conjugated in positive and negative tense. Notice the prefixes and suffixes. The suffix will change depending on the verb, but the last sound (**m, im, m, um,** etc.) is generally consistent.

44

EXAMPLE	Phonetic	Amharic	Prefix / Suffix
I know	awqalehu	አውቃለሁ	
I do not know	**al**awq**m**	አላውቅም	al / qm
You know (m)	tawqaleh	ታውቃለህ	
You do not know (m)	**at**awq**m**	አታውቅም	at / qm
You know (f)	tawqiyalesh	ታውቂያለሽ	
You do not know (f)	**at**awq**im**	አታውቂም	at / qim
He knows	yawqal	ያውቃል	
He does not know	**ay**awq**m**	አያውቅም	ay / qm
She knows	tawqalech	ታውቃለች	
She does not know	**at**awq**m**	አታውቅም	at / qm
We know	ïnawqalen	እናውቃለን	
We do not know	**an**awq**m**	አናውቅም	an / qm
You all know	tawqalachihu	ታውቃላችሁ	
You all do not know	**at**awq**um**	አታውቁም	at /qum
They know	yawqalu	ያውቃሉ	
They do not know	**ay**awq**um**	አያውቁም	ay / qum

The following example shows the verbs *to sit* / **meqemet** / (መቀመጥ) and *to speak* **menager** / (መናገር) conjugated in positive and negative tense. Notice the prefixes in this example are the same as from *to know* / meweq / (ማወቅ) but the suffixes have changed.

To eat	Phonetic	Amharic	Prefix	Suffix
I don't eat.	albelam	አልበላም	al	am
You don't eat.(m)	atbelam	አትበላም	at	am
You don't eat.(f)	atbeym	አትቢይም	at	ym
You all don't eat.	atbelum	አትበሉም	at	um
He doesn't eat.	aybelam	አይበላም	ay	am
She doesn't eat.	atbelam	አትበላም	at	am
We don't eat.	anbelam	አንበላም	an	am
They don't eat.	aybelum	አይበሉም	ay	um

To sit	Phonetic	Amharic	Prefix	Suffix
I don't sit.	alqeme*t*m	አልቀመጥም	al	*t*m
You don't sit. (m)	atqeme*t*m	አትቀመጥም	at	*t*m
You don't sit. (f)	atqeme*chi*m	አትቀመጪም	at	*chi*m
He doesn't sit.	ayqeme*t*m	አይቀመጥም	ay	*t*m
She doesn't sit.	atqeme*t*m	አትቀመጥም	at	*t*m
We don't sit.	anqeme*t*m	አንቀመጥም	an	*t*m
You all don't sit.	atqeme*tu*m	አትቀመጡም	at	*tu*m
They all don't sit.	ayqemetum	አይቀመጡም	ay	*tu*m

To speak	Phonetic	Amharic	Prefix	Suffix
I don't speak.	alnager'm	አልናገርም	al	rm
You don't speak. (m)	atnager'm	አትናገርም	at	rm
You don't speak. (f)	atnagerim	አትናገሪም	at	*r*im
He doesn't speak.	aynager'm	አይናገርም	ay	*r*m
She doesn't speak.	atnager'm	አትናገርም	at	*r*m
We don't speak.	an'nager'm	አንናገርም	an	*r*m
You all don't speak.	atnagerum	አትናገሩም	at	rum
They all don't speak.	aynagerum	አይናገሩም	ay	rum

More examples of negative tense

I want.	ïfelgalehu	እፈልጋለሁ
I don't want.	alfel'gm	አልፈልግም
I go.	ïhiedalehu	እሄዳለሁ
I don't go.	alhiedm	አልሄድም
You think. (m)	tasbaleh	ታስባለህ
You don't think. (m)	atasbm	አታስብም
You sleep. (f)	t'teñi'alesh	ትተኚአለሽ
You don't sleep. (f)	at'teñim	አትተኚም
He is happy. *(irreg verb)*	desteña new	ደስተኛ ነው
He is not happy. *(irreg verb)*	desteña aydelem	ደስተኛ አይደለም
She works.	t'seralech	ትሰራለች
She does not work.	at'seram	አትሰራም
We travel.	ïnguazalen	እንጓዛለን
We do not travel.	anguazm	አንጓዝም
They fight.	ytalalu	ይጣላሉ
They do not fight.	aytalum	አይጣሉም

PAST TENSE NEGATIVE

Note the suffixes for negative past tense are somewhat different. The *I* pronoun form has a **kum** (or a **hum**) suffix and **al** prefix. For example, *I didn't go* is **alhiedkum**. *I didn't come* is tranlsated **almetahum**. See the highlighted in bold for general example of how to say something in the negative past tense.

Past tense positive/negative	Phonetic	Amharic
I won	ashenefku	አሸነፍኩ
I did not win	**alashenefkum**	አላሸነፍኩም
I read	anebebku	አነበብኩ
I did not read	**alanbebkum**	አላነበብኩም
You played (m)	techawet'k	ተጫወትክ
You didn't play (m)	**altechawetkm**	አልተጫወትክም
You cared (f)	astamemsh	አስታmemሽ
You didn't care (f)	**alastamemshm**	አላስታmemሽም
He forgot	resa	ረሳ
He did not forget	**alresam**	አልረሳም

47

She brought the book	me*ts*'hafun ame*tach*	መጽሐፉን አመጣች
She did not bring a book	me*ts*'haf alame*tach*m	መጽሐፍ አላመጣችም
We remembered	astawesn	አስታወስን
We did not remember	alastawesnm	አላስታወስንም
They came	me*tu*	መጡ
They did not come	alme*tu*m	አልመጡም

PAST CONTINUOUS NEGATIVE

To make a past continuous statement negative, such as *I was not thinking*, simply state the past continuous form of the verb, but replace **neber** with **alneberem** (አልነበረም).

I **was not** calling.	ïye*te*rahuh **alneberem.**	እየጠራሁህ **አልነበረም**
She **was not** traveling.	ïyeteguazech **alneberem.**	እየተጓዝች **አልነበረም**
They **were not** selling.	ïyeshe*tu* **alneberem.**	እየሸጡ **አልነበረም**
You **were not** talking (m).	ïyetenager'k **alneberem.**	እየተናገርክ **አልነበረም**

NEGATIVE COMMANDS

The prefix **at** / (አት) can be used as a command such as in *Don't cry*.   See examples.

Example	Phonetic	Amharic
Don't be late (f)	atzegeyi	አትዘገዪ
Don't forget (m)	at'rsa	አትርሳ
Don't come (m)	at'm*ta*	አትምጣ

The prefix **at** / (አት) can also suggest an action to be taken, stated in the form of a polite question. If it precedes **lemn** / (ለምን?) it implies emphasis, but it also makes perfect sense without it. See the following examples.

Why don't you eat? (m)	lemn **at**belam*?*	ለምን አትበላም?
Why don't you eat? (f)	lemn **at**beyim*?*	ለምን አትበዪም?
Why don't you eat? (m/f pl)	lemn **at**belum*?*	ለምን አትበሉም?
Why don't you put on clothes? (m)	lemn **at**lebsm?	ለምን አትለብስም?
Why don't you put on clothes? (f)	lemn **at**lebshim?	ለምን አትለብሺም?
Why don't you put on clothes? (m/f pl)	lemn **at**lebsum?	ለምን አትለብሱም?

These phrases can also be adapted to have past tense meanings such as *Why didn't you go?* (m) **lemn alhiedkm?** / ለምን አልሄድክም?

48

SAYING *WITHOUT*

The word **yelielew** / (የሌለው) means *that doesn't have*. For example, *unsalted food* translates as *che*w **yelielew mgb** / (ጨው የሌለው ምግብ).

salt free	*che*w yelielew	ጨው የሌለው
sugar free	s'kuar yelielew	ስኳር የሌለው

You can also say **kale** / (ካለ) or **yale** / (ያለ) meaning *without*. For example: *I want coffee without sugar.* **buna kale s'kuar ïfelgalehu.** (ቡና ካለ ስኳር እፈልጋለሁ። or **buna yale s'kuar ïfelgalehu** / ቡና ያለ ስኳር እፈልጋለሁ።)

by Eldon Katter

EXPRESSING 'ANTI'

The word *tsere* / ፀረ, meaning *against* can be used like the English prefix *anti*.

anti-American	*tse*re amerikawi	ፀረ-አሜሪካዊ
anti-Communist	*tse*re komyunist	ፀረ-ኮምዩኒስት
anti-establishment	*tse*re sr'at	ፀረ-ስርዓት
anti-government	*tse*re mengst	ፀረ-መንግስት
anti-regulation	*tse*re-*h*gna sr'at	ፀረ-ሕግና ስርዓት

THE IMPERATIVE

The imperative tense expresses a command, such as *Get it. Eat. Go. Take me*, etc. Common imperative phrases are listed on 147. The imperative has different suffixes based on whom one is speaking to ; such as to a male, a female, or a group

49

of people. Like other verb conjugations, there are some irregularities in the way the imperative is expressed, but generally, there are some rules to follow. Take the following for instance:

Give me money (male singular).	genzeb s'*te*ñ.	ገንዘብ ስጠኝ

You will notice the **s't** part is derived from the verb *to give* / **mes*t*et** / (መስጠት). The **ñ** part refers back to oneself. As in English, the object of the sentence follows the imperative form of the verb.

In Amharic, an object can be considered as a male or female. Therefore, the imperative phrase *Try it* can be translated as **mokr<u>e</u>w** or **mokr<u>i</u>w**; from the infinitive form **memoker** / (መሞከር). The **ew** indicates an *it* with a male gender and the **iw** indicates an *it* with a female gender. There are no rules for which objects are male or female.

	Phonetic	Amharic
to listen (infinitive)	mesmat.	መስማት።።
Listen. (m)	s'ma.	ስማ።።
Listen. (f)	s'mi.	ስሚ።።
Listen. (pl)	s'mu.	ስሙ።።
Listen to me. (m)	s'mañ.	ስማኝ።።
Listen to me. (f)	s'miñ	ስሚኝ
Listen to me. (pl)	s'muñ	ስሙኝ
Listen to him. (f)	s'miw.	ስሚው።።
Listen to them. (m)	s'machew.	ስማቸው።።
to catch (infinitive)	meyaz.	መያዝ።።
Catch. (m)	yaz.	ያዝ።።
Catch. (f)	yazi.	ያዚ።።
Catch. (pl)	yazu.	ያዙ።።
Catch it. (m)	yazew.	ያዘው።።
Catch it. (f)	yaziw.	ያዚው።።
Catch it. (pl)	yazut.	ያዙት።።
to take (infinitive)	mewsed.	መውሰድ።።
Take.	wsed	ውሰድ
Take it. (m)	w'sedew.	ውሰደው።።
Take it. (f)	w'sejiw.	ውሰጂው።።
Take it. (pl)	w'sedut.	ውሰዱት።።
Take them. (m)	w'sedachew.	ውሰዳቸው።።

Take them. (f)	w'sejachew.	ውሰጃቸው።
Take them. (pl)	w'seduachew.	ውሰዷቸው።
to tell (infinitive)	menager	መናገር
Tell.	nger	ንገር
Tell me. (m)	ngereñ	ንገረኝ
Tell her. (m)	ngerat	ንገራት
Tell her. (f)	ngeriyat	ንገሪያት
Tell him. (m)	ngererew	ንገረው
Tell them. (f)	ngeriyachew	ንገሪያቸው
Tell them. (pl)	ngeruachew	ንገሯቸው

EXPRESSING OBLIGATION

There are several ways to express obligation, such as *I have to go to work. You have to see a doctor*, etc. A simple way is the following:

- Present tense: (the thing required + **aleb** + suffix)
- Past tense: (the thing required + **nebereb** + suffix)

Present Tense	Phonetic	Amharic
I have to...	... aleb'**ñ**	... አለብኝ
You have to...(m)	... aleb'**h**	... አለብህ
You have to ...(f)	... aleb'**sh**	... አለብሽ
You have to...(pl.)	... aleb**ach'hu**	... አለባችሁ
He has to...	... aleb**et**	... አለበት
She has to...	... aleb**at**	... አለባት
They have to...	... aleb**achew**	... አለባቸው
We have to...	... aleb'**n**	... አለብን

Past Tense	Phonetic	Amharic
I had to...	... nebereb'**ñ**	... ነበረብኝ
You had to...(m)	... nebereb'**h**	... ነበረብህ
You had to ...(f)	... nebereb'**sh**	... ነበረብሽ
You had to...(pl.)	... nebereb**ach'hu**	... ነበረባችሁ
He had to...	... nebereb**et**	... ነበረበት
She had to...	... nebereb**at**	... ነበረባት
They had to...	... nebereb**achew**	... ነበረባቸው
We had to...	... nebereb'**n**	... ነበረብን

I have to practice.	melemamed aleb'ñ.	መለማመድ አለብኝ፡፡
I had to pray.	metseley nebereb'ñ.	መጸለይ ነበረብኝ፡፡
You have to work. (m)	mesrat aleb'h.	መስራት አለብህ ፡፡
You had to fight. (m)	metagel nebereb'h.	መታገል ነበረብህ፡፡
He has to work.	mesrat alebet.	መስራት አለበት፡፡
He needs to get married.	magbat alebet.	ማግባት አለበት፡፡
He had to try.	memoker neberebet.	መሞከር ነበረበት፡፡
She has to come.	memtat alebat.	መምጣት አለባት ፡፡
She had to study.	mat'nat neberebat.	ማጥናት ነበረባት፡፡
We have to sell books.	metshaf't meshet aleb'n.	መጽሃፍት መሸጥ አለብን፡፡
We need to learn Amharic.	amarña memar alebn.	አማርኛ መማር አለብን፡፡
We had to buy food.	m'gb megzat nebereb'n.	ምግብ መግዛት ነበረብን፡፡
They have to vote.	memret alebachew.	መምረጥ አለባቸው፡፡
They need to go to school.	tm'htrt biet mehied alebachew.	ትምህርት ቤት መሄድ አለባቸው፡፡
They had to lie.	mewashet neberebachew.	መዋሸት ነበረባቸው፡፡

Another simple way to express obligation is to use the verb **mefeleg** / መፈለግ

I need these books.	ïnezihn'n metshaf't ïfel'galehu.	እነዚህን መጽሃፍት አፈልጋለሁ፡፡
We need this food.	yhn'n m'gb ïnfel'galen.	ይህንን ምግብ እንፈልጋለን፡፡
You need this job.	y'h sra yasfelg'hal.	ይህ ስራ ያስፈልግሃል፡፡
She needs friends.	guadeñoch yasfelguatal.	ጓደኞች ያስፈልጓታል፡፡

POLITE REQUEST

Previous sections in this book have shown how to express obligation and make imperative commands. A polite request can be made using the verb **mechal** (መቻል) meaning *to be able* or *to be possible*.

Can you give me some food?	m'gb ltseteñ **t'chlaleh?**	ምግብ ልትሰጠኝ ትችላለህ?
Can you (plural) work today?	zarie l'tseru **t'chlalachhu?**	ዛሬ ልትሰሩ ትችላላችሁ?
Can I watch TV?	tivi mayet **ïch'lalehu?**	ቲቪ ማየት እችላለሁ?

There are several verbs to know that are associated with *borrowing* and *lending*:

- መዋስ (**mewas**) – to borrow something for short period of time.
- ማዋስ (**mawas**) – to lend something short term.
- መበደር (**mebeder**)– to borrow a consumable.
- ማበደር (**mabeder**) – to lend a consumable.

Please, can I borrow **this**?	ïbakh **y'hn'n** mewas ich'lalehu?
	እባክህ ይህንን መዋስ እችላለሁ?
Please **lend this to me.**	እባክህ ይህንን አውሰኝ።
	ïbakh **y'hn'n** awseñ.
Please lend me milk. (imp)	እባክህ ወተት አውሰኝ።
	ïbakh wetet awseñ.
Please can I **borrow** some **milk**?	እባክህ የተወሰነ ወተት መበደር እችላለሁ?
	ïbakh yetewesene wetet **mebeder** ich'lalehu?
Please **lend me** a hammer.	እባክህ ፋስ አውሰኝ።
	ïbakh fas **awseñ**.
Please **can I** borrow a hammer?	እባክህ ፋስ መዋስ እችላለሁ?
	ïbakh fas mewas **ich'lalehu**?
Please **can they** borrow a hammer?	እባክህ ፋስ መዋስ ይችላሉ?
	ïbakh fas mewas **y'chlalu**?

LET'S / LET

In English, *Let us / Let's* is used as a suggestion to do something. It's not as strong as a command or as polite as a request, but it is something that is commonly used to direct an action. In Amharic, to say *Let's eat* or *Let's go*, you can simply say them as *We eat* or *We go*.

See the following examples.

Let's be friends.	guadeñoch ïn'hun.	ጓደኞች እንሁን።
Let's help eachother.	ï'ntegagez	እንተጋገዝ።
Let's go.	ï'nhid	እንሂድ።
Let's eat.	ï'nbla	እንብላ።
Let's wait.	ï'ntebq	እንጠብቅ።
Let's get coffee.	buna ï'nteta	ቡና እንጠጣ።

If you want to say *Let me, Let him, Let them etc*, you can make the statement like an imperative but add the prefix '**l**' for first person, '**y**' for him and them, and '**t**' for her. A common phrase is **lstsh** (ልስጥሽ), meaning *Let me give you?*

Let me give (to) you.	l'stsh.	ልስጥሽ።
Let me give to him.	l'stew.	ልስጠው።
Let me give to her.	l'stat.	ልስጣት።
Let me give to them.	l'stachew.	ልስጣቸው።
Let me sit.	l'qemet.	ልቀመጥ።
Let him / her sit. (m/f)	y'qemet / t'qemet.	ይቀመጥ / ትቀመጥ።
Let them eat.	y'b'lu.	ይብሉ።
Let him / her come.	y'mta / t'mta .	ይምጣ / ትምጣ።
Let's see the house.	bietun ï'ny.	ቤቱን እንይ።
Let me help you.	lagz'h.	ላግዝህ።
Let me think about it.	lasb'bet.	ላስብበት።

SENTENCE STRUCTURE

In English, we usually say the object after the subject and the verb. However, in Amharic, the object comes first, followed by the action verb. See the following examples and notice their literal translation.

He picked up the pen.	ïrsu ïskrbitown anesa.
Literally: *He the pen picked up.*	እርሱ እስክርቢቶውን አነሳ።
She gives him money.	ïrsua genzeb t'se*t*ewalech.
Literally: *She money gives him.*	እርስዋ ገንዘብ ትሰጠዋለች።
He gives her money.	ïrsu genzeb yse*t*atal.
Literally: *He money gives her.*	እርሱ ገንዘብ ይሰጣታል።
I am coming with you. (f)	ïnie k'anchi gar ïme*t*alehu.
Literally: *I with you am coming.*	እኔ ካንቺ ጋር እመጣለሁ።
We played yesterday.	ïña t'nant te*ch*awetn.
Literally: *We yesterday played.*	እኛ ትናንት ተጫወትን።
I come from Gonder.	እኔ ከጎንደር መጣሁ።
Literally: *I from Gonder, come.*	ïnie keGonder me*t*ahu.

While the arrangement of sentences in Amharic may be different from English, if you practice this often, it will feel more normal. When you speak like this, your Amharic will sound much more fluent and understandable for native speakers.

COMMON PREPOSITIONS

Following is a list of common prepositions in Amharic.

PREPOSITIONS		
about, with regard to	s'le	ስለ
above	belay	በላይ
across	bashager	ባሻገር
after	behuala	በኋላ
ahead of	befit	በፊት
around (in the area)	akebabi	አከባቢ
at	be	በ
before	befit	በፊት
behind	kehuala	ከኋላ
beneath / below	ketach / s'r	ከታች / ስር
beside	kegon	ከጎን

between / among	mekakel	መካከል
beyond	ke____wedya	ከ____ወድያ
but	gn	ግን
by	be	በ
despite	bihon'm	ቢሆንም
direct / straight	qeṛ'ta	ቀጥታ
during	be'g'zie	በጊዜ
except **this**	**ke'zih** besteqer	ከዚህ በስተቀር
excluding	say*che*mr	ሳይጨምር
to	wede	ወደ
from	ke	ከ
for	le	ለ
here it is	y'khew	ይኸው
in the back	ke'huala	ከኋላ
including	*che*m'ro	ጨምሮ
in front	fit	ፊት
in front of	fit le fit	ፊት ለፊት
like	i'nde	እንደ
near, next to	a*te*geb	አጠገብ
not far away	ruq aydelem	ሩቅ አይደለም
out / outside	w'ch	ውጭ
over / up there	ke'lay / ïza lay	ከላይ / እዛላይ
on	lay	ላይ
straight on	qeṛ'ta	ቀጥታ
(turn) to the left	wede gra (ta*te*f)	ወደ ግራ (ታጠፍ)
(turn) to the right	wede keñ (ta*te*f)	ወደ ቀኝ (ታጠፍ)
to the side of	ke'gon	ከጎን
under / below	betach	በታች
until	ïs'ke	እስከ
with	ke	ከ
without____	kale____	ካለ____
within	ws*t*	ውስጥ

Examples:

We go **after** class.	ketmhr't **behuala** ï'nhid.
	ከትምህርት **በኋላ** እንሄድ።

It is **like** a cat.	ï'**nde** d'met new.
	እንደ ድመት ነው።
It is **near** my house.	bietie **ategeb** new.
	ቤቴ አጠገብ ነው።
It is **on the table**.	tere*piezaw* **lay** new.
	ጠረጴዛው ላይ ነው።
It is **across** the street.	kemengedu **bashager** new.
	ከመንገዱ ባሻገር ነው።
It is **behind** the house.	kebietu **jerba** new.
	ከቤቱ ጀርባ ነው።
From here / From there.	ï''zih / ï'ziya.
	ከዚህ / ከዚያ።
To there	ï'za
	እዛ
Everything, **except** milk.	kewetet **besteqer** hulunm.
	ከወተት በስተቀር ሁሉንም።
Between Gonder and Bahr Dahr.	begonder ï'na bebah'rdar mekakel.
	በጎንደር እና በባህርዳር መካከል።
Not far from Washington DC	kewashngten disi ruq aydelem.
	ከዋሽንግተን ዲሲ ሩቅ አይደለም።

Note that, prepositions don't always translate directly. One of the most common prepositions in English is *in*. For example, *I am in Bole. He is in school. She is in the office*. When speaking Amharic, you would not actually use a preposition. See the following:

I am in Bole.	bolie neñ.	ቦሌ ነኝ።
He is in school.	t'mhrt biet new.	ትምህርት ቤት ነው።
She is in the office.	biro nech.	ቢሮ ነች።

These translate directly as *I am Bole. He is school. She is office*. However, it is understood to mean. *I am at Bole. He is at school. She is at the office*.

PREPOSITION PHRASING

As in English, prepositions are used in Amharic to describe locations or situations. Following are examples that further help to understand how prepositions are used in Amharic. Prepositions in English and Amharic are in bold text.

She went **to the** office.	**wede** biro hiedalech.
Literally: *To the office she went.*	ወደ ቢሮ ሄዳለች።:
He came **from the** farm.	ke'ïrsha bota me*ta*.
Literally: *From farm place, he came.*	ከእርሻ ቦታ መጣ።:
Turn **to the left, after** the river.	kewenzu **behuala wede** gra ta*tef*.
Literally: *From **after** the river, **to the** left turn.*	ከወንዙ በኋላ ወደ ግራ ታጠፍ።:
We are **among** the Amhara people.	ke'amara hzb **mekakel** nen.
Literally: *The Amhara people, **among** we are.*	ከአማራ ህዝብ መካከል ነን።:
The food is **on** the table	mgbu *tere*piezaw **lay** new.
Literally: *The food table on is.*	ምግቡ ጠረጴዛው ላይ ነው።:
During the war, we are **without** peace.	be*tor*net gizie selam **yelen'm**.
Literally: *Of wartime, peace there is not any.*	በጦርነት ጊዜ ሰላም የለንም።:
The man is **under** the bridge.	sewyew kedldyu **betach** new.
Literally: *The man bridge **under** is.*	ሰውየው ከድልድዩ በታች ነው።:

PLURALIZING NOUNS

By making a noun plural, it indicates more than one of a particular object. For
instance, *mouse* becomes *mice*; or *plane* becomes *planes*. Amharic language has
some general ways to make singular nouns into plural. However, the plural nouns
are occasionally irregular, and thus can be confusing. Most commonly, **och** / (**አች**)
is added to the end of a singular noun, to make it plural. If the noun ends in a
vowel sound, it is common to add **woch** / (**ዎች**). For example, see *bed*, *place*, and
mountain in the following table.

English (singular)	Phonetic (singular)	Amharic	English (pl)	Phonetic (plural)	Amharic
book	me*ts*'haf	መፅሐፍ	books	me*tsa*hft	መፃሕፍት
bed	alga	አልጋ	beds	alga**woch**	አልጋዎች
mountain	terara	ተራራ	mountains	terar**och**	ተራሮች
car	mekina	መኪና	cars	mekin**och**	መኪኖች
cat	dmet	ድመት	cats	demet**och**	ድመቶች
country	ager	አገር	countries	ager**och**	አገርች
hand	ïj	አጅ	hands	ïj**och**	አጆች
house	biet	ቤት	houses	biet**och**	ቤቶች
paper	wereqet	ወረቀት	papers	wereqet**och**	ወረቀቶች
person	sew	ሰው	people	sew**och**	ሰዎች
place	bota	ቦታ	places	bota**woch**	ቦታዎች
problem	chigr	ችግር	problems	chigr**och**	ችግሮች
tooth	*tr*s	ጥርስ	teeth	*tr*s**och**	ጥርሶች

58

When attempting to make a singular into a plural, consider that the most likely suffix will be **och** or **woch**. If it is irregular, you may say it the wrong way, but native speakers will very likely understand. For example, a beginner might assume the plural of book me*ts*'haf is me*tsa*hafoch. While me*tsa*hafoch is grammatically incorrect, it is very likely the listener will know what you are trying to say (me*tsa*hft is correct). With time, you can learn the irregular forms and incorporate those into your conversation.

PLURALIZING ADJECTIVES

In Amharic (unlike English), adjectives are adapted to reflect plurals. As with pluralizing nouns, the rules for pluralizing adjectives are often irregular. As with other irregular grammatical situations, you will learn with practice or you can guess the correct way to say it, and hope you will be understood. As with the nouns, the most common suffix for pluralizing is adjectives is **woch** or **och,** but there are exceptions.

English (singular)	Phonetic (singular)	Amharic	Phonetic (plural)	Amharic (plural)
big	tlq	ትልቅ	tla'lq	ትላልቅ
black	*t*qur	ጥቁር	*t*quaqur	ጥቋቁር
dry	dereq	ደረቅ	dereqoch	ደረቆች
fat	wefram	ወፍራም	wefafram	ወፋፍራም
red	qey	ቀይ	qeyay	ቀያይ
small	t'nsh	ትንሽ	t'nansh	ትናንሽ
smart	gobez	ጎበዝ	gobezoch	ጎበዞች
soft	leslasa	ለስላሳ	leslasoch	ለስላሶች
strong	*t*enkara	ጠንካራ	*t*enkaroch	ጠንካሮች
sweet	*t*afach	ጣፋጭ	*t*afachoch	ጣፋጮች

by Eldon Katter

When making a phrase with adjective + noun about a plural subject, it is typical to pluralize both the adjective and noun. This is especially true when the phrase is written, but when spoken it it's also common not to pluralize the adjective; you will still likely be understood. There are some exceptions to adjective pluralization; for instance, in the phrase *strong hands*, **tenkara** is not pluralized.

strong* hands	*t*enkara ïjoch	ጠንካራ እጆች
big mountains	tla'lq teraroch	ትላልቅ ተራሮች
fat cats	wefafram d'metoch	ወፋፍራም ድመቶች
red houses	qeyay bietoch	ቀያይ ቤቶች

*adjective not typically pluralized.

ADJECTIVE / NOUN GENDER

For the most part, adjectives are not changed by gender. However, a noun usually has a gender assignment. For example, a country or city is conjugated using the female verb tense. *Ethiopia has riches.* / **ityo*p*iya habt alat.** / ኢትዮጵያ ሃብት አላት። Most inanimate objects use the third person masculine (*he*) conjugation of verbs. *The table is big.* / *te*repie*zaw tlq new* / ጠረጴዛው ትልቅ ነው። The gender is used however when specifying something in particular as *the*.

EXPRESSING 'THE'/ DEFINATE ARTICAL

In English, *the* is used to specify something, *The dog*, rather than *dog* or *dogs* in general. There are several ways to indicate a specific noun in Amharic. It depends on the situation, so you must learn as you develop your language skills.

Note: In the following examples, *the* adds emphasis to the subject. It is not any subject, but a particular one. A boy is any boy, but *the* boy a specific one. To make this distinction, one adds the suffix **u** to the male subject and **wa** to the female subject.

The boy went to church.	lju wede bietekrstiyan hiede.	ልጁ ወደ ቤተክርስቲያን ሄደ።
The red car is fast.	qeyu mekina fetan new.	ቀዩ መኪና ፈጣን ነው።
I don't like **the** movie.	filmun alwededkutm.	ፊልሙን አልወደድኩትም።
What is **the** problem?	chgru mndnew?	ችግሩ ምንድነው?
Where is **the** food?	mgbu yet ale?	ምግቡ የት አለ?
The sun is out. (f)	*ts*ehaywa we*t*ach!	ፀሃይዋ ወጣች።
We missed **the** train. (f)	baburwa amele*t*echn.	ባቡርዋ አመለጠችን።
That is not **the** ball.(f)	kuaswa yach aydelechm.	ኳስዋ ያች አይደለችም።
This is **the** teacher. (f)	astemariwa yhch nat.	አስተማሪዋ ይህች ናት።

Additional examples:

That is a girl.	yachi siet l'j nat.	ያቺ ሴት ልጅ ናት።
The girl is smart.	l'jtua b'l*t* nat	ልጅቷ ብልጥ ናት።
You need **a job**.	s'ra yas'felghal	ስራ ያስፈልግሃል።
The job has a good salary.	sraw *t*'ru demoz alew.	ስራው ጥሩ ደሞዝ አለው።
We have **mountains**.	teraroch alun.	ተራሮች አሉን።
I want to climb the mountain	teraraw'n mez'lel ïfel'galehu.	ተራራውን መዝለል አፈልጋለሁ።
I like **food**.	m'gb ïwedalehu.	ምግብ እወዳለሁ።
I like the food.	m'gbun ïwedewalehu.	ምግቡን እወደዋለሁ.
I don't like going to **class**.	wede k'fl mehied alwed'm.	ወደ ክፍል መሄድ አልወድም።
The class is boring.	k'flu aselchi new.	ክፍሉ አሰልቺ ነው።

EXPRESSING *WHEN* or *WHILE*

The following table shows examples of how to express particular moments in time. In English, *when* or *while* expresses a moment in the present, past, or future. For example, *When I was young* (past), *When I get rich* (future), etc. In Amharic, one introduces the action (or location) first, followed by the phrase **ïyale**... followed by its pronoun-appropriate suffix. See the following table and examples.

When I ...	...ïyalehu	... እያለሁ
When you ...(m)	... ïyaleh	... እያለህ
When you ...(f)	... ïyalesh	... እያለሽ
When he (it) ...	... ïyale	... እያለ
When she ...	... ïyalech	... እያለች
When they ...	... ïyalu	... እያሉ
When we ...	... ïyalen	... እያለን

| **While we** were traveling... | guzo lay **ïyalen** ... | ጉዞ ላይ **እያለን** ... |
| **When I** was in school.... | tmhrt biet **ïyalehu** ... | ትምህርት ቤት **እያለሁ** ... |

EXPRESSING PREFERENCE

The verb **meshal** / (መሻል) is used to express something is preferable or better than something else.

| I prefer... | ...yshaleñal. | ...ይሻለኛል። |
| You prefer... (m) | ...yshalahal. | ...ይሻልሃል። |

You prefer... (f)	...yshalshal.	...ይሻልሻል።
He prefers...	...yshalewal.	...ይሻለዋል።
She prefers...	...yshalatal.	...ይሻላታል።
They prefer...	...yshalachewal.	...ይሻላቸዋል።
We prefer...	...yshalenal.	...ይሻለናል።

Marriage is **preferable to her**.	tdar **yshalatal**.	ትዳር ይሻላታል።
I prefer Addis to Hawasa.	keHawasa, Adis **yshaleñal**.	ከሃዋሳ አዲስ ይሻለኛል።
I prefer Ambo **to** Bahrdar.	keBahrdar, Ambo yshaleñal.	ከባህርዳር አንቦ **ይሻለኛል**።

COMPARING THINGS

In English, when something is compared, -er is added to the adjective; for example, *shorter than, happier, bigger*, etc. There is no direct translation of these comparisons, but equivalent phrasing is described below. The word **yebelete** can be used before a positive adjective to show it is greater than others compared.

To compare to something to other things, you can use the preposition **ke**, meaning *from*. For example, **kehulum** (*from all*); **ke ïrsua** (*from her*); **ke ïnersu** (*from them*), **ke'Haimanot** (*from Haimanot*).

They are slower	zegemteña nachew.
Lit: *Slow they are.*	ዘገምተኛ ናቸው።
She is taller (from all others).	ï'sua **kehulum** yebelete rejim nat.
Lit: *She **more** tall is.*	እሷ ከሁሉም የበለጠ ረጅም ናት።
She is clever. (from all others)	ï'sua **kehulum** gobez nat.
Lit: *She **from all**, clever is.*	እሷ ከሁሉም ጎበዝ ናት፡፡
She is the **most pretty of everyone**.	ïsua **kehulum** qonjo nat.
Lit: *She from all pretty is.*	እሷ ከሁሉም ቆንጆ ናት፡፡
I am bigger **than before**.	**kebefitu** ahun tl'q neñ.
Lit: *From before, now big I am.*	ከበፊቱ አሁን ትልቅ ነኝ።
You are stronger **than I am**.	**k'enie** ante *te*nkara neh.
Lit: *From me, you strong are.*	ከኔ አንተ ጠንካራ ነህ።

The word **belay** is also used to give emphasis to an adjective, meaning *more*.

Wine is **more expensive** than beer.	wey'n ke'bira **belay w'd** new.
Lit: Wine from beer than expensive is.	ወይን ከቢራ በላይ ውድ ነው፡፡

62

Bahir Dahr is **bigger than** Lalibela.	bah'rdar ke'lalibela **belay t'lq** new
Lit: Bahir Dahr from Lalibala more big is.	ባህርዳር ከላሊበላ በላይ ትልቅ ነው::

To say something is *the best*, use **mrt** / ምርጥ.

You are the best (m/f)	mrt neh / nesh.
Lit: Best you are.	ምርጥ ነህ / ነሽ::

To express something is *worse*, you can use the word for weak (**dekama**) or *bad* (**metfo**). There is no direct translation for the words *worse* or *worst*. The word **yebase** can be placed before a negative word to show its worst of the two or more things.

At football, he is more weak than she.	be'ïgre kuas ïrsu ke ï'rsua **yebase dekama** new.
Lit: *Of football, from her, more weaker he is.*	በእግር ኳስ እርሱ ከእርሷ የባሰ ደካማ ነው::
Crime has become worse.	Wenjel **metfo** iyehone new.
Lit: Crime bad become has.	ወንጀል መጥፎ እየሆነ ነው::
You are the worst. (m)	betam met'fo neh.
Lit. You are very bad.	በጣም መጥፎ ነህ::

The word **ïnde** is also used to express *like* or *similar*. Both words are used between the nouns they are comparing:

Berhan is like Selam.	b'rhan **ï'nde** Selam new.	ብርሃን እንደ ሰላም ነው::

THE VERB *TO MISS*

In English, the verb *to miss* is used in several different ways. These are incongruous with Amharic and aren't translated the same way. Following are some examples of how to express *miss* in Amharic.

- If you are missing a person, use the verb **menafeq** / መናፈቅ.
- If you missed a bus, plane, or appointment, use the verb **mamlet** / ማምለጥ.
- If you missing a material item like a shoe or a dog, you can use **matat** / ማጣት meaning to search for. Alternatively, you can use **met'fat** / መጥፋት mean lost.

I miss **my mom.**	**ïnatien** nafekuat.	እናቴን ናፈኳት::
I miss my husband.	balien **nafekut.**	ባሌን ናፈኩት::
I missed the bus.	awtobisu **ameleteñ.**	አውቶቢሱ አመለጠኝ::
I am missing (searching for) my shoe.	*cha*mayien **atahut.**	ጫማዬን አጣሁት::
My dog is missing (**lost**).	wshayie **tefa.**	ውሻዬ ጠፋ::

63

SAYING ABOUT

In a previous section on prepositions it is shown that *about me / about you* etc is expressed using **s'le + pronoun**. In English, the word *about* has several meanings which you may want to express in Amharic. Here are some examples to help you directly translate phrases using *about*.

- **s'le** - usually is used to express *about* something (a book, film, person, etc).
- **akobabi** - means *about* or *around* something such as a number for comparison ($100, 32 degrees, 10 meters, etc).

What is the film **about**?	filmu **s'le** m'ndn new?	ፊልሙ ስለ ምንድን ነው?
The film is **about** Ethiopia	filmu **s'le** ityop*i*ya new.	ፊልሙ ስለ ኢትዮጲያ ነው::
Who are you talking about?	**s'le** man new ïyawerah yalekew?	ስለ ማን ነው እያወራህ ያለከው?
It's **about** $100.	meto dolar **akababi** new.	መቶ ዶላር አካባቢ ነው::

EXPRESSING *OR*

The word **weym** / (ወይም) is a direct translation of the word *or* and is used similar to English to indicate a choice between two or more things.

This **or** that?	yh **weym** ya?	ይህ ወይም ያ?
Black **or** white?	*t*qur **weym** nech?	ጥቁር ወይም ነጭ?
Tea **or** coffee?	shay **weym** buna?	ሻይ ወይም ቡና?

LISTING ITEMS

The Amharic equivalent of the word *and* is **ïna** (እና). It is used as a suffix to separate one or more words.

mother **and** child	ïnat **ïna** lj	እናት እና ልጅ
bread **and** tea	dabo **ïna** shay	ዳቦ እና ሻይ
cars **and** horses.	mekinoch **ïna** feresoch	መኪኖች እና ፈረሶች
I want eggs, milk, **and** bread.	ïnkulal, wetet **ïna** dabo ïfel'galehu.	እንቁላል፤ወተት እና ዳቦ አፈልጋለሁ::

The word for *also*, is **degmo** / ደግም or **betechemri** / በተጨማሪ.

I am **also** ill.	**degmo** / *betechemari* tamem'ku.	ደግም / በተጨማሪ ታመምኩ::
Also, we need butter.	**degmo** / **betec**hemari qbie ïnfelgalen.	ደግም / በተጨማሪ ቅቤ አንፈልጋለን::

by Brittany Franck

GREETINGS	Selamta	ሰላምታ
Welcome (m)	ïnkuan dehna metah	እንኳን ደህና መጣህ
Welcome (f)	ïnkuan dehna metash	እንኳን ደህና መጣሽ
Hello / Hi	selam / tadiyas	ሰላም / ታዲያስ
How are you? (m)	ïndemn neh?	እንደምን ነህ?
How are you? (f)	ïndemn nesh?	እንደምን ነሽ?
(alt) How are you (m)	dehna neh?	ደህና ነህ?
(alt) How are you? (f)	dehna nesh?	ደህና ነሽ?
How is your family? `	biete seb ïndiet new?	ቤተሰብ እንዴት ነው?
How's life?	h'ywet indiet new?	ህይወት እንዴት ነው?
How's it going?	ïndiet new?	እንዴት ነው?

| Fine / I am fine. | dehna / dehna neñ. | ደህና / ደህና ነኝ |
| Praise be to God | ïgzi'abhier ymesgen | እግዚአብሄር ይመስገን |

Note: You can generally say *How are you?* by saying *ïndemn* followed by the word for *You are*; **neh/nesh/nachihu**. For persons of respect, such as elders, you can use **dehna newot** (ደህና ነዎት?).

As an alternative to *How are you?* (ïndemn neh?) you can say **dehna neh / nesh** etc? This literally translates to *Are you fine?*

When saying *Good morning* you are literally asking *How did you spend your night?* (**ïndemn adersh**) or *Was your night fine?* **dehna aderk?** (ደህና አደርh?).

Good morning (m)	ïndemn aderk?	እንደምን አደርh?
Good morning (f)	ïndemn adersh?	እንደምን አደርሽ?
Good afternoon (m)	ïndemn walk?	እንደምን ዋልh?
Good afternoon (f)	ïndemn walsh?	እንደምን ዋልሽ?
Good evening (m)	ïndemn amesheh?	እንደምን አመሽh?
Good evening (f)	ïndemn ameshesh?	እንደምን አመሸሽ?
Good night (m)	dehna ïder	ደህና እደር
Good night (f)	dehna ïderi	ደህና እደሪ

How was your night? (m.)	ïndemn aderk?	እንደምን አደርh?
How was your night? (f)	ïndemn adersh?	እንደምን አደርሽ?
How was your day? (m.)	ïndemn walk?	እንደምን ዋልh?
How was your day? (f)	ïndemn walsh?	እንደምን ዋልሽ?
How was your evening?(m)	ïndemn amesheh?	እንደምን አመሽh?
How was your evening?(f)	ïndemn ameshesh?	እንደምን አመሸሽ?

Good bye (m)	dehna hun	ደህና ሁን
Good bye (f)	dehna huñi	ደህና ሁኚ
Have a good day (m)	dehna wal / melkam qen	ደህና ዋል / መልካም ቀን
Have a good day (f)	dehna way / melkam qen	ደህና ዋይ / መልካም ቀን
See you later.	behuala ïngenañalen.	በኋላ እንገናኛለን
I'm happy to meet you	sletewaweqn desteña neñ	ስለ ተዋወቅን ደስተኛ ነኝ
May God give you health	tiena ystlñ	ጤና ይስጥልኝ።
May God give you health (f)	tiena ys'tsh.	ጤና ይስጥሽ።
What is your name (m/f)?	s'mh (smsh) manew?	ስምህ (ስምሽ) ማነው?
What's her name?	s'mua man new?	ስሟ ማን ነው?

66

What's his name?	s'mu man new?	ስሙ ማን ነው?
My name is ____.	____ ïbalalehu .	____ እባላለሁ፡፡
name	sm	ስም
Pardon me please (m)	ïbakh yqrta adrglñ	እባክህ ይቅርታ አድርግልኝ፡፡
I forgot your name (f)	s'mshn resahut.	ስምሽን ረሳሁት

MAKING CONVERSATION

Where are you from? (m)	keyet neh?	ከየት ነህ?
What are you doing here?	ïzih mn t'seraleh?	እዚህ ምን ትሰራለህ?
Are you adjusting? (m)	ïyelemed'k new?	እየለመድክ ነው?
Are you adjusting? (f)	ïyelemed'sh new/?	እየለመድሽ ነው?
I'm adapting to it.	lemjalehu / tesmamtoñal	ለምጃለሁ/ተስማምቶኛል
How old are you? (m)	ïdmieh snt new?	ዕድሜህ ስንት ነው?
How old are you? (f)	ïdmiesh snt new?	ዕድሜሽ ስንት ነው?
How long have you been here? (m)	ïzih mn yahl gizie qoytehal?	እዚህ ምን ያህል ጊዜ ቆይተሃል?
How long have you been here? (f)	ïzih mn yahl gizie qoyteshal?	እዚህ ምን ያህል ጊዜ ቆይተሻል?
Where have you been? (m)	yet neberk?	የት ነበርክ?
Where have you been? (f)	yet nebersh?	የት ነበርሽ?
You've been missing? (m)	tefah.	ጠፋህ፡፡
You've been missing? (f)	tefash.	ጠፋሽ፡፡
I am here.	alehu.	አለሁ፡፡

BASIC PHRASES	meseretawi haregat	መሠረታዊ ሀረጋት
Yes / No	awo / aydel'm	አዎ / አይደለም
Can you? (m/f)	tchlaleh? tchyalesh?	ትችላለህ? ትችያለሽ?
Congratulations! (m/f)	ïnkuan des aleh! (alesh!)	እንኳን ደስ አለህ! (አለሽ!)
Do you agree? (m/f)	tesmamtehal? tesmamteshal?	ተስማምተሃል? / ተስማምተሻል?
Do you speak English_? (m)	ïng'lizeña tnageraleh?	እንግሊዘኛ ትናገራለህ?
Do you speak ___? (f)	____ tnageri'alesh?	____ ትናገሪአለሽ?
good / bad	t'ru / metfo	ጥሩ / መጥፎ
How do I find ___?	____ ïndiet ageñalehu?	____ እንዴት አገኛለሁ?
How do you say ___?	____ ïndiet ybalal?	____ እንዴት ይባላል?
However	yhun'na	ይሁንና
I am ___	____ neñ.	____ ነኝ
I am slowly learning	qes beqes ïyetemarku new.	ቀስበቀስ እየተማርኩ ነው.
I am not ____.	____ aydelehum.	____ አይደለሁም፡፡
I can ____	____ ïchlalehu	____ እችላለሁ

67

I cannot.	alchlm.	አልችልም፡፡
I don't care.	gd yeleñm.	ግድ የለኝም፡፡
I have___	___aleñ	____ አለኝ
I don't have___	___yeleñm	____የለኝም
I want___	___ïfelgalehu	____እፈልጋለሁ
I don't want ___	___alfel'gm	____አልፈልግም
I like ___very much	___betam ïwedalehu	___በጣም እወዳለሁ
I don't like ___	___alwedm	____አልወድም
I love ___	___afeqralehu	____አፈቅራለሁ
I speak___	ïnie___ïnageralehu	እኔ____ እናገራለሁ
I don't speak___	ïnie___alnager'm	እኔ____አልናገርም
I prefer___	ïnie ___ yshaleñal	እኔ____ይሻለኛል
It doesn't matter.	lew't yelewm	ለውጥ የለውም
It is ___	___ new	____ነው
It is not ___	___ aydelem	____ አይደለም
It is very good.	betam t'ru new.	በጣም ጥሩ ነው፡፡
like that	ïndeziya	እንደዚያ
like this	ïndezih	እንደዚህ
Okay	ïshi	እሺ
Please (m/f)	ïbakh / ïbak'sh	እባኩህ / እባክሽ
Speak slowly (m)	qes b'leh tenager.	ቀስ ብለህ ተናገር፡፡
Speak slowly (f)	qes b'lesh tenageri.	ቀስ ብለሽ ተናገሪ፡፡
Sure.	ïrgteña.	እርግጠኛ፡፡
Thank you	amesegnalehu	አመሰግናለሁ
Thanks to God.	ïgziabhier ymesgn.	እግዚአብሄር ይመስገን
There is ___.	___ale.	____አለ፡፡
You're welcome.	m'nm aydelem.	ምንም አይደለም፡፡
There is not / none.	yelem.	የለም፡፡
What are you doing? (m)	mn ïyaderegh new?	ምን እያደረግህ ነው?
What are you doing? (f)	mn ïyaderegsh new?	ምን እያደረግሽ ነው?

MORE BASICS

Are you ready? (m/f)	zgju neh? zgju nesh?	ዝግጁ ነህ? ዝግጁ ነሽ?
Are you sure? (m/f)	ïrgteña neh? ïrgteña nesh?	እርግጠኛ ነህ? እርግጠኛ ነሽ?
By the way...	be'negerachn lay...	በነገራችን ላይ...
Can I help you? (m)	lrdah wey?	ልርዳህ ወይ?
Excuse me. (Pardon me) (f)	yqrta adrgilñ.	ይቅርታ አድርጊልኝ፡፡

Forgive me (m).	yqrta adrglñ.	ይቅርታ አድርግልኝ።
I agree with you.	be'ante hasab ïsmamalehu.	በአንተ ሀሳብ እስማማለሁ ።
I believe...	...amnalehu	...አምናለሁ።
I am busy /I don't have time.	s'ra ybezabñal	ስራ ይበዛብኛል።
I am drinking.	ïyetetahu new.	እየጠጣሁ ነው።
I gave you. (f)	setchieshalehu.	ሰጥቼሻለሁ።
I know her / him.	awqatalehu / awqewalehu.	አውቃታለሁ / አውቀዋለሁ
I promised.	qal gebchalehu.	ቃል ገብቻለሁ
I can see it.	ytayeñal.	ይታየኛል
I will help you.(m)	ïredahalehu.	እረዳሃለሁ
I will wait for you. (f)	ïtebqsh'alehu.	እጠብቅሻለሁ።
I'm coming____.	____ ïyametahu new.	____ እያመጣሁ ነው።
I'm bringing ____.	____ lameta new.	... ላመጣ ነው።
I'm waiting.	ïyetebeqku new.	እየጠበቅኩ ነው።
if...	...kehone	...ከሆነ
if not...	...kalhone	...ካልሆነ
If I come...	kemetahu...	ከመጣሁ ...
If there is...	... kale	.... ካለ
if so	ïndih kehone	...እንዲህ ከሆነ
instead of ____	be ____mtk	በ ____ ምትክ
Bring beer instead of wine.	be'weyn fanta bira amta.	በወይን ፋንታ ቢራ አምጣ።
Its not a problem.	chgr yelewm.	ችግር የለውም።
Introduce me. (m/f)	astewawqeñ / astewawqiñ.	አስተዋውቀኝ / አስተዋውቂኝ።
Is it possible?	ychalal?	ይቻላል?
It is not possible.	aychal'm.	አይቻልም።
Let me think about it.	las'b'bet	ላስብበት።
Me too.	ïniem.	እኔም።
my favorite	yenie mrcha	የኔ ምርጫ
my opinion	yenie hasab	የኔ ሃሳብ
In my opinion...	ïndenie hasab	እንደኔ ሃሳብ
Not now.	ahun aydelem	አሁን አይደለም
One moment.	and gizie.	አንድ ጊዜ።
Sorry, I'm late.	s'le'zegeyehu yqrta	ስለዘገየሁ ይቅርታ
Thank you for helping me. (m)	s'le'redaheñ amesegnalehu.	ስለረዳሀኝ አመሰግናለሁ።
Thank you for helping me. (f)	s'le'redashñ amesegnalehu.	ስለረዳሽኝ አመሰግናለሁ።

69

Thank you for coming. (m)	s'le'me*ta*h amesegnalehu.	ስለመጣህ አመሰግናለሁ።
Thank you for coming. (f)	s'le'me*ta*sh amesegnalehu.	ስለመጣሽ አመሰግናለሁ።
Thank you for everything.	s'le'hulum neger amesegnalehu.	ለሁሉም ነገር አመሰግናለሁ።
Thank you	amesegnalehu	አመሰግናለሁ
Wait for me. (m/f)	tebqeñ / *te*bqiñ.	ጠብቀኝ / ጠብቂኝ።
Let us share.	ïnkafel.	እንካፈል።
Will you bring __? (m)	____ tame*ta*leh?	____ ታመጣለህ?
Will you help me? (m)	t'redañaleh?	ትረዳኝአለህ?
Is that suitable?	ymechal / ysmamal	ይመቻል / ይስማማል
That works for me.	lïnie ymecheñal	ለእኔ ይመቸኛል።
That doesn't work for me.	lïnie aymecheñm	ለእኔ አይመቸኝም።
What do you think? (m)	mn tasbaleh?	ምን ታስባለህ?

CONFUSION	g'ra megabat	ግራ መጋባት
I am confused.	g'ra gebtoñal	ግራ ገብቶኛል
Are you confused? (m)	g'ra gebtohal ïndie?	ግራ ገብቶሃል እንዴ?
Do you know... (f)	taw'qiyalesh?	ታውቂያለሽ?
Do you remember? (f)	tastawshalesh?	ታስታውሻለሽ?
Do you understand? (m)	gebtohal wey? / gebah?	ገብቶሃል ወይ? / ገባህ?
Do you understand? (f)	gebtoshal wey? / gebash?	ገብቶሻል ወይ? / ገባሽ?
Don't you remember? (m)	atastawsm?	አታስታውስም?
I didn't forget.	alresahum.	አልረሳሁም።
I don't know.	alawqm.	አላወቅም።
I don't understand.	algebañ'm.	አልገባኝም
I forgot.	res'chalehu	ረስቻለሁ።

70

You forgot.	res'tehal	ረስተሃል፡፡
I did not forget.	alresahum.	አልረሳሁም፡፡
I remember.	astawsalehu.	አስታውሳለሁ፡፡
I don't remember.	alastaws'm	አላስታውስም፡፡
I'm not sure.	ïrgteña aydelehum.	እርግጠኛ አይደለሁም፡፡
I know / I don't know	awqalehu / alawqm	አውቃለሁ / አላውቅም
I'm thinking	ïyasebku new	እያሰብኩ ነው
misunderstanding	ale megbabat	አለ መግባባት
Please repeat (f)	ïbaksh dgemiw.	እባክሽ ድገሚው፡፡
What did you say? (m)	mn alk?	ምን አልክ?
What does it mean?	yh mn malet new?	ይህ ምን ማለት ነው?
What is it?	mndnew?	ምንድነው?
Yes, I understand.	awo gebañ.	አዎ ገባኝ
You speak very fast.	betam beftnet new ymtaweraw.	በጣም በፍጥነት ነው የምታወራው

EMOTION	s'miet	ስሜት
affection	fqr masayet	ፍቅር ማሳየት
afraid	frhat	ፍርሃት
angry / *I am angry.*	ndiet / tenadjalehu.	ንዴት / ተናድጃለሁ
anxious	chnqet	ጭንቀት
boring / *It is boring.*	aselchi / yselechal	አሰልቺ/ ይሰለቻል
cry	leqso	ለቅሶ
despair	tesfa mequret	ተስፋ መቁረጥ
fear	frhat	ፍርሃት
fearless	defar	ደፋር
feeling	s'miet	ስሜት
frightening	asferi	አስፈሪ
funny	as'qiñ	አስቂኝ
happiness / joy	desta	ደስታ
hope	tesfa	ተስፋ
hopeful	balemulu tesfa	ባለ ሙሉ ተስፋ
hopeless	tesfa bis	ተስፋ ቢስ
laugh	saq	ሳቅ
love	fqr	ፍቅር
loneliness	bcheña	ብቸኛ
sadness	hazen	ሐዘን

71

scary	ye'miyasfera	የሚያስፈራ
smile	fegegta	ፈገግታ
stress	ch'nq / chnqet	ጭንቅ / ጭንቀት
stressful	aschenaqi	አስጨናቂ
tiresome	adkami	አድካሚ
unhappy	desteña yalhone	ደስተኛ ያልሆነ
worry	merebesh	መረበሽ
Are you crying? (f)	ïyaleqesh new?	እያለቀስሽ ነው?
Are you sad? (m)	az'nehal?	አዝነሃል?
Are you lonely? (m)	bcheña neh?	ብቸኛ ነህ?
Be happy. (m)	tedeset.	ተደሰት።
Don't cry. (f)	atalqsh.	አታልቅሽ።
Don't worry. (m)	atasb.	አታስብ።
I am angry.	teqotchalehu.	ተቆጥቻለሁ።
I am happy.	desteña neñ.	ደስተኛ ነኝ.
I feel happy.	des bloñal	ደስ ብሎኛል።
I am sad.	azñalehu.	አዝኛለሁ።
I am scared	ferchalehu.	ፈርቻለሁ
I am worried.	techenqie'alehu.	ተጨንቄአለሁ
That is funny.	des yemil new.	ደስ የሚል ነው።
That is interesting (fun)	yasqal / ygermal	ያስቃል / ይገርማል
You look happy today (m).	zarie desteña tmes'laleh.	ዛሬ ደስተኛ ትመስላለህ።
You look sad (f).	yazensh t'mesyalesh.	ያዘንሽ ትመስያለሽ።

'Mary and G'day' by Andrew Tadross

COLOR	qelem	ቀለም
black	*t*qur	ጥቁር
blue	semayawi	ሰማያዊ
brown	bunama	ቡናማ
gray	gra*cha*	ግራጫ
green	arenguadie	አረንጓዴ
orange	brtukanama	ብርቱካናማ
pink	roz	ሮዝ
purple	ham'rawi	ሃምራዊ
red	qey	ቀይ
white	ne*ch*	ነጭ
yellow	bi*cha*	ቢጫ

NUMBER	qu*t*r	ቁጥር
0 – zero	bado / ziero	ባዶ / ዜሮ
1 – one	and	አንድ
2 – two	hulet	ሁለት
3 – three	sost	ሶስት
4 – four	arat	አራት
5 – five	amst	አምስት
6 – six	sdst	ስድስት
7 – seven	sebat	ሰባት
8 – eight	s'mnt	ስምንት
9 – nine	ze*te*ñ	ዘጠኝ
10 – ten	asr	አስር
11 – eleven	asra and	አስራ አንድ
12 – twelve	asra hulet	አስራ ሁለት
13 – thirteen	asra sost	አስራ ሶስት
14 – fourteen	asra arat	አስራ አራት
15 – fifteen	asra amst	አስራ አምስት
16 – sixteen	asra sdst	አስራ ስድስት
17 – seventeen	asra sebat	አስራ ሰባት
18 – eighteen	asra smnt	አስራ ስምንት
19 – nineteen	asra ze*te*ñ	አስራ ዘጠኝ
20 – twenty	haya	ሃያ

21 – twenty-one	haya and	ሃያ አንድ
25 – twenty-five	haya amst	ሃያ አምስት
30 – thirty	selasa	ሰላሳ
32 – thirty-two	selasa hulet	ሰላሳ ሁለት
40 – forty	arba	አርባ
50 – fifty	hamsa	ሃምሳ
60 – sixty	sdsa	ስድሳ
70 – seventy	seba	ሰባ
80 – eighty	semanya	ሰማንያ
90 – ninety	ze*t*ena	ዘጠና
100 – one hundred	and meto	አንድ መቶ
156	meto hamsa sdst	መቶ ሃምሳ ስድስት
(one) thousand	(and) shi	(አንድ) ሺ
million	milyon	ሚሊዮን
billion	bilyon	ቢልዮን
first	ye'mejemerya	የመጀመርያ
second	huleteña	ሁለተኛ
third	sosteña	ሶስተኛ
fourth	arateña	አራተኛ
fifth	amsteña	አምስተኛ
both	huletum	ሁለቱም
single	and / we*t*	አንድ / ወጥ
double	drb	ድርብ
triple	sost ïtf	ሶስት እጥፍ
quadruple	arat ïtf	አራት እጥፍ
multiple	bzu gizie	ብዙ ጊዜ
one half	gmash / and huleteña	ግማሽ / አንድ ሁለተኛ
one third	and sosteña	አንድ ሶስተኛ
one fourth	rub / and arateña	ሩብ / አንድ አራተኛ
one tenth	and asreña	አንድ አስረኛ
one whole	and mulu	አንድ ሙሉ
all	hulum	ሁሉም
a lot	bzu	ብዙ
almost	a*t*egeb	አጠገብ
almost ready	ïyederese new	እየደረሰ ነው

already	huneña / yehone	ሁነኛ / የሆነ
finally	bemecheresha	በመጨረሻ
not yet	gena	ገና
previously	asqedmo	አስቀድሞ
recently	be'qrb	በቅርብ
Give me some time. (m)	gizie s'teñ.	ጊዜ ስጠኝ።
Give me some time. (f)	gizie s'chiñ.	ጊዜ ስጪኝ።

TIME EXPRESSIONS

What time is it?	snt se'at new?	ስንት ሰዓት ነው?
It is 10:00.	asr se'at.	አስር ሰዓት።
*It is a **quarter after** 10:00.*	asr se'at **ke'rub**.	አስር ሰዓት ከሩብ።
It is 10:30.	asr se'at tekul.	አስር ሰዓት ተኩል።
It is 10:45.	asr se'at ke'arbamst.	አስር ሰዓት ከአርባ አምስት።
It is a quarter to 2:00.	le'hulet se'at **rub guday**.	ለሁለት ሰዓት ሩብ ጉዳይ።
At ____ o'clock.	lk ____ se'at.	ልክ ____ ሰዓት።

The Ethiopian timetable is unique. It runs six hours off from traditional time norms used throughout the world. For example, people wake up at 1:00 in the morning, eat lunch at 6:00, and eat dinner at 12:00 in the evening. This would be the equivalent of 7:00AM, 12:00 noon, and 6:00 PM, respectively. Notice in the following examples, the time has been adjusted by six hours, but the time of day can be understood by the words for morning/afternoon before the time.

CONVERTING TIME

It is 10:00 **in the morning**.	**ketewatu** arat se'at. (4:00)	ከጠዋቱ አራት ሰዓት (4:00)
It is 3:00 **in the afternoon**.	**keqenu** zeteñ se'at. (9:00)	ከቀኑ ዘጠኝ ሰዓት (9:00)
Its 9:00 **in the evening**.	**kemsh'tu** sost se'at. (3:00)	ከምሽቱ ሶስት ሰዓት (3:00)
Its 1:00 **at night**.	**kelielitu** sebat se'at. (7:00)	ከሌሊቱ ሰባት ሰዓት (7:00)

To express minutes before or after the hour, **ke/ħ** (*from*) is used for after the hour, and **guday** (*until/remaining*) is used for before. The word **tekul** (ተኩል) means half hour (30 min); and **rub** (ሩብ) means a quarter hour. Use the following to express the time of day: **ketwetu** (ከጠዋቱ) – in the morning. **keqenu** (ከቀኑ) – in the afternoon. **kemsh'tu** (ከምሽቱ) – in the evening. **ke'lielitu** (ከሌሊቱ) – at night.

ETHIOPIAN TIME

| *It is 2:10.* | hulet se'at ke'asr. | ሁለት ሰዓት ከአስር። |

It is a **quarter** after 2:00. (2:15).	hulet se'at kerub.	ሁለት ሰዓት ከሩብ።
It is 2:30. (half past).	hulet se'at tekul.	ሁለት ሰዓት ተኩል።
It is a quarter to 3:00. (2:45).	rub guday le'sost.	ሩብ ጉዳይ ለሶስት።
At ___ --- ___ o'clock	lk _ --- _ se'at.	ልክ ___ ሰዓት፥

wall clock	yeg'dgda se'at	የግድግዳ ሰዓት
watch	ye'ï'j se'at	የአጅ ሰዓት

UNITS OF TIME	gizie melekiya	ጊዜ መለኪያ
second	sekend	ሰከንድ
minute	deqiqa	ደቂቃ
half hour	gmash se'at	ግማሽ ሰዓት
hour	se'at	ሰዓት
day	qen	ቀን
daily	beye qenu	በየቀኑ
every day	hulu qen	ሁሉ ቀን
week	samnt	ሳምንት
weekly	beye samntu	በየ ሳምንቱ
month	wer	ወር
monthly	beye weru	በየ ወሩ
year	amet	አመት
annual / yearly	beye ametu	በየ አመቱ
decade	asr amet	አስር አመት
era / generation	zemen / twld	ዘመን / ትውልድ
century	meto amet	መቶ አመት

CALENDAR	qen mequterya	ቀን መቁጠርያ
date	ïlet	እለት
yesterday	tnant	ትናንት
today	zarie	ዛሬ
tonight	zarie mata	ዛሬ ማታ
tomorrow	nege	ነገ
day after tomorrow	ke'nege wedya	ከነገ ወድያ
day before yesterday	ke'tnant wedya	ከትናንት ወድያ
day to day	qen beqen	ቀን በቀን
early	qedem b'lo	ቀደም ብሎ
every	hulum	ሁሉም

first	ye'mejemerya	የመጀመርያ
next week	ye'miqetlew samnt	የሚቀጥለው ሳምንት
last	ye'mecheresha	የመጨረሻ
last year	balefew amet	ባለፈው አመት
last week	yalefew samnt	ያለፈው ሳምንት
late	zegyto	ዘግይቶ
nowadays	be'ahunu gizie	በአሁኑ ጊዜ
up coming	mechi gizie	መጪ ጊዜ
soon	be'qrb qen	በቅርብ ቀን
Come early every time.	hul gizie qedmeh na.	ሁል ጊዜ ቀድመህ ና።

TIMES OF DAY	yeqenu gziyat	የቀኑ ግዜያት
daybreak	wegagen	ወጋገን
morning	tewat	ጠዋት
early in the morning	betam betewat.	በጣም በጠዋት
every morning	tewat tewat	ጠዋት ጠዋት
noon	ïkule qen	እኩለ ቀን
afternoon	ke'se'at behuala	ከሰዓት በኋላ
evening	mata	ምሽት
night	lielit	ሌሊት
At night	be'msht	በምሽት
midnight	ïkule lielit	እኩለ ሌሊት
time	gizie	ጊዜ

TIME RELATED		
period / time / duration	gizie / qoyta	ጊዜ / ቆይታ
latest / most recent	zemenawi / beq'rb	ዘመናዊ / በቅርብ
after	behuala	በኋላ
after this	kezih behuala	ከዚህ በኋላ

77

after that	keziya behuala	ከዚያ በኋላ
already	derese	ደረሰ
at the end	bemecheresha	በመጨረሻ
before	befit	በፊት
before that	keziya befit	ከዚያ በፊት
during	begizie	በጊዜ
future	wede fit	ወደፊት
last time	balefew gizie	ባለፈው ጊዜ
last	mecheresha	መጨረሻ
next	qetay	ቀጣይ
previous	yalefew / befit	ያለፈው / በፊት
later	behaula	በኋላ
then	keziya	ከዚያ
past	yalefe	ያለፈ
present time / currently	be'ahunu gizie	በአሁኑ ጊዜ
until	ïske	እስከ
Until I return	ïskem'meles	እስከምመለስ
until now	ïske'ahun	እስከአሁን
until then	ïskeziya	እስከዚያ
since then	keziyan gizie je'mro	ከዚያን ጊዜ ጀምሮ

START / FINISH	mejemeriya / mecheresha	መጀመሪያ / መጨረሻ
final	mecheresha	መጨረሻ
The end	ye'mecheresha	የመጨረሻ
At first	be'mejemeriya	በመጀመሪያ
beginner	jemari	ጀማሪ
beginning	ye'mejemeriya	የመጀመሪያ
Almost finished	tegebadual.	ተገባዷል።
Are you finished? (m)	cheresk?	ጨረስክ?
Are you finished? (f)	cheres'sh?	ጨረስሽ?
I am not finished.	alchereskum.	አልጨረስኩም።
Is it finished?	techersual?	ተጨርሷል።
Not finished.	alcheresem.	አልተጨረሰም።
I began ...	jemerku	ጀመርኩ
I begin ...	ïjemralehu	እጀምራለሁ
The first time	ye'mejemeriya gizie	የመጀመሪያ ጊዜ
The last time	ye'mecheresh gizie	የመጨረሻ ጊዜ

78

MONTHS	werat	ወራት
January	ṭr	ጥር
February	yekatit	የካቲት
March	megabit	መጋቢት
April	miyaziya	ሚያዝያ
May	gnbot	ግንቦት
June	senie	ሰኔ
July	hamlie	ሃምሌ
August	nehasie	ነሃሴ
September (first month)	meskerem	መስከረም
October	ṭqmt	ጥቅምት
November	hdar	ህዳር
December	tahsas	ታህሳስ
13th month (Ethiopian Calendar)	pagumien	ጳጉሜን

Note: The Ethiopian calendar is associated with the Orthodox/Coptic churches. There are 13 months, and the year runs 7-8 years behind the western calendar. When it is January 1, 2016 by the western calendar, it will be ሚያዝያ 4, 2008 in Ethiopia. Ethiopian Airlines provides schedules by the Western calendar.

DAYS OF THE WEEK	yesamntu qenat	የሳምንቱ ቀናት
Monday	seño	ሰኞ
Tuesday	makseño	ማክሰኞ
Wednesday	rebuï	ረቡእ
Thursday	hamus	ሃሙስ
Friday	arb	አርብ
Saturday	qdamie	ቅዳሜ
Sunday	ïhud	እሁድ
weekend	yesamntu mechresha qanat	የሳምንቱ መጨረሻ ቀናት

FREQUENCY	hunatie	ሁናቴ
once	and gizie	አንድ ጊዜ
twice	hulet gizie	ሁለት ጊዜ
always	hul gizie	ሁል ጊዜ
every time	ïyandandu gizie	እያንዳንዱ ጊዜ
frequently	betedegagami	በተደጋጋሚ

never	ftsum	ፍፁም
often	bzu gizie	ብዙ ጊዜ
seldom / rarely	alfo alfo	አልፎ አልፎ
sometimes	andandie	አንዳንዴ
time after time	beyegiziew	በየጊዜው
usually	bzuwn gizie	ብዙውን ጊዜ

GENDER	tsota	ፆታ
person / people	sew / sewoch	ሰው / ሰዎች
human	yesew zer	የሰው ዘር
male	teba'ït / wend	ተባእት / ወንድ
female	anst / siet	አንስት / ሴት
man / men	sew / wend //wendoch	ሰው/ ወንድ // ወንዶች
woman / women	siet / sietoch	ሴት / ሴቶች
men **and** women	wendoch ïna sietoch	ወንዶች እና ሴቶች
boy / boys	wend lj / wend ljoch	ወንድ ልጅ / ወንድ ልጆች
girl / girls	siet lj / set ljoch	ሴት ልጅ / ሴት ልጆች
boyfriend	yewend guadeña	የወንድ ጓደኛ
girlfriend	yesiet guadeña	የሴት ጓደኛ
Mr.	ato	አቶ
Mrs.	weyzero	ወይዘሮ
Ms.	weyzerit	ወይዘሪት

FAMILY	bieteseb	ቤተሰብ
husband	bal	ባል
wife	mist	ሚስት
father	abat	አባት
mother	ïnat	እናት
son / sons	wend lj / wend ljoch	ወንድ ልጅ / ወንድ ልጆች
daughter / daughters	siet lj / siet ljoch	ሴት ልጅ / ሴት ልጆች
brother / brothers	wendm / wendmoch	ወንድም / ወንድሞች
sister / sisters	ïht / ïhtoch	እህት / እህቶች
uncle	agot	አጎት
aunt	akst	አክስት
cousin	ye'akst lj / ye'agot lj	የአክስት ልጅ / የአጎት ልጅ
mother-in-law	amat	አማት
father-in-law	amat	አማት

brother-in-law	warsa	ዋርሳ
son-in -law	amach	አማች
daughter-in-law	mrat	ምራት
step son	ye'ïnjera lj	የእንጃራ ልጅ
step daughter	ye'ïnjera lj	የእንጃራ ልጅ
grandfather	ayat	አያት
grandmother	ayat	አያት
grandchildren	ye lj lj	የልጅ ልጅ
baby	h*ts*an	ህጻን
children	ljoch	ልጆች
family	bieteseb	ቤተሰብ
parent / parents	welaj / welajoch	ወላጅ / ወላጆች
relative	zemed	ዘመድ
twins	menta ljoch	መንታ ልጆች
best friend	ye qrb guadeña	የቅርብ ጓደኛ
friend	guadeña	ጓደኛ
friendship	guadeñnet	ጓደኝነት
neighbor / neighbors	gorebiet / gorebietoch	ጎረቤት / ጎረቤቶች
widow	mebelet	መበለት

MARRIAGE	**tdar**	**ትዳር**
bride	mushrit	ሙሽሪት
bridesmaids	yesiet miziewoch	የሴት ሚዜዎች
couple	*t*nd	ጥንድ
divorce	fch	ፍች
engagement	qelebet maser	ቀለበት ማሰር
fiancé (m/f)	ïcho*ñ*a	እጮኛ
groom	mushra	ሙሽራ
groomsmen	yewend miziewoch	የወንድ ሚዜዎች
married person	yageba sew	ያገባ ሰው
not married (m/f)	yalageba / yalagebach	ያላገባ / ያላገባች
spouse	yetdar guadeña	የትዳር ጓደኛ
wedding	gabcha	ጋብቻ
wedding ring	yegabcha qelebet	የጋብቻ ቀለበት
vows	qale-mehala	ቃለ-መሃላ

81

ROMANCE / LOVE	fqr	ፍቅር
Do you love me? (m)	t'wedeñaleh?	ትወደኛለህ?
Do you love me? (f)	t'wejiñalesh?	ትወጃኛለሽ?
Do you miss me? (f)	nafekush?	ናፈኩሽ?
I love you. (m)	ïwedhalehu.	እወድሃለሁ።
I love you. (f)	ïwedshalehu.	እወድሻለሁ።
I am in love.	fqr yzoñal.	ፍቅር ይዞኛል።
I admire you. (m)	adenqhalehu.	አደንቅሃለሁ።
I respect you. (m)	akebrhalehu.	አከብርሃለሁ።
Are you married? (f)	agbteshal?	አግብተሻል?
Are you married? (m)	agbtehal?	አግብተሃል?
Give me your number.	qutrshn s'chñ.	ቁጥርሽን ስጭኝ።
I have a boyfriend / girlfriend.	fqreña aleñ.	ፍቅረኛ አለኝ።
I am divorced.	fetchalehu.	ፈትቻለሁ።
I am married.	agbchalehu.	አግብቻለሁ።
I am not married.	alagebahum.	አላገባሁም።
I am single.	latie neñ.	ላጤነኝ።
I miss you. (m/f)	nafekeñ / nafeq'shñ.	ናፈከኝ / ናፈቅሽኝ።
You are beautiful. (f)	qonjo nesh. / tamriyalesh.	ቆንጆ ነሽ። / ታምሪያለሽ።
You are handsome. (m)	shebela neh. / tamraleh.	ሽበላ ነህ። / ታምራለህ።
You are sweet	tafach nesh	ጣፋጭ ነሽ፡፡

SEXUAL	gbre-sgawi	ግብረ-ሥጋዊ
abstinence	meqoteb	መቆጠብ
birth control	ye welid meqotateriya	የወሊድ መቆጣጠሪያ
circumcision	grzat	ግርዛት
condom	kondom	ኮንዶም
ejacuation	merchet	መርጨት
homosexual	gbre sedom	ግብረሰዶም
kiss / hug	mesam / maqef	መሳም / ማቀፍ
menstruation	yewer abeba	የወር አበባ
monogamy	mewesen	መወሰን
pregnant / pregnancy	ïrguz / ïrgzna	እርጉዝ / እርግዝና
lover / sweetheart	afqari	አፍቃሪ
rape	as'ged'do med'fer	አስገድዶ መድፈር
sexual intercourse	ye gbre-sga g'n'ñunet	የግብረ-ሥጋ ግንኙነት
unprotetected sex	lq yehone ygbre sga g'n'ñunet	ልቅ የሆነ የግብረ ስጋ ግንኙነት

English	Transliteration	Amharic
virgin	ljagered	ልጃገረድ
Use a condom. (m)	kondom te*t*eqem.	ኮንዶም ተጠቀም።
I don't want sex.	gbre-sga gnñunet alfelgm	ግብረ-ስጋ ግንኙነት አልፈልግም።

THE HEAD	*ch*nqlat	ጭንቅላት
beard	*ts*im	ጺም
cheek	gun*ch*	ጉንጭ
chin	age*ch*	አገጭ
ear / ears	joro / jorowoch	ጆሮ / ጆሮዎች
eye / eyes	ayn / aynoch	አይን / አይኖች
eye brows	q'nd'boch	ቅንድቦች
eye lash	sh'fash'ft	ሽፋሽፍት
forehead	gnbar	ግንባር
head	ras	ራስ
hair	*ts*egur	ጸጉር
jaw	mengaga	መንጋጋ
lip / lips	kenfer / kenaf'rt	ከንፈር / ከናፍርት
moustache	*ts*im	ጺም
mouth	af	አፍ
nose	afn*ch*a	አፍንጫ
skull	ye'ras q'l	የራስ ቅል
teeth / tooth	*t*rs / *t*rsoch	ጥርስ / ጥርሶች
throat	guroro	ጉሮሮ
tongue	mlas	ምላስ

THE BODY	gela (sewnet)	ገላ (ሰውነት)
abdomen	hod	ሆድ
ankle	qur*ch*m*ch*mit	ቁርጭምጭሚት
arm / arms	ql*t*m	ቅልጥም
arm pit	b'bt	ብብት
back	jerba	ጀርባ
bone	a*t*nt	አጥንት
breast / breasts	*t*ut / *t*utoch	ጡት / ጡቶች
buttocks	qi*t*	ቂጥ
calf	bat	ባት
chest	deret	ደረት
finger / fingers	ta*t* / ta*t*och	ጣት / ጣቶች

83

finger nail / finger nails	tfr / t'froch	ጥፍር / ጥፍሮች
hand / hands	ïj / ïjoch	እጅ / እጆች
hip / pelvis	dalie	ዳሌ
knee	gulbet	ጉልበት
leg / legs	ïgr / ïgroch	እግር / እግሮች
muscle	tuncha	ጡንቻ
neck	anget	አንገት
nipple	yetut chaf	የጡት ጫፍ
penis	yewend blt	የወንድ ብልት
scar	tebasa	ጠባሳ
shoulder	tkesha	ትከሻ
skin	qoda	ቆዳ
spine	akerkari	አከርካሪ
testicle	qolet	ቆለጥ
thigh	tafa	ታፋ
toe / toes	ye ïgr tat / tatoch	የእግር ጣት / ጣቶች
vagina	ye siet blt	የሴት ብልት
wrist	knd	ክንድ

ORGANS	**yewust hwasat**	የውስጥ ህዋሳት
bladder	fiña	ፊኛ
brain	angol	አንጎል
heart	lb	ልብ
intestine	anjet	አንጀት
kidney	kulalit	ኩላሊት
liver	gubet	ጉበት
lung	sanba	ሳንባ
stomach	cheguara	ጨጓራ
uterus	mah'tsen	ማህጸን

MEDICAL TERMS	**hkmna nek qalat**	ህክምና ነክ ቃላት
anesthesia	madenzezha	ማደንዘዣ
antibiotic	tsere bakterya	ጸረ-ባክተርያ
antiseptic	tsere bklet	ጸረ-ብከለት
bandage	fasha	ፋሻ
bed pan	shnt meqebeya	ሽንት መቀበያ
body temperature	ye sewnet muqet	የሰውነት ሙቀት

84

cure / medicine	medhanit	መድኃኒት
diagnosis	ye mrmera w*t*iet	የምርመራ ውጤት
doctor	hakim	ሃኪም
examination	mrmera	ምርመራ
fetus	*ts*n's	ጽንስ
food poisoning	ye'mgb memerez	የምግብ መመረዝ
health	*t*ien'net	ጤንነት
healthy	*t*ieneña	ጤነኛ
hospital	hospital	ሆስፒታል
massage	metashet	መታሸት
medication	hkmna	ህክምና
needle / injection	merfie	መርፌ
patient	beshteña / takami	በሽተኛ / ታካሚ
pharmacy	medhanit medebr	መድኃኒት መደብር
poisonous / toxic	merzama	መርዛማ
Red Cross	qey mesqel	ቀይ መስቀል
scale	mizan	ሚዛን
stitches	s'fiet	ስፌት
stretcher	beshteña meshekemya	በሽተኛ መሸከምያ
tablet / pill	ïnkbl	እንክብል
treatment	hkmna	ህክምና
to examine (v)	memermer	መመርመር
to get worse (v)	mebabas	መባባስ
to improve (v)	mashashal	ማሻሻል
to treat (v)	makem	ማከም

MEDICAL CONDITIONS	**ke hkmna gar yeteyayazu**	ከህክምና ጋር የተያያዙ
abortion	maswered	ማስወረድ
AIDS	AIDS	ኤድስ
allergic	allergic	አለርጂክ
bleeding	medmat	መድማት
bloody nose	men'ser	መንሰር
blood pressure	ye'dem g'fit	የደም ግፊት
bruise	mebelez	መበለዝ
cancer	neqersa	ነቀርሳ
chill	b'rd b'rd malet	ብርድ ብርድ ማለት
cleft lip	yeken'fer mesen*t*eq	የከንፈር መሰንጠቅ

85

cleft palate	yelanqa mesenteq	የላንቃ መሰንጠቅ
cold	gunfan	ጉንፋን
constipation	hod d'rqet	ሆድ ድርቀት
contagious	telalafi beshta	ተላላፊ በሽታ
cough	sal	ሳል
dehydration	d'rqet	ድርቀት
diarrhea	teq'mat	ተቅማጥ
digestion	mgb madqeq	ምግብ ማድቀቅ / መፍጨት
disease	be'shta	በሽታ
dizziness	rasn mesat	ራስን መሳት
fever	tkusat	ትኩሳት
food poisoning	ye mgb memerez	የምግብ መመረዝ
gastritis	ye cheguara hmem	የጨጓራ ህመም
goiter	inqrt	እንቅርት
head ache	ras mtat	ራስ ምታት
HIV	HIV	ኤችአይቪ
hunger	rehab	ረሃብ
infection	qus'l	ቁስል
itchy	ye'miyasak'k	የሚያሳከክ
lice	q'mal	ቅማል
malaria	weba	ወባ
migraine	kebad ye ras hmem	ከባድ የራስ ህመም
nausea	maqleshlesh	ማቅለሽለሽ
pain	s'qay	ስቃይ
poison	merz	መርዝ
pregnancy	irgzna	እርግዝና
rabies	ye'i'bd w'sha besh'ta	የእብድ ውሻ በሽታ
sexually transmitted disease	begbre sga gnñunet yemitelalef beshta	በግብረ ስጋ ግንኙነት የሚተላለፍ በሽታ
sick / ill	yetameme	የታመመ
sore	qus'let / hmem	ቁስለት / ህመም
sprain	welemta	ወለምታ
stomach ache	yehod qurtet	የሆድ ቁርጠት
swelling	ïbtet	እብጠት
surgery	qedo tgena	ቀዶ ጥገና
tapeworm	koso	ኮሶ
tuberculosis (tb)	sanba neqersa	ሳንባ ነቀርሳ
tumor	ïti	እጢ

tooth ache	*t*rs hmem	ጥርስ ህመም
vaccination	ktbat	ክትባት
wound	qus'l	ቁስል

BODILY FUNCTION	**ye sewnet tegbarat**	የሰውነት ተግባራት
belch / burp	magsat	ማግሳት
breath	tnfash	ትንፋሽ
fart	fes	ፈስ
give birth	mew'led	መውለድ
sleep	meteñat	መተኘት
snore	mankorafat	ማንኮራፋት
whistle	mafuachet	ማፉጨት
sneeze	masne*t*es	ማስነጠስ
yawn	mazagat	ማዛጋት

BODILY FLUIDS	**ye sewnet fesash**	የሰውነት ፈሳሽ
blood	dem	ደም
breast milk	yïnat *tut* wetet	የእናት ጡት ወተት
mucus	lgag	ልጋግ
pee / urine	shnt	ሽንት
poop / feces	ar / segera	ኣር / ሰገራ
pus	megl	መግል
saliva / spit	mraq	ምራቅ
sperm / semen	yewend yezer frie	የወንድ የዘር ፍሬ
sweat	lab	ላብ
tears	ïnba	እንባ
vagina fluids	yesiet merabiya akal fesash	የሴት መራቢያ አካል ፈሳሽ
vomit	te'wket	ተውከት

HEALTH COVERSATION

Are you sick? (f)	amoshal?	ኣሞሻል?
Are you better? (m/f)	teshlohal / tesh'loshal?	ተሽሎሃል / ተሽሎሻል?
I feel better.	teshloñal.	ተሽሎኛል።
I am sick.	amoñal.	ኣሞኛል።
He is not well?	dehna aydelem?	ደህና ኣይደለም?
He doesn't feel well.	*t*ru s'miet aysemawm.	ጥሩ ስሜት አይሰማውም።
I'm not feeling well.	*t*ru s'miet aysemañm.	ጥሩ ስሜት አይሰማኝም።

87

I have a burn.	yaq*t*leñal.	ያቅጥለኛል።
I have cut myself.	rasien qore*t*kut.	ራሴን ቆረጥኩት።
I feel dizzy.	rasien azoreñ.	ራሴን አዞረኝ።
I need to be examined.	bedokter metayet alebñ.	በዶክተር መታየት አለብኝ።
What hurts? (m)	m'nhn ysemahal?	ምንህን ይሰማሃል።
Take me to a clinic.	hekim biet wsdñ.	ሀኪም ቤት ውስዱኝ
I have pain here.	ïzih gar yameñal.	እዚህ ጋር ያመኛል።
I was sick.	tam'mie neber.	ታምሜ ነበር።
What's wrong with you? (m)	mn honehal?	ምን ሆነሃል?
Don't you feel well? (f)	dehna aydeleshm?	ደህና አይደለሽም?
Get well. (m/f)	*t*ena ys*t*'h	ጤና ይስጥህ.
Where is the pain? (m)	yet yamahal?	የት ያምሃል?
In my stomach.	hodien yameñal.	ሆዴን ያመኛል።
When did it start? (m/f)	mechie jemereh/sh?	መቼ ጀመረህ/ሽ?
After eating.	kebelahu behuala.	ከበላሁ በኋላ።
Take this for a week (m/f)	yhn le'and samnt wsed/j.	ይህን ለአንድ ሳምንት ውሰድ/ጅ።
Take rest. (m/f).	ïreft adrg/gi.	እረፍት አድርግ/ጊ።

DISABILITIES	**ye akal meguadel**	የአካል መጓደል
blind	ayne swur	አይነ ስውር
crippled	lms	ልምስ
deaf	denqoro	ደንቆሮ
deformity	me*t*amem	መጣመም
dementia	ye aïmro zgmet	የአእምሮ ዝግመት
disability	akal megudel	አካል መጉደል
disabled	akalu yegodele / akales'nkul	አካሉ የጎደለ / አካለ ስንኩል
dwarf	dnk	ድንክ
injured	qusleña / gudateña	ቁስለኛ / ጉዳተኛ
injury	gudat	ጉዳት
insane	yabede	ያበደ

88

limp (n)	ankasa	አንካሳ
paralyzed	yesewnet kfl simot / Sh'ba	የሰውነት ክፍል ሲሞት / ሽባ
wheel chair	maguaguazha wenber	በሽተኛ ማጓጓዣ ወንበር

SENSES — s'mietoch — ስሜቶች

It stinks (smells bad).	metfo shta yshetal	መጥፎ ሽታ ይሽታል
fragrance	me'aza	መዓዛ
hearing (v)	mesmat	መስማት
odor / smell	teren	ጠረን
sense	s'miet	ስሜት
sight / vision	iyta	ዕይታ
taste (v)	meq'mes	መቅመስ
touch (v)	men'kat	መንካት

BUSINESS TERMINOLOGY — ngd nek qalat — ንግድ ነክ ቃላት

asset	nbret	ንብረት
bank	bank	ባንክ
bankruptcy	wdqet	ውድቀት
boss	aleqa	አለቃ
budget	bejet	በጀት
business	ngd	ንግድ
cargo	yechnet	የጭነት
career	muya	ሙያ
cent	santim	ሳንቲም
change (money returned)	mel's	መልስ
change (small amount)	zr'zr	ዝርዝር
cheap	rkash	ርካሽ
coin	santim	ሳንቲም
commerce / trade	ngd	ንግድ
corporation / company	kubanya	ኩባንያ
credit	blcha	ብልጫ
customer	denbeña	ደንበኛ
customer service	yedenbeña agelglot	የደንበኛ አገልግሎት
debt	ïda	እዳ
debtor	bale ïda	ባለ እዳ
deposit	teqemach	ተቀማጭ
discount	qnash	ቅናሽ

English	Transliteration	Amharic
economy	yehabt ateqaqem	የሃብት አጠቃቀም
employee	serateña	ሰራተኛ
employer	aseri	አሰሪ
expensive	wd	ውድ
export	wede wch ye'milak ngd	ወደ ውጭ የሚላክ ንግድ
fee	k'fya	ከፍያ
import	kewch ye'migeba ngd	ከውጭ የሚገባ ንግድ
income	gebi	ገቢ
invention	fetera	ፈጠራ
investment (cognate)	habtn le'ngd sra masemarat	ሃብትን ለንግድ ስራ ማሰማራት
items	zr'zr ïqawoch	ዝርዝር እቃዎች
job / work	sra	ስራ
loan	bdr	ብድር
lucrative / profitable	atrafi	አትራፊ
manager	astedadari	አስተዳዳሪ
market	gebeya	ገበያ
money	genzeb	ገንዘብ
office	biro	ቢሮ
office building	yebiro hntsa	የቢሮ ህንፃ
price / cost / worth	waga	ዋጋ
profession	yesra aynet / muya	የስራ አይነት / ሙያ
professional support	bqat yalew dgaf / muyawi dgaf	ብቃት ያለው ድጋፍ / ሙያዊ ድጋፍ
profit	trf	ትርፍ
qualifications	bqat	ብቃት
quality	t'rat	ጥራት
receipt	dereseñ	ደረሰኝ
rent	kiray	ኪራይ
salary	demoz	ደሞዝ
shop	suq	ሱቅ
shopping	gbyt	ግብይት
shortage	ïtret	እጥረት
tax	gbr	ግብር
total	teqlala	ጠቅላላ
value	tqm / waga	ጥቅም / ዋጋ
valuable	teqami	ጠቃሚ

90

BUSINESS PHRASES	ngd nek ababaloch	ንግድ ነክ አባባሎች
Bring the bill. (m)	hisab s'teñ.	ሂሳብ ስጠኝ።
I bought	gezahu	ገዛሁ
I buy	ïgezalehu	እገዛለሁ
You will buy? (m)	tgezaleh?	ትገዛለህ?
Can you lower the price?	waga meqenes tchlaleh?	ዋጋ መቀነስ ትችላለህ?
Do you have ____? (m)	____aleh?	____አለህ?
Final price?	ye mecheresha waga	የመጨረሻ ዋጋ
Is this the real price?	tkkleña wagaw new?	ትክክለኛ ዋጋው ነው?
Give me the change.	mels s'teñ.	መልስ ስጠኝ።
How much is it?	snt new?	ስንት ነው?
You owe me.	yenie ïda alebh.	የኔ እዳ አለብህ።
I owe you.	yante ïda alebñ.	ያንተ እዳ አለብኝ።
It is cheap.	rkash new.	ርካሽ ነው።
It is expensive.	wd new.	ውድ ነው።

OCCUPATION	muya	ሙያ
What is your job?	s'rah mndn new?	ስራህ ምንድን ነው?
I am a _...__.	ïnie ____ neñ.	እኔ ____ ነኝ።
actor	tewanañ	ተዋናኝ
agent	wekil	ወኪል
architect	qeyash / arktiekt	ቀያሽ / አርከቴክት
artist	s'net 'beb balemuya	ስነጥበብ ባለሙያ
baker	gagari	ጋጋሪ
barber	tsegur astekakay	ፀጉር አስተካካይ
bartender	barista	ባሪስታ
bureaucrat / govt worker	ye'mengst serateña	የመንግስት ሰራተኛ
butcher	araj	አራጅ
builder / construction worker	gnbeña	ግንበኛ
businessman / merchant	negadie	ነጋዴ
carpenter	ïnchet s'ra / anatsi	እንጨት ስራ / አናጺ
chef	absay	አብሳይ
chemist	qemami	ቀማሚ
consultant / advisor	amakari	አማካሪ
cook	wet biet serateña	ወጥ ቤት ሰራተኛ
craftsman	ïde tbebeña	እደ ጥበበኛ
customer service	yedenbeña agelglot	የደንበኛ አገልግሎት

dancer	dansena / chefari	ዳንሰኛ / ጨፋሪ
dentist	yetrs hakim	የጥርስ ሃኪም
doctor (medical)	hakim / dokter	ሃኪም / ዶክተር
driver	shofier	ሾፈር
electrician	ieliektrik serateña	ኤሌክትሪክ ሰራተኛ
engineer	mehandis	መሃንዲስ
entrepreneur	s'ra fetari	ስራ ፈጣሪ
farmer / peasant	geberie	ገበሬ
fisherman	asa atmaj	አሳ አጥማጅ
gardener	atklteña	አትክልተኛ
guard	zebeña	ዘበኛ
hunter	adañ	አዳኝ
interpreter	asterguami	አስተርጓሚ
judge	daña	ዳኛ
lawyer	tebeqa	ጠበቃ
mason	gnbeña	ግንበኛ
mechanic	mekanik	መካኒክ
merchant	negadie	ነጋዴ
midwife	awalaj	አዋላጅ
musician	muziqeña	ሙዚቀኛ
nurse	ners	ነርስ
organizer	azegaj	አዘጋጅ
painter	qelem qebi	ቀለም ቀቢ
peace corps	yeselam guad	የሰላ ም3ድ
pilot (airplane)	awroplan abrari	አውሮፕላን አብራሪ
plumber	buanbua serateña	ቧንቧ ሰራተኛ
politician	poletikeña	ፖለቲከኛ
prostitute	sietña adari	ሴትኛ አዳሪ
repair man	tgena serateña	ጥገና ሰራተኛ
retirement / retired	trota	ጥሮታ
salesman	shach	ሻጭ
secretary	tsehafi	ፀሃፊ
servant (domestic worker)	yebiet serateña	የቤት ሰራተኛ
shepherd	ïreña	እረኛ
singer	zefañ	ዘፋኝ
shopkeeper	suq tebaqi	ሱቅ ጠባቂ
tailor	lbs sefi	ልብስ ስፊ

92

teacher	astemari	አስተማሪ
trainer	aseltañ	አሰልጣኝ
translator	terguami	ተርጓሚ
veterinarian	ye ïns'sat hakim	የእንስሳት ሃኪም
volunteer	bego feqadeña	በጎ ፈቃደኛ
weaver	shemanie	ሸማኔ
worker	serateña	ሰራተኛ
writer / author	tsehafi / derasi	ጸሃፊ / ደራሲ

FIELD OF STUDY	**ye tnat aynet**	**የጥናት አይነት**
architecture	s'ne hntsa	ስነ-ህንፃ
agriculture	gbrna	ግብርና
art	s'ne tbeb	ስነ-ጥበብ
biology	s'ne hiwet	ስነ-ህወት
business	ngd	ንግድ
chemistry	s'ne qmema	ስነ-ቅመማ
communication / language	megbabiya / quanqua	መግባቢያ / ቋንቋ
design	ndf	ንድፍ
economics	ngd	ንግድ
engineering	mhndsna	ምህንድስና
English	ïnglizeña quanqua	እንግሊዘኛ ቋንቋ
geography	s'ne mh'dar	ስነ-ምህዳር
history	tarik	ታሪክ
law / civics	hg / s'ne hg	ህግ / ስነ-ህግ
management	astedader	አስተዳደር
math	hisab	ሂሳብ
medicine	hkmna	ህክምና
natural resources	yetefet 'ro habt	የተፈጥሮ ሃብት
nursing	nersing	ነርሲንግ
philosophy	flsfna	ፍልስፍና
physics	fiziks	ፊዚክስ
political science	poletikal sayns	ፖለቲካል ሳይንስ
psychology	s'ne lbona	ስነ-ልቦና
sociology	ye'mahbereseb tnat	የማህበረሰብ ጥናት
science	sayns	ሳይንስ
teaching	memh'rnet	መምሀርነት

EDUCATION	tmhrt	ትምህርት
answer	mels	መልስ
assignment	ye'm'db s'ra	የምድብ ስራ
attention / concentration	tkuret	ትኩረት
behavior / character	tsebay / bah'ri	ፀባይ / ባህሪ
book	mets'haf	መፅሃፍ
break / rest	ïreft	እረፍት
chalk	temenie	ጠመኔ
class room	memariya kfl	መማርያ ከፍል
class work	yekfl s'ra	የከፍል ስራ
college	koliej	ኮሊጅ
discipline	s'ne sr'at / teg'sats	ስነ-ስርአት / ተግሳጽ
graduation	mreqa	ምረቃ
homework	yebiet sra	የቤት ስራ
knowledge	ïwqet	እውቀት
library	biete metsa'heft	ቤተ መፃህፍት
memorization	matnat	ማጥናት
notebook	debter	ደብተር
page	gets	ገፅ
paper	wereqet	ወረቀት
pen	ïskripto	ስክርፒቶ
pencil	ïrsas	እርሳስ
principal (head teacher)	r'ïse mem'hr	ርዕስ መምህር
question	tyaqie	ጥያቄ
school	tmhrt biet	ትምህርት ቤት
scissors	meqes	መቀስ
student	temari	ተማሪ
study (v)	mat'nat	ማጥናት
teach (v)	mastemar	ማስተማር
test	fetena	ፈተና
uneducated	yaltemare	ያልተማረ
wisdom	tsega	ፀጋ

I have a question.	*t*yaqie aleñ.	ጥያቄ አለኝ።
What is your question?	*t'*yaqieh m'ndn new?	ጥያቄህ ምንድን ነው?
*I **learned** Amharic.*	amarña **temarku.**	አማርኛ ተማርኩ።
I will learn Tigrinya.	tgrña ïmaralehu.	ትግርኛ እማራለሁ።

I teach English.	ïnglizeña **astemralehu.**	እንግሊዘኛ አስተምራለሁ።

BUILDING MATERIALS	yehn*t*sa mesariyawoch	የህንፃ እቃ መሳሪያዎች
asphalt	rienj / asfalt	ሬንጅ / አስፋልት
block / brick	blokiet	ብሎኬት
ceramic	ïb'nebered	እብነበረድ
concrete (dry)	dereq siminto	ደረቅ ሲሚንቶ
concrete (wet) - mortar	ïr*t*b siminto	እርጥብ ሲሚንቶ
construction	gnbata	ግንባታ
bronze	nehas	ነሃስ
copper	medab	መዳብ
glass	*t*ermus	ጠርሙስ
glue	ma*t*abeqiya	ማጣበቂያ
gravel	*t*ete*r*	ጠጠር
metal	b'ret	ብረት
pipe	tubo	ቱቦ
plastic	goma	ጎማ
rebar	ye'armata b'ret	የአርማታ ብረት
rock / stone	alet	አለት
sand	ashewa	አሸዋ
string	gemed	ገመድ
The project is complete.	projektu te*t*enaqual.	ፕሮጀክቱ ተጠናቋል።
The project is not complete.	projektu alte*t*enaqeqem.	ፕሮጀክቱ አልተጠናቀቀም።

TOOLS	mesariyawoch	መሳሪያዎች
axe	fas / me*t*'rebiya	ፋስ / መጥረቢያ
bucket	baldi	ባልዲ
hammer	medosha	መዶሻ
ladder	meselal	መሰላል
nail	mismar	ሚስማር
pliers	pinsa	ፒንሳ
saw	megaz	መጋዝ
screw	b'lon	ብሎን
screw driver	b'lon mefcha	ብሎን መፍቻ
shovel	akafa	አካፋ
sickle	ma*ch*d	ማጭድ
wrench	bulen mef'cha	ቡለን መፍቻ

95

TRANSPORTATION	meguaguazha	መጓጓዣ
arrive (v)	med'res	መድረስ
arrival	medresha	መድረሻ
bridge	dldy	ድልድይ
depart	menesha	መነሻ
destination	medresha bota	መድረሻ ቦታ
flight	berera	በረራ
delay	mezegyet	መዘግየት
journey	guzo	ጉዞ
landing	mewred / meriet menkat	መውረድ / መሬት መንካት
passenger	tesafari	ተሳፋሪ
path	menged	መንገድ
public transportation	yeh'zb mamelalesha	የህዝብ ማመላለሻ
road	menged / godana	መንገድ / ጎዳና
seat	meqemecha	መቀመጫ
short cut	aquarach	አቋራጭ
take off	menesat / mebrer	መነሳት / መብረር
toll road	yek'fya menged	የከፍያ መንገድ
traffic	t'rafik	ትራፊክ
traffic jam	ye'menged mechenaneq	የመንገድ መጨናነቅ
transportation	meguaguazha	መጓጓዣ
tunnel	metelalefiya / washa	መተላለፊያ / ዋሻ

VEHICLES	ye'meguaguazha zediewoch	የመጓጓዣ ዘዴዎች
airplane	awroplan	አውሮፕላን
bicycle	bskliet	ብስክሌት
boat	jelba	ጀልባ
bus / minibus	awtobs / minibas	አውቶብስ / ሚኒባስ
car / automobile	mekina	መኪና
horse cart	gari	ጋሪ
pickup truck	kamiyon	ካሚዮን
ship	merkeb	መርከብ
taxi	tak'si	ታክሲ
train	babur	ባቡር
truck	yech'net mekina	የጭነት መኪና

The word *taxi* can mean the blue or yellow cars that are used for private transportation (usually a rickety Toyota Corolla or a Lada). But taxi also means the public transportation line taxis (minibuses) that are on fixed routes.

BUS TERMINOLOGY

bus station	awtobus *ta*biya / menahariya	አውቶቡስ ጣብያ / መናሃሪያ
seat	meqeme*cha*	መቀመጫ
slowly	beqesta / bezgta	በቀስታ / በዝግታ
slow	qes / rega / zg	ቀስ / ረጋ / ዝግ
Stop. (get off bus)	weraj!	ወራጅ
Do you go to____? (m)	wede____t'hiedaleh?	ወደ____ትሄዳለህ?
Is there a space?	bota ale?	ቦታ አለ?
(Please) drive slowly.	(ïbakh) qes bleh nda.	(እባኩህ) ቀስ ብለህ ንዳ።
What time does it depart?	snt se'*at* ynesal?	ስንት ሰዓት ይነሳል?
What time does it arrive?	snt se'*at* ydersal?	ስንት ሰዓት ይደርሳል?
Watch out!	temelket!	ተመልከት!
Slow down!	qes bel!	ቀስ በል!

AUTOMOBILE TERMINOLOGY

automatic (shift)	aw'tomatik	አውቶማቲክ
standard / stick shift	ba'lemarsh	ባለማርሽ
brake	frien	ፍሬን
break down	blsht	ብልሽት
car	mekina	መኪና
car accident	ye'mekina adega	የመኪና አደጋ
car owner	bale mekina	ባለ መኪና
crack	sn*t*q	ስንጥቅ
engine	moter	ሞተር
flat tire	yetenefese goma	የተነፈሰ ጎማ
hood	kofen	ኮፈን
gasoline	naf*ta*	ናፍጣ
gas station	nedaj madeya	ነዳጅ ማደያ
motor	moter	ሞተር
speed	f*t*net	ፍጥነት
tire	goma	ጎማ
trunk	sa*t*'n	ሳጥን
wheel	cherkyo / ye'mishkereker	ቸርኪዮ / የሚሽከረከር
wind shield	parab'rie*tsa*	ፓራብሪጻ

TOURISM	yeturist mes'hbnet	የቱሪስት መስህብነት
hike	ye ïgr guzo	የእግር ጉዞ
hotel	hotiel	ሆቴል
map	karta	ካርታ
reservation	yetekelele bota	የተከለለ ቦታ
suitcase / luggage	shanta / borsa	ሻንጣ / ቦርሳ
tour	gub'ñt	ጉብኝት
travel	guzo	ጉዞ
traveler	mengedeña / teguazh	መንገደኛ / ተጓዥ
to take a picture	foto mansat	ፎቶ ማንሳት
print photo	foto matem	ፎቶ ማተም
souvenir	mastawesha	ማስታወሻ
Show me ___.	… asayeñ	… አሳየኝ.
Are you homesick? (f)	ager'sh nafqoshal?	አገርሽ ናፍቆሻል?
Can I take a picture of you? (f)	foto lanesash ïch'lalehu?	ፎቶ ላነሳሽ እችላለሁ?
Can you show me on map? (m)	karta lay ltasayeñ tchlaleh?	ካርታ ላይ ልታሳየኝ ትችላለህ?
Take a picture. (m/f)	foto ansa / anshi	ፎቶ አንሳ / አንሺ.
Have a good trip.	melkam menged.	መልካም መንገድ::
It is near / far.	ruq / qrb new.	ቅርብ / ሩቅ ነው::

by Brittany Franck

EATING	meblat	መብላት
breakfast	qurs	ቁርስ
lunch	m'sa	ምሳ
dinner	ïrat	እራት
bill	hisab	ሂሳብ
bowl	godguada sah'n	ጎድጓዳ ሳህን
café	buna biet	ቡና ቤት
carbohydrate	hey'l se*chi*	ሀይል ሰጪ
customer	denbeña	ደንበኛ
delicious food	*tafach* mg'b	ጣፋጭ ምግብ
appetite	ye'mgb f'lagot	የምግብ ፍላጎት
drink / beverage	me*tet*	መጠጥ
enough / sufficient	beqa / beqi	በቃ / በቂ
fatty food	*cho*mama m'gb	ጮማማ ምግብ
food / meal	mg'b	ምግብ
fork	shuka	ሹካ
glass	br*ch*qo	ብርጭቆ
hunger	rehab	ረሃብ
hungry	merab	መራብ
knife	bila	ቢላ
napkin	me*t*regia / soft	መጥረጊያ / ሶፍት
nutritious	yeteme*tate*ne m'gb	የተመጣጠነ ምግብ

99

packaged food	yetaxege m'gb	የታሸገ ምግብ
plate	sa'hn	ሳህን
protein	p'rotin	ፕሮቲን
restaurant	m'gb biet	ምግብ ቤት
servant	yebiet serateña	የቤት ሰራተኛ
snack	mekses	መክሰስ
spoon	mankiya	ማንኪያ
stew (wot)	wet	ወጥ
tip (gratuity)	gursha	ጉርሻ
vegetarian	at'k'l't temegabi	አትክልት ተመጋቢ
waitress / waiter	as'tenagaj	አስተናጋጅ
with	ke	ከ
without	yale	ያለ

When eating at an Ethiopian restaurant you will always be using ïnjera (እንጀራ), a spongy, sour, pan-cake like bread, as your utensil. Eat with your right hand only. You will use the ïnjera to scoop up *t*bs (ጥብስ) (grilled lamb, goat or beef), **shiro** (spicy chickpea stew), salad, or **wet** (ወጥ) (stewed sauces – actually sounds more like **wot**). Raw meat is a specialty called **kitfo**. If you don't want your food spicy, ask for **ali*ch*a**. If you do like spicy, put some **mi*t*mi*t*a** on it. This word also describes a spicy personality. **Berbere** is the spice used most in cooking.

Note that it is hard to find fresh meat on Orthodox fasting (*tso*m /ፆም) days. Make sure to eat only with your right hand as dictated by custom. If you are liked very much, your friends might feed you by hand!

BEVERAGE	me*t*et	መጠጥ
alcohol	alkol	አልኮል

100

alcohol free	alkol yelielew	አልኮል የሌለው
beer (cold)	(qezqaza) bira	(ቀዝቃዛ) ቢራ
bottle	termus	ጠርሙስ
bottle cap opener	mekfecha	መክፈቻ
bottled water	yetashege w'ha	የታሸገ ውሃ
can	tasa / qorqoro	ጣሳ / ቆርቆሮ
(hot) coffee	(tkus) buna	(ትኩስ)ቡና
honey wine	tej	ጠጅ
ice	beredo	በረዶ
juice	chmaqi	ጭማቂ
milk	wetet	ወተት
soft drink / soda	leslasa	ለስላሳ
tea / tea pot	shay / yeshay manqorqoriya	ሻይ / የሻይ ማንቆርቆሪያ
water	w'ha	ውሃ
wine	weyn	ወይን
without ice	yale beredo	ያለ በረዶ
with ice	keberedo gar	ከበረዶ ጋር

by Brittany Franck

COFFEE CEREMONY RELATED

coffee cup	yebuna s'ni	የቡና ስኒ
coffee pot	jebena	ጀበና
coffee organizer	rekebot	ረከቦት
cup	s'ni	ስኒ

fan (for fanning fire)	margebgebiya	ማርገብገቢያ
incense	ïtan	እጣን
incense holder	ïtan ïqa	እጣን እቃ
to make coffee (v)	buna maflat	ቡና ማፍላት
popcorn	fendisha	ፈንዲሻ
pottery	shekla	ሸክላ
stool	berchuma / duka	በርጮማ / ዱካ
snack	buna qurs	ቡና ቁርስ
tea spoon	yeshay mankiya	የሻይ ማንኪያ

EATING / DRINKING PHRASES

Are you hungry? (m/f)	rbohal? / rboshal?	ርቦሃል? / ርቦሻል?
I am hungry.	rboñal.	ርቦኛል።
I am not hungry.	alrabeñm.	አልራበኝም።
Are you full? (m/f)	tegbehal? / tegbeshal?	ጠግበሃል? / ጠግበሻል?
I am full.	teg'bie'alehu.	ጠግቤአለሁ።
Bring me / Give me (m)	amtalñ / amchilñ	አምጣልኝ / አምጪልኝ
Can I give you? (f)	lstsh?	ልስጥሽ?
Do you eat...? (m/f)	... t'belaleh? / ... t'beyalesh?	... ትበላለህ? / ... ትበያለሽ?
Do you have...?	____aleh?	____አለህ?
Do you like...? (m/f)	...t'wedaleh? / t'wejalesh?	...ትወዳለህ? / ትወጃለሽ?
Do you want? (m/f)	tfelgaleh? / tfelgiyalesh?	ትፈልጋለህ? / ትፈልጊያለሽ?
Give me. (m/f)	s'teñ / s'chiñ.	ስጠኝ / ስጪኝ።
Here it is.	y'khew	ይኸው
Here you are (take). (m/f)	ïnka /ïnki /wused / wuseji	እንኸ ውሰድ / እንኪ ውሰጂ
How much is it?	snt new?	ስንትነው?
I am thirsty.	temtoñal.	ጠምቶኛል።
I don't drink alcohol.	alkol altetam	አልኮል አልጠጣም።
I don't eat meat.	s'ga albelam.	ስጋ አልበላም።
I don't like.	alwedm.	አልወድም።
I don't want anything.	m'nm alfelg'm.	ምንም አልፈልግም።
I like ____.	____ ïwedalehu.	____ እወዳለሁ።
Is there anything to eat?	*ye'mibela neger ale?*	የሚበላ ነገር አለ?
More stew please. (m)	ïbakh ch'mare wet	እባክህ ጮማሬ ወጥ
Pass me ____.	____ aqebleñ.	____ አቀብለኝ።
Tastes good.	ytaftal	ይጣፍጣል
What do you want to drink? (m)	ye'miteta mn tfelgaleh?	የሚጠጣ ምን ትፈልጋለህ?

102

What do you want? (f)	mn tfelgiyalesh?	ምን ትፈልጊያለሽ?
What is there to drink?	ye'mi*teta* mn ale?	የሚጠጣ ምን አለ?
Yes, I like ____.	awo____ ïwedalehu	አዎ____ እወዳለሁ።
I am cooking.	mgb ïyeserahu new	ምግብ እየሰራሁ ነው።
Is the food ready?	mgb derswal?	ምግብ ደርስዋል?
Yes, it is ready.	awo derswal.	አዎ ደርስዋል።

INGREDIENTS	n*t*re neger	ንጥረ ነገርር
beef	yeberie s'ga	የበሬ ስጋ
bread	dabo	ዳቦ
butter	qbie	ቅቤ
cake	kiek	ኬክ
candy	keremiela	ከረሜላ
cheese	ayb	አይብ
chicken	doro	ዶሮ
cooking oil	ye mgb zeyt	የምግብ ዘይት
egg	ïnqulal	እንቁላል
fish	asa	አሳ
flour	duqiet	ዱቄት
honey	mar	ማር
injera	injera	እንጀራ
meat	s'ga	ስጋ
pork	asama	አሳማ
porridge	genfo	ገንፎ
salt	*che*w	ጨው
soup	shorba	ሾርባ
spice	qmem	ቅመም
stew / sauce	we*t* / s'go	ወጥ / ስጎ
sugar	s'kuar	ስኳር
yogurt	ïrgo	እርጎ

FOOD PREPARATION	ye'mgb zgjt	የምግብ ዝግጅት
baked	yebesele	የበሰለ
bitter	merara	መራራ
bland	mef*ch*et	መፍጨት
boiled	yeteqeqele	የተቀቀለ
cold / hot	qez'qaza / muq	ቀዝቃዛ / ሙቅ

container	mgb meyazha	ምግብ መያዣ
delicious / sweet	*tafach*	ጣፋጭ
fresh	tkus	ትኩስ
fried	yete*t*ebese	የተጠበሰ
kitchen	ma*i*d biet	ማዕድ ቤት
oven	mdja	ምድጃ
pan	me*t*besha	መጥበሻ
pot	ïnsra	እንስራ
raw	*t*'rie / yalbesele	ጥሬ / ያልበሰለ
refrigerated	yeqezeqeze	የቀዘቀዘ
ripe	yebesele	የበሰለ
salty	*che*w yebezabet	ጨው የበዛበት
unsalted	*che*w yelielew	ጨው የሌለው
spicy	yeteqememe / qmem yalew	የተቀመመ / ቅመም ያለው
stove	ye'aieliektrik mdja	የኤሌክትሪክ ምድጃ
stove (gas)	yegaz mdja	የጋዝ ምድጃ
sweet	tafach	ጣፋጭ

VEGETABLES	**atklt**	**አትክልት**
bean / pea	baqiela / ater	ባቄላ / አተር
beets	qey sr	ቀይስር
cabbage	gomen	ጎመን
cauliflower	abeba gomen	አበባ ጎመን
carrot	karot	ካሮት
chickpea / garbanzo	shmbra	ሽምብራ
corn	beqolo	በቆሎ
cucumber	kyar	ክያር
eggplant	deber'jan	ደበርጃን
garlic	ne*ch* shnkurt	ነጭ ሽንኩርት
lentils / pulses	msr	ምስር
lettuce	sela*t*a	ሰላጣ
mushroom	ïnguday	እንጉዳይ
okra	bamiya	ባሚያ
olive	ye'weyra f'rie	የወይራ ፍሬ
onion	shnkurt	ሽንኩርት
peanut	lewz	ለውዝ
peas	ater	አተር

104

pepper	berberie	በርበሬ
potato	dnch	ድንች
spinach	qos*ta*	ቆስጣ
tomato	timatim	ቲማቲም
pumpkin	duba	ዱባ
zuchini	zukini	ዙኪኒ

FRUIT	frafrie	ፍራፍሬ
apple	pom	ፖም
avocado	avocado	አቮካዶ
banana	muz	ሙዝ
berries	injori	ኢንጆሪ
cucumber	kyar	ክያር
grape	wey'n	ወይን
mango	mango	ማንጎ
papaya	papaya	ፓፓያ
guava	zeytun	ዘይቱን
orange	brtukan	ብርቱካን
raisin	zebib	ዘቢብ
watermelon	habab	ሃባብ
zuchini	zukini	ዙኪኒ

GRAINS	*t'*rie ïhloch	ጥሬ እህሎች
barley	gebs	ገብስ
oats	aja	አጃ
rice	ruz	ሩዝ
sorghum	mashla	ማሽላ
teff	*teff*	ጤፍ
wheat	sndie	ስንዴ

FARMING	ïrsha	እርሻ
agriculture	gbrna	ግብርና
agroforestry	den l'mat	ደን ልማት
animal enclosure	beret	በረት
conservation terracing	ïr'ken	እርከን
crop	ïhl	እህል
dried cow dung	kubet	ኩበት

cow dung	ïbet	እበት
dry land	dereq meriet	ደረቅ መሬት
dung / fertilizer	madaberiya	ማዳበሪያ
farm	ïrsha	እርሻ
farmland	ye'mitares meriet	የሚታረስ መሬት
fertile	lem	ለም
field	mieda	ሜዳ
food security	ye mgb wastna	የምግብ ዋስትና
garden	ye guaro atklt	የጓሮ አትክልት

hay	sar / drqosh	ሳር / ድርቆሽ
hay stack	ye gtosh kmr	የግጦሽ ክምር
infertile land	yal'lema meriet	ያልለማ መሬት
irrigated land	w'ha yeteta meriet	ውሃ የጠጣ መሬት
irrigation	bemesno w'ha matetat	በመስኖ ውሃ ማጠጣት
mill	wefcho	ወፍጮ
pasture / grazing land	gtosh / yegtosh meriet	ግጦሽ / የግጦሽ መሬት
pesticide	tsere-tebay	ጸረ-ተባይ
plow man	arash	አራሽ
seed	yetekl zer	የተከል ዘር
topsoil	delel afer	ደለል አፈር
weeding	marem	ማረም
yield / harvest	ye ïhl mrt	የእህል ምርት

ANIMAL TERMS	ïnsesa nek	እንሰሳ ነክ
animal	ïnsesa	እንሰሳ
endangered species	bemet'fat lay yale z'rya	በመጥፋት ላይ ያለ ዝርያ
endemic species	ager bekel z'rya	አገር በቀል ዝርያ
extinct species	yetefa z'rya	የጠፋ ዝርያ
feather	laba	ላባ
fish	asa	አሳ
hoof	yekebt tfr	የከብት ጥፍር
horn	qend	ቀንድ
livestock	ye qend kebtoch	የቀንድ ከብቶች
mammal	tut atbi	ጡት አጥቢ
mating	g'n'ñunet	ግንኙነት
reptile	tesabi ïns'sat	ተሳቢ እንስሣት
slaughter (v)	mared	ማረድ
species	z'rya	ዝርያ
udder	gt	ግት
wool	yebeg tsegur / suf	የበግ ፀጉር / ሱፍ

DOMESTIC ANIMALS	yebiet ïnsesat	የቤት እንሰሳት
baby cow (calf)	tja	ጥጃ
camel	gmel	ግመል
cat	dmet	ድመት
cattle	kebtoch	ከብት
chicken	doro	ዶሮ
cow	lam	ላም
dog	wsha	ውሻ
donkey	ahya	አህያ
goat	fyel	ፍየል

horse	feres	ፈረስ
kitten	g'lgel	ግልገል
mouse / rat	ay*t*	አይጥ
mule	beqlo	በቅሎ
ox	berie	በሬ
pet	lemada ïnsesa	ለማዳ እንስሳ
pig	asama	አሳማ
puppy	buchla	ቡችላ
sheep / lamb	beg	በግ

WILD ANIMALS	yedur ïnsesat	የዱር እንስሳት
ape	*tota*	ጦጣ
baboon	gurieza	ጉሬዛ
crocodile	azo	አዞ
elephant	z'hon	ዝሆን
fox	qebero	ቀበሮ
giraffe	qe*ch*nie	ቀጭኔ
hyena	jb	ጅብ
hippopotamus	gumarie	ጉማሬ
lion	anbesa	አንበሳ
monkey	zhenjero	ዝንጀሮ
rabbit	*t*nchel	ጥንቸል
snake	ïbab	እባብ
tiger (puma, cheetah, etc.)	nebr	ነብር
whale / shark	asa nebari	አሳ ነባሪ
wolf	tekula	ተኩላ
zebra	ye'mieda ahya	የሜዳ አህያ

SMALL ANIMALS	tnansh ïnsesat	ትናንሽ እንስሳት
ant	gundan	ጉንዳን
bat	yelielit wef	የሌሊት ወፍ
bed bug	t'huan	ትኋን
bee	nb	ንብ
bird	wef	ወፍ
butterfly	birabiro	ብራብሮ
cockroach	berero	በረሮ
dove	ïrg'b	እርግብ

108

flea	quncha	ቁንጫ
fly	znb	ዝንብ
frog	ïnqurarit	እንቁራሪት
lizard	ïnsh'lalit	እንሽላሊት
mosquito	yeweba tn'ñ	የወባ ትንኝ
snail	qend awta	ቀንድ አውጣ
spider	shererit	ሸረሪት
turtle	ieli	ኤሊ
vulture	tnb ansa	ጥምብ አንሳ
worm	tl	ትል

HOLIDAY	be'al	በአል
birthday	ye l'det qen	የልደት ቀን
celebration	akebaber	አከባበር
Christmas	gena	ገና
culture	bahl	ባህል
Easter	fasika	ፋሲካ
Ethiopian shoulder dance	ïsksta	እስክስታ
feast	dgs	ድግስ
gift	s'tota	ስጦታ
Happy Birthday!	melkam ldet	መልካም ልደት
Happy holiday!	melkam be'al / ïnkuan aderesachu	መልካም በአል / እንኳን አደረሳችሁ
Happy Easter!	melkam fasika	መልካም ፋሲካ
Merry Christmas!	melkam gena	መልካም ገና
New Year	adis amet	አዲስ አመት
tradition	bahl	ባህል
Ethiopian holidays	ye ityopiya be'alat	የኢትዮጲያ በአላት

RELIGION	haymanot	ሃይማኖት
amen	amien	አሜን
ancient	ye'tnt	የጥንት
angel	melak	መልአከ
atheist	haymanot yelielew	ሃይማኖት የሌለው
belief / trust	ïmnet	እምነት
Bible	mets'haf qdus	መፅሃፍ ቅዱስ
Catholic	katolik	ካቶሊክ

109

Christian	krstiyan	ክርስቲያን
church	biete krstiyan	ቤተ ክርስትያን
cross / crucifix	mesqel	መስቀል
fasting	tsom	ፆም
forgiveness	yqrta	ይቅርታ
God	ïgziabhier	እግዚአብሄር
heaven / paradise	genet	ገነት
hell	gehanem	ገሃነም
holy / sacred	yetebareke	የተባረከ
Islamic	ye ïslam	የእስላም
Jesus	ïyesus	የየሱስ
Jewish	yhuda	ይሁዳ
missionary	yehaymanot sebaki	የሃይማኖት ሰባኪ
monastery	gedam	ገዳም
moral	gbregeb	ግብረገብ
morality	gbregebnet	ግብረገብነት
mosque	mesgid	መስጊድ
Muslim	ïslam	እስላም
myth / story / legend	tarik	ታሪክ
Orthodox	ortodoks	ኦርቶዶክስ
pope	papas	ጳጳስ
prayer	tselay	ጸላይ
priest	qies	ቄስ
prophet	neby	ነቢይ
Protestant	protiestant	ፕሮቴስታንት
ramadan	remedan	ረመዳን
religion	haymanot	ሃይማኖት
Satan	Sey'tan	ሰይጣን
sin	hatyat	ሃጥያት
spirit	menfes	መንፈስ

by Brittany Franck

GOVERNMENT / KINGDOM	mengst	መንግስት
administration	astedader	አስተዳደር
against	teqawami / antsar	ተቃዋሚ / አንፃር
association / union	mahber	ማህበር
authority / power	sltan	ስልጣን
campaign	zemecha	ዘመቻ
capitalism	kapitalizm	ካፒታሊዝም
chairman	liqe menber	ሊቀመንበር
communism	komuniz'm	ኮሙኒዝም
conflict	gcht	ግጭት
corruption	musna	ሙስና
crown	zewd	ዘውድ
democracy	dimokrasi	ዲሞክራሲ
dictator	ambagenen	አምባገነን
district	wereda	ወረዳ
election	mrcha	ምርጫ
emperer	ngus	ንጉስ
firm / organization	drjt	ድርጅት

111

king	ngus	ንጉስ
leader	meri	መሪ
leadership	amerar	አመራር
mayor	kentiba	ከንቲባ
monarchy	zewdawi	ዘውዳዊ
NGO	mengstawi yalhone	መንግስታዊ ያልሆነ
politics	poletika	ፖለቲካ
prohibited	yetekelekele	የተከለከለ
propaganda	propoganda	ፕሮፓ,ጋንዳ
queen	ngst	ንግስት
regime	gezhiw	ገቢው
regulation	denb	ደንብ
respect	kbr	ክብር
speech	n'g'gr	ንግግር
socialism	mah'berawi	ማህበራዊ
stability	meregagat	መረጋጋት
the main issue	wanaw guday	ዋናው ጉዳይ
tyrant	chequañ	ጨቋኝ
vote	mrcha	ምርጫ
voter	merach	መራጭ
zone	akababi	አካባቢ

by Meron Bekele

SOCIETY	hbreteseb	ሀብረተሰብ
anarchy	sr'at alba	ስርአት አልባ
crowd	yesewoch chnqnq	የሰዎች ጭንቅንቅ
demonstration (peaceful)	selamawi self	ሰላማዊ ሰልፍ
discrimination	adlwo	አድልዎ
equality	ïkulnet	እኩልነት
freedom / liberty	netsanet	ነፃነት
freedom of speech	ye'menager netsanet	የመናገር ነፃነት
group	sb'sb	ስብስብ
human	ye'sew zer	የሰው ዘር
humanity	seb-awinet	ሰብ-አዊነት
human rights	ye'sewoch mebt	የሰዎች መብት
ignorance	maglel	ማግለል
individual	g'leseb	ግለሰብ
inequality	lyunet	ልዩነት
injustice	i-ft'hawinet	ኢ.-ፍትሃዊነት
justice	ft'h	ፍትሃዊ
labor	ye'sew hay'l	የሰው ሃይል
orphan	ye'mut lj / welaj alba	የሙት ልጅ / ወላጅ አልባ
orphanage	yewelaj alba merja tequam	የወላጅ አልባ መርጃ ተቋም
people	hzb	ህዝብ
population	yehzb bzat	የህዝብ ብዛት
protest	teqawmo	ተቃውሞ
protester	teqawami	ተቃዋሚ
racism	zereñ'net	ዘረኝነት
racist	zereña	ዘረኛ
revolution	abyot	አብዮት
riot / disturbance	rebsha	ረብሻ
rich / poor	habtam / d'ha	ሃብታም / ድሃ
segregation	belyunet mekefafel	በልዩነት መከፋፈል
sexism	tsotawi adlwo	ፆታዊ አድልዎ
stereotype	yejmla amelkaket	የጅምላ አመለካከት

113

MEDIA	megenaña	መገናኛ
argument	chqchq	ጭቅጭቅ
controversy	alemesmamat	አለመስማማት
controversial	ashami	አሻሚ
debate	krkr	ክርክር
event	hunieta	ሁኔታ
film / movie	film	ፊልም
freedom of press	yep'ries netsanet	የፕሬስ ነጻነት
issue	guday	ጉዳይ
journalist / reporter	gazieteña	ጋዜጠኛ
magazine	mets'hiet	መጽሄት
mass media	yeziena masercha	የዜና ማሰራጫ
news	ziena	ዜና
newspaper	gazieta	ጋዜጣ
scandal	werie / hamiet	ወሬ / ሃሜት
truth / honesty	ïwnet / haqeñ'net	እዉነት / ሃቀኝነት

IMMIGRATION / NATIONALITY	sdet / ziegnet	ስደት / ዜግነት
adoption	teqebaynet	ተቀባይነት
application	tgbera	ትግበራ
birth date	ldet qen	የልደት ቀን
birth place	yetwld bota	የትውልድ ቦታ
cheap labor	rkash gulbet	ርካሽ ጉልበት
citizen	ziega	ዜጋ
colony	qñ gzat	ቅኝ ግዛት
customs	gum'ruk	ጉምሩክ
ethnicity	b'hiereseb	ብሄረሰብ
immigration office	yesdeteñoch biro	የስደተኞች ቢሮ
flag	bandira	ባንዲራ
foreigner	yewch ziega	የዉጭ ዜጋ
foreign aid	yewch ïrdata	የዉጭ እርዳታ
identification	metaweqiya	መታወቂያ
immigrant	sdeteña	ስደተኛ

114

immigration	sdet	ሰደት
language	quanqua	ቋንቋ
national	agerawi	አገራዊ
nationality	ziegnet	ዜግነት
race	zer	ዘር
signature	firma	ፊርማ
surname (last name)	ye'abat sm	የአባት ስም
visa / passport	ylef wereqet	ይለፍ ወረቀት
xenophobia	t'lacha	ጥላቻ
I am American.	amerikawi neñ.	አሜሪካዊ ነኝ፡፡
I come from America.	ke'amerika metahu.	ከአሜሪካ መጣሁ፡፡
I live in America.	amerika ïnoralehu.	አሜሪካ እኖራለሁ፡፡

CONFLICT	**g*ch*t**	**ግጭት**
ally	degafi / tebabari	ደጋፊ / ተባባሪ
ammunition	*t*yt / mesariya	ጥይት / መሳሪያ
army	*to*r serawit	ጦር ሰራዊት
battle	wgiyaw	ውጊያው
bomb	fenji	ፈንጂ
bullet	*t*yt	ጥይት
combat (fighting)	wgiya	ውጊያ
coup d'état	mefenqle mengst	መፈንቅለ መንግስት
chaos	rebsha	ረብሻ
enemy	*te*lat	ጠላት
explosive material	teqe*tata*y qus	ተቀጣጣይ ቁስ
genocide	yehzb ïlqit	የህዝብ እልቂት
gun	*te*bmenja	ጠብመንጃ
hatred	t'lacha	ጥላቻ
invasion	werera	ወረራ
military / soldier	*to*r serawit / wetader	ጦር ሰራዊት
peace	selam	ሰላም
pistol	shgu*t*	ሽጉጥ
reconciliation	ïrq / megbabat	እርቅ / መግባባት
slavery	barnet	ባርነት
struggle	tgl	ትግል
sword	seyf	ሰይፍ
terrorism	shbr	ሽብር

115

terrorist	ashebari	አሸባሪ
torture	sqay	ስቃይ
victory	dl	ድል
war	*to*rnet	ጦርነት
weapon	mesariya	መሳሪያ
world peace	ye'alem selam	የአለም ሰላም

CRIME	**wenjel**	**ወንጀል**
burglary	zrfiya	ዝርፊያ
child abuse	yel'joch *t'*qat	የልጆች ጥቃት
criminal	wenjeleña	ወንጀለኛ
domestic / spousal abuse	yebiet w'st *t'*qat	የቤት ውስጥ ጥቃት
fraud	ma*ch*berber	ማጭበርበር
guilt / guilty	*t*fat / *t*fateñ'net	ጥፋት / ጥፋተኝነት
inmate / prisoner	ïsreña	እስረኛ
innocent	*t*fat yelielew	ጥፋት የሌለው
killer	geday	ገዳይ
murder	gdiya	ግድያ
police	polis	ፖሊስ
police station	polis *ta*biya	ፖሊስ ጣቢያ
prison / jail	wehni biet / ïsr biet	ወህኒ ቤት / እስር ቤት
prisoner	ïs'reña	እስረኛ
rape	as'ged'do med'fer	አስገድዶ መድፈር
robbery	zerefa	ዘረፋ
sexual abuse	*tso*tawi *t'*qat	ጾታዊ ጥቃት
shooting	tekus	ተኩስ
thief	lieba	ሌባ
threat	mas'ferariya	ማስፈራሪያ
vandalism	mawdem / ma*t*fat	ማውደም / ማጥፋት
victim	*t*qat yederesebet	ጥቃት የደረሰበት
violence	huket / b*t*b*t*	ሁከት / ብጥብጥ

116

LEGAL TERMS	hg nek	ሕግ ነክ
bribe	gubo	ጉቦ
contract	wl / kontrat	ውል / ኮንትራት
court	frd biet	ፍርድ ቤት
guilty	tfateña	ጥፋተኛ
innocent	tfat yelielew	ጥፋት የሌለው
illegal	h'ge - wet	ሕገ - ወጥ
legal	hgawi	ሕጋዊ
law	hg	ሕግ
lawyer / advocate	tebeqa	ጠበቃ
penalty	qtat	ቅጣት
punishment	qtat	ቅጣት
rule	denb	ደንብ
trial	yefrd biet guday	የፍርድ ቤት ጉዳይ
unjust	i-ft'hawi	ኢ-ፍትሃዊ
violation	t'set	ጥሰት

URBAN GEOGRAPHY		
bridge	d'ldy	ድልድይ
building	hntsa	ሕንፃ
capital city	wana ketema	ዋና ከተማ
city	ketema	ከተማ
city center (downtown)	mahal ketema	ማሃል ከተማ
community	hbreteseb	ሕብረተሰብ
demographics	s'nehz'b	ስነህዝብ
development	lmat	ልማት
dweller / resident	newari	ነዋሪ
factory	fabrika	ፋብሪካ

117

gutter	tbo	ትቦ
location	megeña	መገኛ
market	gebeya	ገበያ
monument	hawlt	ሃውልት
neighbor	gorebiet	ጎረቤት
neighborhood	sefer	ሰፈር
park	menafesha	መናፈሻ
place / location	bota	ቦታ
population density	yhzb bzatna kmcht	የህዝብ ብዛትና ክምችት
port	wedeb	ወደብ
rural	geter	ገጠር
shopping center	yegebeya maïkel	የገበያ ማእከል
side walk	ye'ïg'r menged	የእግር መንገድ
slaughter house	qiera	ቄራ
society / community	mah'bereseb	ማህበረሰብ
suburb	geter / ketema akababi	ገጠር / ከተማ አካባቢ
station	tabiya	ጣቢያ
swimming pool	ye'mewaña genda	የመዋኛ ገንዳ
train	babur	ባቡር
urban	ye ketema	የከተማ
urban plan	ye ketema ïqd	የከተማ እቅድ
warehouse	makemacha sfra	ማከማቻ ስፍራ
village	yegeter mender	የገጠር መንደር
villager	yegeter sew	የገጠር ሰው

118

ACCIDENT	mtfo agatami	መጥፎ ኢጋጣሚ
alive	yeterefe / yalmote	የተረፈ / ያልሞተ
ambulance	ambulans	አምቡላንስ
broken	yetesebere	የተሰበረ
damaged (messed up)	yetebelashe	የተበላሸ
coffin / casket	yeriesa satn	የሬሳ ሳጥን
collision	gcht	ግጭት
corps	riesa	ሬሳ
dangerous	adegeña	አደገኛ
dead	yemote	የሞተ
death	mot	ሞት
emergency	dnget	ድንገት
funeral	qebr	ቀብር
grief	leqso	ለቅሶ
injury	gudat	ጉዳት
life	hywet	ህይወት
passenger	tesafari	ተሳፋሪ
safe	astemamañ	አስተማማኝ
tomb / grave	meqabr	መቃብር
tragedy	asazañ	አሳዛኝ
tragic	askefi / asazañ	አስከፊ / አሳዛኝ
urgent	aschekuay	አስቸኳይ

SOCIAL ISSUES	yehbreteseb gudayoch	የህብረተሰብ ጉዳዮች
addict	suseña	ሱሰኛ
alcoholic	ye'alkol suseña	የአልኮል ሱሰኛ
alcoholism	ye'alkol	የአልኮል መጠጥ በሽታ
bad habit / addiction	metfo lmad	መጥፎ ልማድ
beggar	lemañ	ለማኝ
charity	bego adragot	በጎ አድራጎት
child labour	yeh'tsanat gul'bet	የህጻናት ጉልበት
cigarette	sigara	ሲጋራ
depression	dbrt	ድብርት
donation	s'tota / mewacho	ስጦታ / መዋጮ
drug (illicit)	adenzazh ïts	አደንዛዥ እጽ
drunk	sekaram	ሰካራም
gambling	qumar	ቁማር

119

homeless	biet yelielew	ቤት የሌለው
inequality	lyunet	ልዩነት
infant mortality	yeh*ts*anat mot	የህጻናት ሞት
illiteracy	mehaymnet	መሃይምነት
insane / crazy	ïbd	እብድ
mental health	ye'aïmro *ti*ena	የአእምሮ ጤና
poverty	d'hnet	ድህነት
prostitution	sieteña adarinet	ሴተኛ አዳሪነት
suicide	rasn ma*t*fat	ራስን ማጥፋት
unemployed (adj/noun)	s'ra a*t*	ስራ አጥ
unemployment	s'ra a*t*net	ስራ አጥነት

COMPETITION	**w'd'dr**	**ውድድር**
1st	andeña	አንደኛ
2nd	huleteña	ሁለተኛ
3rd	sosteña	ሶስተኛ
medal	miedaliya	ሜዳሊያ
gold	werq	ወርቅ
silver	br	ብር
bronze	nehas	ነሃስ
advantage	*t*qm	ጥቅም
average	mekakeleña	መካከለኛ
better	yeteshale	የተሻለ
best	mr*t*	ምርጥ
effort	*t*'ret	ጥረት
loser	teshenafi	ተሸናፊ
prize / award	shlmat	ሽልማት
winner	ashenafi	አሸናፊ
bad	me*t*fo	መጥፎ
worse	be*t*am me*t*fo	በጣም መጥፎ
worst	ïjg be*t*am me*t*fo	እጅግ በጣም መጥፎ
He is better.	ïsu yshalal.	እሱ ይሻላል።
It's the worst.	me*t*fow	መጥፎው
You are the worst.	metfow neh / nesh	መጥፎው ነህ / ነሽ።
You are the best (m/f)	mr*t* neh / nesh.	ምርጥ ነህ / ነሽ።

by Eldon Katter

SPORTS		ስፖርት
athlete	sporteña	ስፖርተኛ
audience	temelkach	ተመልካች
ball	kuas	ኳስ
basketball	qr*ch*at kuas	ቅርጫት ኳስ
coach	asel*ta*ñ	አሰልጣኝ
champion	ashenafi	አሸናፊ
endurance	*t*nkarie / *ts*'nat	ጥንካሬ / ፅናት
football	ïgr kuas	እግር ኳስ
fan	degafi	ደጋፊ
game	*che*wata	ጨዋታ
goal	gb	ግብ
kick (imperative) (m/f)	Mta / M*chi*	ምታ / ምቺ
marathon	maraton	ማራቶን
onlookers / spectators	temelkach	ተመልካች
opponent	teqawami	ተቃዋሚ
penalty	q*ta*t	ቅጣት
player	te*cha*wach	ተጫዋች
practice / exercise	l'm'm'd	ልምምድ
race / running	w'd'dr / ru*cha*	ውድድር / ሩጫ
referee	daña	ዳኛ
runner	rua*ch*	ሯጭ
score	masqo*t*er	ማስቆጠር
sport	sport	ስፖርት
stadium	stadiyom	ስታዲዮም
stamina	brtat	ብርታት
swimming	wana	ዋና

team	budn	ቡድን
tie	acha	አቻ
track and field	ye'trak ïna ye'mesk	የትራክ እና የመስክ
World Cup	ye'alem wan*cha*	የአለም ዋንጭ
wrestling	tgl	ትግል

Do you play football? (m)	ïgr kuas t*cha*wetaleh?	እግር ኳስ ትጫወታለህ?
I watch football.	ïgr kuas ïmeleketalehu.	እግር ኳስ እመለከታለሁ።
Who are you a fan of?	man'n tdegfaleh?	ማንን ትደግፋለህ?
Who is your favorite team? (m)	yeman degafi neh?	የማን ደጋፊ ነህ?
Who is playing?	manew ye'michawetew?	ማነው የሚጫወተው?
Ethiopia vs. Nigeria	ityo*pi*a ke nayjieriya	ኢ.ትዮጲያ ከ ናይጄሪያ

HOUSE	biet	ቤት
At ____ house.	be ____biet	በ ____ ቤት
bed	alga	አልጋ
bedroom	meñta kfl	መኝታ ከፍል
bench	agdami	አግዳሚ
broom	me*t*regiya	መጥረጊያ
carpet / rug	mn*t*af	ምንጣፍ
ceiling	kornis	ኮርኒስ
chair	wenber	ወንበር
compound	gbi	ግቢ
curtain	megareja	መጋረጃ
desk	ye *ts*'hfet *te*re*pi*eza	የፅህፈት ጠረጴዛ
door	ber / mezgiya	በር / መዝጊያ
drawer	mesabiya	መሳቢያ
enclosure / fence	kebabi / gbi / a*t*r	ከባቢ / ግቢ / አጥር

floor	welel	ወለል
furniture	yebiet qusaqus	የቤት ቁሳቁስ
hut	gojo	ጎጆ
house	biet	ቤት
house (mud walled)	yechqa biet	የጭቃ ቤት
house work	yebiet s'ra	የቤት ስራ
inside / interior	wst	ውስጥ
key / lock	qulf	ቁልፍ
kitchen	maïd biet	ማዕድ ቤት
land holder	baleyzota	ባለ ይዞታ
land lord / renter	akeray / tekeray	አከራይ / ተከራይ
living room	salon	ሳሎን
mansion	t'lq biet	ትልቅ ቤት
outside / exterior	wch	ውጭ
owner	balebiet	ባለቤት
possession	balebietnet	ባለቤትነት
property	nbret	ንብረት
rental house	yekiray biet	የኪራይ ቤት
roof	tariya	ጣሪያ
roof (corrugated metal)	qorqoro	ቆርቆሮ
room	kf'l	ክፍል
shelf	mederderiya	መደርደሪያ
stairs	dereja	ደረጃ
stool	duka	ዱካ
storeroom	ïqa biet	እቃ ቤት
table	terepieza	ጠረጴዛ
telephone	slk	ስልክ
wall	gdgda	ግድግዳ
window	meskot	መስኮት
yard (back)	guaro	ጓሮ

by Eldon Katter

BATHROOM	**shnt biet**	ሽንት ቤት
blade (razor)	mla*ch*	ምላጭ
bath tub	yeshawer biet genda	የሻወር ቤት ገንዳ
comb	mabe*t*eriya / mido	ማበጠሪያ / ሚዶ
cold water	qezqaza w'ha	ቀዝቃዛ ውሃ
warm water	leb yale w'ha	ለብ ያለ ውሃ
hot water	muq w'ha	ሙቅ ውሃ
mirror	mestewat	መስተዋት
plumbing	buanbua s'ra	ቧንቧ ስራ
shower	gela meta*t*ebiya	ገላ መታጠብ
sink	w'ha meqebeya	ውሃ መቀበያ
soap	samuna	ሳሙና
toilet	me*ts*edaja biet / shnt biet	መፀዳጃ ቤት / ሽንት ቤት
toilet paper	soft	ሶፍት
tooth paste	*t*rs samuna	ጥርስ ሳሙና
toothbrush	*t*rs brush	ጥርስ ብሩሽ
towel	fo*t*a	ፎጣ
water	w'ha	ውሃ
wet / moist	ïr*t*b	እርጥብ
clean	n*ts*u*h	ንፁህ
dust	abuara	አቧራ
hygenic	n*ts*'hnawn ye*t*ebeqe	ንፅህናውን የጠበቀ
unhygenic	n*ts*'hnawn yal*t*ebeqe	ንፅህናውን ያልጠበቀ
I washed...	...a*t*bie'alehu.	...አጥቤአለሁ።

124

| Go to the bathroom. (f) | wede shnt biet hji. | ወደ ሽንት ቤት ሂጂ። |
| Wash your hands. (m) | ïjoch'hn tateb. | እጆችሀን ታጠብ። |

SLEEP	**ïnqlf**	**እንቅልፍ**
alarm clock	qesqash se'at	ቀስቃሽ ሰዓት
blanket	brd lbs	ብርድ ልብስ
dream	hlm	ሀልም
insomnia	ye ïnqlf ïtot	የእንቅልፍ እጦት
mattress	f'rash	ፍራሽ
nap (short sleep)	t'nsh ï'nqlf	ትንሽ እንቅልፍ
nightmare	qzhet	ቅዠት
overnight	adar	አዳር
pillow	t'ras	ትራስ
sheet	ansola	አንሶላ
sleepy	ïnqlfam	እንቅልፋም
snoring (v)	mankorafat	ማንኮራፋት

Are you tired? (m/f)	dek'mohal? / dekmoshal?	ደክሞሃል? / ደክሞሻል?
I'm not tired.	aldekemeñm.	አልደከመኝም።
I'm tired.	dekmoñal.	ደክሞኛል።
I am sleepy.	ïnql'fie meta.	እንቅልፊ መጣ።

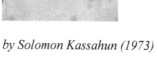

by Solomon Kassahun (1973)

CLOTHING	lbs	ልብስ
belt	qebeto	ቀበቶ
bra	*tu*t mas'yazha	ጡት ማስያዣ
bracelet	ambar	አምባር
braid	sh'ruba	ሽሩባ
cosmetics / makeup	yequnjna s'ra	የቁንጅና ስራ
cotton	*t't*	ጥጥ
diamond	almaz	አልማዝ
dress	qemis	ቀሚስ
earing	yejero gie*t*	የጆሮ ጌጥ
eye glasses	mene*t*sr	መነፅር
fashion	fashn	ፋሽን
fashion / style	fash'n	ፋሽን
hat (priest/Muslim style)	qob	ቆብ
hat / cap	kof'ya / bar'nie*ta*	ኮፍያ / ባርኔጣ
huge	tlq	ግዙፍ
jewelry	gie*ta*gie*t*	ጌጣጌጥ
laundry	lbs ma*t*ebiya	ልብስ ማጠቢያ
leather	qoda	ቆዳ
lingerie	yesiet yews*t* lbs	የሴት የውስጥ ልብስ
material / cloth	*che*rq	ጨርቅ
neck tie	karabat	ከራባት
necklace	ye anget habl	የአንገት ሃብል
pants	suri	ሱሪ
perfume	shto	ሽቶ
purse (women's)	yesiet yegenzeb borsa	የሴት የገንዘብ ቦርሳ
ring	qelebet	ቀለበት
sack / bag	borsa	ቦርሳ
scarf	shash	ሻሽ
shirt	shemiz	ሸሚዝ
shoes	*cha*ma	ጫማ
shorts	qum *'ta*	ቁምጣ
size	me*t*en	መጠን
skirt	gurd qemis	ጉርድ ቀሚስ
sock	kalsi	ካልሲ
suit	suf	ሱፍ
tattoo	nqsat	ንቅሳት

126

underpants	yewst suri	የውስጥ ሱሪ
wallet (men's)	yewend yekis borsa	የወንድ የኪስ ቦርሳ
wrist watch	ye ïj se'at	የእጅ ሰዓት
loose	leqeq yale	ለቀቅ ያለ
tight	tebeq yale	ጠበቅ ያለ
narrow	tebab	ጠባብ
new clothes	adis lbs	አዲስ ልብስ
old clothes	arogie lbs	አሮጌ ልብስ
wide	sefi	ሰፊ

What are you wearing? (m)	mn lebsehal?	ምን ለብሰሃል?
What did you wear? (m)	mn lebseh neber?	ምን ለብሰህ ነበር?
*I am **wearing** yellow pants.*	bicha suri **lebshalehu.**	ቢጫ ሱሪ ለብሻለሁ።
I will wear white socks.	nech kalsi adergalehu.	ነጭ ካልሲ አደርጋለሁ።
I'm wearing a red shirt.	qey shemiz lebshalehu.	ቀይ ሸሚዝ ለብሻለሁ።
I'm wearing black shoes.	tqur chama adrgie'alehu.	ጥቁር ጫማ አድርጌአለሁ።
I'm wearing brown pants.	buni suri lebshalehu.	ቡኒ ሱሪ ለብሻለሁ።
It fits.	l'k new.	ልክ ነው።
It doesn't fit.	l'k aydelem.	ልክ አይደለም።
Its not my size.	l'kie aydelem	ልኬ አይደለም።
Its nice.	t'ru new	ጥሩ ነው።
Let me try it on.	l'lekaw	ልለካው።
It's too big (small) for me.	le'inie betam t'lq / (t'nsh) new	ለእኔ በጣም ትልቅ / ትንሽ ነው።

* Note: The verb for wearing clothes is matleq/madreg. The verb for wearing socks is madreg.

masinqo the one string musical
instrument. ማሲንቆ

bv Solomon Kassahun

127

PHONE CONVERSATION

Call me. (m)	dew'l'lñ.	ደው·ልልኝ.
Can I call you? (m)	l'dewul'lh ïch'lalehu?	ልደው·ልልህ እችላለሁ?
Can I talk to ____?	____ menager ïch'lalehu?	____ መናገር እችላለሁ?
Hold just a minute.	and deqiqa qoy.	አንድ ደቂቃ ቆይ::
I am in ____.	____ new yalehut.	____ ነው· ያለሁ·ት::
I called you. (f)	dewuyielsh neber.	ደው·ዬልሽ ነበር::
I can't hear you. (f)	l'se'mash alchalkum.	ልሰማሽ አልቻልኩ·ም::
I don't hear you. (m)	alsemahuhm.	አልሰማሁ·ህም::
I left a message.	melïkt t'chalehu.	መልዕክት ትቻለሁ·::
I'm talking on the phone.	slk ïyanegagerku new.	ስልክ እያነጋገርኩ· ነው·::
I will call you. (f)	ïdewl'lshalehu.	እደው·ልልሻለሁ·::
There was no answer.	m'nm mels alneberem.	ምንም መልስ አልነበረም::
Who is speaking?	man l'bel?	ማን ልበል?
What did you say? (m/f)	m'n alk? / alsh?	ምን አልክ? / አልሽ?

NOISE / MUSIC   dm*ts* / muziqa   ድምፅ / ሙ·ዚቃ

disturbance / bother	rebsha	ረብሻ
drum	kebero	ከበሮ
guitar	gitar	ጊታር
loud	kef yale dm*ts*	ከፍ ያለ ድምፅ
music	muziqa	ሙ·ዚቃ
musical instrument	ye'muziqa mesariya	የሙ·ዚቃ መሳሪያ
noise	dm*ts*	ድምፅ
party	dgs	ድግስ
recording	meq're*ts*	መቅረጽ
scream / shout	*chu*het	ጩኸት
silence / quiet	tse't'ta	ፀጥታ
song	zefen	ዘፈን
sound	dm*ts*	ድምፅ
stereo	steriyo	ስተሪዮ
voice / volume	dm*ts*	ድምፅ
Lower the volume. (m)	dm*ts* qen's	ድምፅ ቀንስ

by Brittany Franck

ELECTRICITY / POWER	mebrat hayl	መብራትኀይል
bright	demaq	ደማቅ
charcoal	kesel	ከሰል
dark	chelema	ጨለማ
electric wire	ye'elektrik gemed	የኤሌክትሪክ ገመድ
gas	gaz	ጋዝ
kerosene	nech gaz	ነጭ ጋዝ
lamp	mebrat	መብራት
light	brhan	ብርሃን
light bulb	ampol	አምፖል
power outage	mebrat metfat	መብራት መጥፋት

power plant / station	hayl makemachana makefafeya	ሃይል ማከማቻና ማከፋፈያ
switch	mab'riya mat'fiya	ማብሪያ ማጥፊያ
Turn it on. (m)	mebratun abraw.	መብራቱን አብራው።
Turn it off. (f)	mebratun atfiw.	መብራቱን አጥፊው።

WATER RESOURCES	**yew'ha habt**	**የውሃ ሃብት**
contaminated / polluted	ye'tebekele	የተበከለ
dam	gdb	ግድብ
drinking water	ye'metet w'ha	የመጠጥ ውሃ
drainage	fesash meqotateriya	ፈሳሽ መቆጣጠሪያ
ground water	ye'meriet wst w'ha	የመሬት ውስጥ ውሃ
hose	ye'w'ha tubo	የውሃ ቱቦ
plumbing	ye'buanbua s'ra	የቧንቧ ስራ
spring / water source	ye'w'ha mnch	የውሃ ምንጭ
tap water	ye'buanbua w'ha	የቧንቧ ውሃ
water	w'ha	ውሃ
water pump	ye'w'ha matecha	የውሃ ማጠጫ
water supply	ye'w'ha srcht	የውሃ ስርጭት
well	ye'w'ha gudguad	የውሃ ጉድጓድ

POST OFFICE	**posta biet**	**ፖስታ ቤት**
address	adrasha	አድራሻ
box	satn	ሳጥን
envelope / mail	posta	ፖስታ
letter	debdabie	ደብዳቤ
message	melïkt	መልእክት
package	ïshg	እሽግ
stamp (postage)	tiembr	ቴምብር
I want to send this package.	yhn ïshg melak ïfelgalehu.	ይህን እሽግ መላክ አፈልጋለሁ።
I am waiting for a package.	and ïshg ïyetebeqku new.	አንድ እሽግ እየጠበኩ ነው።
Has my package arrived?	yenie ïshg der'sual?	የኔ እሽግ ደርሷል?

THE WORLD	**alem**	**አለም**
atmosphere	kebabi ayer	ከባቢ አየር
ground / land	meriet	መሬት
moon	chereqa	ጨረቃ
planet	planiet	ፕላኔት

sky	semay	ሰማይ
star	kokeb	ኮከብ
sun	*tse*hay	ፀሀይ
universe / outer space	hwa	ህዋ

DIRECTIONS / LOCATION	**aq*tacha* / bota**	**አቅጣጫ / ቦታ**
here	ïzih	እዚህ
from here	kezih	ከዚህ
there	ïziya	እዚያ
to there	ïs'keziya	እስከዚያ
far	ruq	ሩቅ
near	qrb	ቅርብ
Cross the road.	mengedun teshager.	መንገዱን ተሻገር።
Go this way.	bezih menged hid.	በዚህ መንገድ ሂድ።
I'm taking a walk.	ïyeteramedku new.	እየተራመድኩ ነው።
To the left.	wede gra.	ወደ ግራ።
To the right.	wede qeñ.	ወደ ቀኝ።
Straight ahead.	qet'tawedefit.	ቀጥታ ወደፊት።
Up there.	ïza lay.	እዛ ላይ።
Down there.	ïza tach.	እዛ ታች።
Over there.	ïza gar.	እዛ ጋር።
This way	bezih bekul.	በዚህ በኩል።
Where are you going? (m)	yet ïyehedk new?	የት እየሄድክ ነው?
Where are you? (f)	yet nesh?	የትነሽ?
Where did you come from?(f)	keyet me*ta*sh?	ከየት መጣሽ?
Where is the place located?	botaw yet new?	ቦታው የት ነው?
Where is it?	yet new?	የት ነው?
Where was he? (m)	yet nebere?	የት ነበረ?
Where was she? (f)	yet neberech?	የት ነበረች?
Where were you? (m/f)	yet neberk? / yet nebersh?	የት ነበርክ? / የት ነበርሽ?
Which direction is it?	beyet aq*tacha* new?	በየት አቅጣጫ ነው?
Which way is it?	yetñaw menged new?	የትኛው መንገድ ነው?

GEOGRAPHY	**melk'a mdr**	**መልከአ ምድር**
altitude / elevation	kef'ta	ከፍታ
border / limit	dnber / dar	ድንበር / ዳር
border / edge / boundary	awasañ	አዋሳኝ

131

continent	ahgur	አህጉር
country	ager	አገር
direction	aqtacha	አቅጣጫ
equator	ye'mdr wegeb	የምድር ወገብ
latitude	yekentros mesmeroch	የኬንትሮስ መስመሮች
location / place	megeña / bota	መገኛ / ቦታ
longitude	yekiekros mesmeroch	የኬክሮስ መስመሮች
map	kar'ta	ካርታ
region	akababi	አካባቢ
EAST	msraq	ምስራቅ
WEST	mïrab	ምዕራብ
NORTH	semien	ሰሜን
SOUTH	debub	ደቡብ
SOUTHWEST	debubmïrab	ደቡብምዕራብ

COUNTRIES

In Amharic, certain countries are pronounced similar to English. Some are quite different. Here is a sampling of country names in Amharic. If you don't know the Amharic version, try the English word with an 'Amharic' accent.

English	ye'ageroch sm	የአገሮች ስም
Africa (continent)	af'rika	አፍሪካ
America	amierika	አሜሪካ
Australia	awstraliya	አውስትራሊያ
Brazil	brazil	ብራዚል
Canada	kanada	ካናዳ
China	chayna	ቻይና
Egypt	gbts	ግብፅ
England	ïngliz	እንግሊዝ
Eritrea	iertra	ኤርትራ
Ethiopia	ityopia	ኢትዮጵያ
France	ferensay	ፈረንሳይ
Germany	jermen	ጀርመን
Greece	grik	ግሪክ
India	hnd	ሀንድ
Israel	ïsra'iel	እስራኤል

132

Italy	taliyan	ጣሊያን
Jamaica	jamayka	ጃማይካ
Japan	japan	ጃፓን
Kenya	kienya	ኬንያ
Korea	koriya	ኮሪያ
Netherlands	niezerland	ኔዘርላንድ
Nigeria	nayjieriya	ናይጄሪያ
Poland	poland	ፖላንድ
Russia	rusiya	ሩሲያ
South Africa	debub af'rika	ደቡብ አፍሪካ
Sudan	sudan	ሱዳን
Sweden	swidn	ስዌድን
Turkey	turk	ቱርክ

To indicate the nationality of a person one uses a suffix, typically **awi** for a male, and **awit** for a female.

English	Phonetic	Amharic
American (m)	amierikawi	አሜሪካዊ
American (f)	amierikawit	አሜሪካዊት
Brazillian (m)	brazilawi	ብራዚላዊ
Brazillian (f)	brazilawit	ብራዚላዊት
Chinese (m)	chaynawi	ቻይናዊ
Chinese (f)	chaynawit	ቻይናዊት
Eritrean (m)	iertrawi	ኤርትራዊ
Eritrean (f)	iertrawit	ኤርትራዊት
English (m)	ïnglizawi	እንግሊዛዊ
English (f)	ïnglizawit	እንግሊዛዊት
Ethiopian (m)	ityopiyawi	ኢትዮጵያዊ
Ethiopian (f)	ityopiyawit	ኢትዮጵያዊት
German (m)	jermanawi	ጀርመናዊ
German (f)	jermanawit	ጀርመናዊት
What country are you from?	keyet ager new?	ከየት አገር ነህ?
I am Ethiopian.	ityopiyawi neñ.	ኢትዮጵያዊ ነኝ።
I come from Ethiopia.	keityopiya metahu.	ከኢትዮጵያ መጣሁ

ENVIRONMENT	akababi	አካባቢ
barren	yeteraqote	የተራቆተ
biodiversity	bz'ha hy'wet	ብዝሃ ህይወት
climate change	ye'ayer nb'ret lew't	የአየር ንብረት ለውጥ
conservation	tbeqa	ጥበቃ
consumption	fjota	ፍጆታ
desert	bereha	በርሃ
desertification	berhamanet	በርሃማነት
ecosystem	akababiyawi sr'ate zmdna	አካባቢያዊ ስርአተ ዝምድና
environmental resources	akababiyawi habt	አካባቢያዊ ሃብት
forest	chaka / den	ጫካ / ደን
forestry	yeden tbeqa	የደን ጥበቃ
garbage / rubbish	qoshasha materaqemiya	ቆሻሻ ማጠራቀሚያ
lumber	tawla / ïnchet	ጣዉላ / እንጨት
log	gnd	ግንድ
deforestation	yeden meraqot	የደን መራቆት
reforestation	melso madan	መልሶ ማዳን
man-made	sew serash	ሰዉ ሰራሽ
natural	yetefetro	የተፈጥሮ
natural resource	yetefetro habt	የተፈጥሮ ሃብት
pollution	bklet	ብከለት
seedling	f'rie zer	ፍሬ ዘር
tree nursery	chgñ tabiya	ችግኝ ጣቢያ
habitat	menoriya	መኖሪያ
sustainable	qetaynet yalew	ቀጣይነት ያለዉ

134

wildlife	yedur arawit	የዱር አራዊት
wilderness	bereha / chaka	በረሃ / ጫካ
wildfire	seded ïsat	ሰደድ እሳት
wood	ïnchet	እንጨት

PLANTS — tekloch — ተክሎች

branch	qrnchaf	ቅርንጫፍ
bush / shrub	qutquato	ቁጥቋጦ
eucalyptus	bahr zaf	ባህር ዛፍ
exotic tree (non-native)	yebaïd hager zaf	የባእድ ሃገር ዛፍ
flower	abeba	አበባ
fruit tree	ye'frie zaf	የፍሬ ዛፍ
grass	sar	ሳር
indigenous tree	ager beqel zaf	አገር በቀል ዛፍ
juniper / cedar	td	ጥድ
leaf	qtel	ቅጠል
olive tree	weyra zaf	ወይራ ዛፍ
plant	atklt	አትክልት
root	sr	ስር
sunflower	suf	ሱፍ
stem	gnd	ግንድ
thorn	ïshoh	እሾህ
tree	zaf	ዛፍ
trunk	gnd	ግንድ
vine / climber	hareg	ሃረግ
weed	arem	አረም

GEOLOGY — qrtse mdr — ቅርፀ ምድር

cave	washa	ዋሻ
downhill	qulqul	ቁልቁል

erosion	ye'afer meshersher	የአፈር መሸርሸር
flat	teftafa	ጠፍጣፋ
highland	dega	ደጋ
hill	korebta	ኮረብታ
hole	gudguad	ጉድጓድ
hole (deep)	t'lq gudguad	ጥልቅ ጉድጓድ
hole (shallow)	qrb gudguad	ቅርብ ጉድጓድ
land	meriet	መሬት
lowland	qola	ቆላ
mine (gold)	(yewerq) qufaro	(የወርቅ) ቁፋሮ
mineral	ma'ïdn	ማእድን
mountain	terara	ተራራ
mountain peak / apex	yeterara chaf	የተራራ ጫፍ
mud	chqa	ጭቃ
pile	kmr	ክምር
rocky	aletama	አለታማ
sand	ashewa	አሸዋ
semi high land	weynadega	ወይናደጋ
slope	daget / qulqulet	ዳገት / ቁልቁለት
soil	afer	አፈር
steep	qetyale	ቀጥያለ
stone / rock	dngay	ድንጋይ
topography	s'ne-mdr	ስነ-ምድር
underground	meriet wst	መሬት ውስጥ
uphill	daget	ዳገት

BODIES OF WATER

beach	yebahr darcha	የባህር ዳርቻ
cliff	gedel	ገደል
creek / stream	zh'ret	ዥረት
deep water	tlq w'ha	ጥልቅ ውሃ
fresh water	n'tsuh w'ha	ንፁህ ውሃ
island	desiet	ደሴት
lake	hayq	ሀይቅ
peninsula	bahre-geb meriet	ባህረ-ገብ መሬት
pond	kurie	ኩሬ

reservoir	w'ha materaqemiya	ዉ.ሃ ማጠራቀሚያ
river	wenz	ወንዝ
salt water	chewama w'ha	ጨዋማ ዉ.ሃ
shallow water	qrb w'ha	ቅርብ ውሃ
waterfall	fuafuatie	ፏፏቴ
waves	maïbel	ማእበል
wetland	ïrtbetama meriet	እርጥብታማ መሬት

by Andrew Tadross

DISASTERS	**adega**	**አደጋ**
ash	amed	አመድ
burn (v)	meqatel	መቃጠል
collapse (failure)	wdqet	ውድቀት
destroy (v)	mawdem	ማውደም
disaster	adega	አደጋ
disaster prevention	adega mekelakel	አደጋ መከላከል
drainage	mafsesha	ማፍሰሻ
earthquake	ye'meriet menqetqet	የመሬት መንቀጥቀጥ
famine / starvation	rehab	ረሃብ
fire	ïsat	እሳት
flame	nebelbal	ነበልባል
flood	gorf	ጎርፍ
hazardous / dangerous	adegeña	አደገኛ
hurricane	awlo nefas	አውሎ ነፋስ
monsoon	yekremt znab	የክረምት ዝናብ
natural disaster	yetefet'ro adega	የተፈጥሮ አደጋ
rescue	madan	ማዳን

137

safety	dehn'net	ደህንነት
smoke	*chi*s	ጭስ
volcano	ïsate gomora	እሳተ ጎmorራ

WEATHER	**ye'ayer hunieta**	**የአየር ሁኔታ**
dry season	bega	በጋ
cloud / cloudy	demena / demenama	ደመና / ደመናማ
cold / cool	qzqazie	ቅዝቃዜ
condition	hunieta	ሁኔታ
drought	drq	ድርቅ
dry	dereq	ደረቅ
fog	gum	ጉም
heat	muqet	ሙቀት
hot	ye'miyaqa*t*l	የሚያቃጥል
humidity	ïr*t*bet	እርጥበት
ice	beredo	በረዶ
light rain shower	kafiya	ካፊያ
lightning	mebreq	መብረቅ
moisture	ïr*t*bet	እርጥበት
rain	znab	ዝናብ
rainbow	qestedemena	ቀስተደመና
rainy season	kremt	ክረምት
snow	beredo	በረዶ
season	weqt	ወቅት
storm	ma'ïbel	ማእበል
sunlight	ye*tse*hay brhan	የፀሃይ ብርሃን
sun / sunny	*tse*hay / *tse*hayama	ፀሃይ / ፀሃያማ
tropical	moqatama	ሞቃታማ በታ
thunder	negodguad	ነጎድጓድ
temperature	muqet	ሙቀት
warm	moqat	ሞቃት
weather	ye'ayer hunieta	የአየር ሁኔታ
wind / windy	nefas / nefashama	ነፋስ / ነፋሻማ
sunset	*tse*hay megbat	ፀሃይ መግባት
sunrise	*tse*hay mewtat	ፀሃይ መውጣት
What a beautiful day.	des yemil new.	ደስ የሚል ቀን።
It's cold / hot.	y'qezqzal / y'mqal.	ይቀዘቅዛል / ይሞቃል።

| Its raining. | ïyezeneb new. | እየዘነብ ነው፡፡ |

MATH / SCIENCE	hisab / sayns	ሂሳብ / ሳይንስ
addition / add (pl)	medemer / dem'ru	መደመር / ደምሩ
analysis	mrmera	ምርመራ
chemical	ntre-neger	ንጥረ-ነገር
division / divide (pl)	makafel / akaflu	ማካፈል / አካፍሉ
gas	tnet	ትነት
liquid / fluid	fesash	ፈሳሽ
math	hisab	ሂሳብ
multiplication / multiply (pl)	mabazat / abazu	ማባዛት / አባዙ
organic	yetefetro	የተፈጥሮ
percent	kemeto	ከመቶ
physical	techebach	ተጨባጭ
powder	duqiet	ዱቄት
ratio	temezazañ / zmdna	ተመዛዛኝ ዝምድና
scientific	saynsawi	ሳይንሳዊ
solid	tenkara	ጠንካራ
subtraction / subtract (pl)	meqenes / qensu	መቀነስ / ቀንሱ

SHAPE / MEASUREMENT	qrts / melekiya	ቅርፅ / መለኪያ
100 kilos	and kuntal	አንድ ኩንታል
amount	meten	መጠን
angle	ïyta	እይታ
area	sfat	ስፋት
arrow	qest	ቀስት
center	mahal	ማሃል
circle	kb	ክብ
corner	megenaña	መገናኛ
curve	matefiya	ማጠፊያ
depth	tlqet	ጥልቀት
distance	rqet	ርቀት
dot / point	netb	ነጥብ
elevation / altitude	kef'ta	ከፍታ
height	qumet	ቁመት
insufficient / shortage	ïtret	እጥረት
length	rzmet	ርዝመት

139

line	mesmer	መስመር
linear	mesmer yetebeqe	መስመር የጠበቀ
measurement	melekiya	መለኪያ
rectangle	arat me'azn	አራት መአዝን
round	zuriya	ዙርያ
shape	qrts	ቅርፅ
square	ïkul arat me'azn	እኩል አራት መአዝን
triangle	sost me'azn	ሶስት መአዝን
volume	yzota	ይዞታ
weight	kbdet	ክብደት
width	rzmet	ርዝመት

LANGUAGE	**quanqua**	**ቋንቋ**
accent	ye'anegager tqsha	የአነጋገር ጥቅሻ
adjective	qtsl	ቅፅል
adverb	tewsake gs	ተውሳከ ግስ
alphabet / script	fidel	ፊደል
antonym	teqarani	ተቃራኒ
comma	netela serez	ነጠላ ሰረዝ
definition	meglecha	መግለጫ
dictionary	mezgebe qalat	መዝገበ ቃላት
foreign language	yewch quanqua	የውጭ ቋንቋ
grammar	sewasew	ሰዋሰው
meaning / translation	trgum	ትርጉም
noun	sm	ስም
paragraph	anqets	አንቀጽ
plural	yebzu qutr	የብዙ ቁጥር
preposition	mes'tewaded	መስተዋደድ
pronunciation	anebabeb / dmts aweta't	አነባበብ / ድምፅ አወጣጥ
question mark	tyaqie mlkt	ጥያቄ ምልከት
sentence	arefte neger	አረፍተ ነገር
spelling	yeqalat fideloch atsa'tsaf	የቃላት ፊደሎች አፃፃፍ
synonym	temesasay	ተመሳሳይ
verb	gs	ግስ

ADVERBS	**gs**	**ግስ**
accidentally	be'dnget	በድንገት

as	ïnde	እንደ
approximately	be'gmt	በግምት
barely	letnsh	ለትንሽ
basically	bemeseretu	በመሰረቱ
carefully	be'tnqaqie	በጥንቃቄ
easily	beqelalu	በቀላሉ
exactly	be't'k'kl	በትክክል
finally	be'mecheresha	በመጨረሻ
generally	be'teqlala	በጠቅላላ
honestly	be ïwnet	በእውነት
however	yhun'ïna	ይሁን እና
individually / separately	ïyandandu / bemeleyayet	እያንዳንዱ / በመለያየት
jointly / together	be'hbret / and lay	በህብረት / አንድ ላይ
lately	be'qrb gizie	በቅርብ ጊዜ
luckily / by chance	be'ïdl / be'agatami	በእድል / በአጋጣሚ
mainly / especially	be'waneñanet	በዋነኛነት
more than / extremely	be'ybelt	በይበልጥ
obviously	be'gltsnet	በግልፅነት
precisely / perfectly	be't'kkl	በትክክል
primarily / mostly	be'qdmiya	በቅድሚያ
quickly	be'ftnet	በፍጥነት
repeatedly	be'tedegagami	በተደጋጋሚ
sadly	be'hazen	በሃዘን
seriously	be'kebadnet / be'asasabinet	በከባድነት / በአሳሳቢነት
slightly	be'tnsh	በትንሽ
suddenly	be'dnget	በድንገት
surprisingly / unexpectedly	baltetebeqe hunieta	ባልተጠበቀ ሁኔታ
surely / certainly	be'ïrgteñanet	በእርግጠኛነት
thankfully	be'msgana	በምስጋና
unfortunately	be'ïdlebisnet	በእድለቢስነት
unlikely	ye'maymesl	የማይመስል

POSITIVE DESCRIPTIONS	awontawi agelaletsoch	አዎንታዊ አገላለፆች
accurate	t'k'kl	ትክክል
alert / active	nqu / tgu	ንቁ / ትጉ
astonishing	asgerami	አስገራሚ
beautiful	konjo	ቆንጆ

141

brave	defar	ደፋር
calm	*tset* yale	ፀጥ ያለ
challenging	aschegari	አስቸጋሪ
clever	gobez	ጎበዝ
comfortable	mchu	ምቹ
curious	asasabi	አሳሳቢ
dependable / reliable	tamañ	ታማኝ
determined	yeteleye	የተለየ
diligent	tguh / t'guri	ትጉህ
educated	yetemare	የተማረ
effective	wu*ti*etama	ውጤታማ
efficient	bqat yalew	ብቃት ያለው
enthusiastic	gugu / tesfeña	ጉጉ / ተስፈኛ
essential / necessary	asfelagi	አስፈላጊ
exciting	ye'miyaneqaqa	የሚያነቃቃ
flawless / perfect	ïnken yelielew	እንከን የሌለው
flexible	ye'mite*tate*f / ye'mitazez	የሚተጣጠፍ / የሚታዘዝ
fresh	adis	አዲስ
friendly	tegbabi	ተግባቢ
funny / hilarious	asqiñ	አስቂኝ
generous	cher / deg	ቸር / ደግ
gentle	yeteregaga	የተረጋጋ
good	*t*'ru	ጥሩ
great	g'rum	ግሩም
handsome	shebela	ሸበላ
helpful	tebabari	ተባባሪ
honest	tamañ	ታማኝ
humorous	te*cha*wach / asqiñ	ተጫዋች / አስቂኝ
important	asfelagi	አስፈላጊ
impressive	asgerami	አስገራሚ
independent	ne*tsa* mehon	ነፃ መሆን
intelligent	blh / bruh	ብልህ / ብሩህ
interesting	des yemil	ደስ የሚል
lovely	tewedaj	ተወዳጅ
loyal	tamañ	ታማኝ
lucky	ïdleña	እድለኛ
memorable	ye'mayresa	የማይረሳ

nice	*t*'ru	ጥሩ
open minded	besfat ye'mi'asb	በስፋት የሚያስብ
ordinary / normal	tera	ተራ
patient	t'ïgst	ትዕግስት
polite	t'hut	ትሁት
popular	tawaqi	ታዋቂ
positive	qena	ቀና
powerful	hayleña	ኃይለኛ
precise	be'tk'kl	በትክክል
proud	bekurat	በኩራት
reliable	ye'mitamen	የሚታመን
sane	ye'miyamezazn	የሚያመዛዝን
sensitive	s'mietawi	ስሜታዊ
sexy	maraki	ማራኪ
smart / clever	gobez	ጎበዝ
special	lyu	ልዩ
solid	*teta*r	ጠጣር
strong	hayleña / *t*enkara	ኃይለኛ / ጠንካራ
sturdy	*t*enkara	ጠንካራ
stylish	zena*ch*	ዘናጭ
sympathetic	asazañ	አሳዛኝ
tranquil	yeteregaga	የተረጋጋ
unforgettable	ye'mayresa	የማይረሳ
useful	*t*eqami	ጠቃሚ
wise	blh	ብልህ

NEGATIVE DESCRIPTIONS	**alutawi agelale*ts***	አሉታዊ አገላለፅ
annoying	ye'miyanad'd	የሚያናድድ
awful	ye'miyas*t*ela	የሚያስጠላ
bad	me*t*fo	መጥፎ
bastard	diqala	ዲቃላ
boring	aselchi	አሰልቺ
careless	gd yelesh	ግድ የለሽ
clumsy	qezhaqaza / denbara	ቀዥቃዛ / ደንባራ
corrupt	museña	ሙሰኛ
coward	feri	ፈሪ
decayed	yebesebese	የበሰበሰ

143

disgrace	qel'b - bis	ቀልብ - ቢስ
disgusting	ye'miyastela	የሚያስጠላ
evil	kfu / seytanawi	ክፉ / ሰይጣናዊ
goof / fool	moñ	ሞኝ
horrible	betam metfo	በጣም መጥፎ
idiot	dedeb	ደደብ
illiterate	mehaym	መሃይም
isolated	kelielaw yeraqe	ከሌላው የራቀ
jealous	qenateña	ቀናተኛ
lazy	senef	ሰነፍ
liar	w'sh'tam	ውሸታም
meaningless	trgum yelesh	ትርጉም የለሽ
nasty	chekañ / kfu	ጨካኝ / ክፉ
rude	balegie / sd	ባለጌ / ስድ
quarrelsome	negereña	ነገረኛ
selfish	s'gb'gb / ras wedad	ስግብግብ / ራስ ወዳድ
senseless	trgum yelielew	ትርጉም የሌለው
shame	hafret	ሃፍረት
shameful	asafari	አሳፋሪ
shameless	ayn'awta	አይን አውጣ
strange	leyet yale	ለየት ያለ
stupid	dedeb	ደደብ
taboo	ye'tekelekele	የተከለከለ
unclear	glts yalhone	ግልፅ ያልሆነ
unacceptable	teqebaynet yelielew	ተቀባይነት የሌለው
undesirable	ye'mayfeleg	የማይፈለግ
unlucky	ïdle bis	እድለ ቢስ
unnecessary	alasfelagi	አላስፈላጊ
unusual / unfamiliar	yaltelemede	ያልተለመደ
wasteful	betañ	በታኝ
weak	dekama	ደካማ
worthless / futile	tqm yelielew / waga bis	ጥቅም የሌለው / ዋጋ ቢስ

DESCRIBING PEOPLE	**agelalets**	**አገላለፅ**
attractive / beautiful	maraki / qonjo	ማራኪ / ቆንጆ
bald	melata	መላጣ
dark (skin, hair)	tqur	ጥቁር

144

elderly	sh'maglie	ሽማግሌ
elders	sh'magliewoch	ሽማግሌዎች
fat / obese	wefram	ወፍራም ወፍረት
healthy	tieneña	ጤነኛ
gray hair	shbetam	ሽበታም
naked	raqut	ራቁት
old woman	arogit	አሮጊት
old man	shmaglie	ሽማግሌ
short	achr	አጭር
strong	tenkara	ጠንካራ
tall	rejim	ረጅም
thin	qechin	ቀጭን
ugly	ye'miyastela	የሚያስጠላ
young	wetat	ወጣት

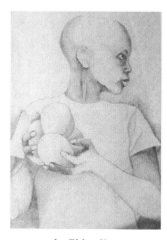

by Eldon Katt

COMPARISON	**nts'tsr**	**ንፅፅር**
easy / light	qelal	ቀላል
difficult / heavy	kebad	ከባድ
big / large	t'lq / gzuf	ትልቅ / ግዙፍ
bigger	teleq yale	ተለቅ ያለ
smaller	yanese	ያነስ
high	kef yale	ከፍ ያለ

145

medium	mekakeleña	መካከለኛ
low	zq yale	ዝቅ ያለ
alike	ye'mimesasel	የሚመሳሰል
as much / as many	yan'nu yahl	ያንኑ ያህል
different (unique)	lyu	ልዩ
even / equal	temetatañ	ተመጣጣኝ
identical	ïkul / temesasay	እኩል / ተመሳሳይ
main	wana	ዋና
mainly	bewananet	በዋናነት
majority	ab'lacha	አብላጫ
many	bzu	ብዙ
massive	betam gzuf	በጣም ግዙፍ
opposite / reverse	teqarani	ተቃራኒ
similar	temesasay	ተመሳሳይ
the same	and aynet / temesasay	አንድ አይነት / ተመሳሳይ

BAD BEHAVIOUR	**metfo tsebay**	**መጥፎ ፀባይ**
crazy person	qews sew	ቀውስ ሰው
dishonest	ye'maytamen	የማይታመን
harassment	tqat	ጥቃት
insult	sdb	ስድብ
thief	lieba	ሌባ
Catch him!	yazew!	ያዘው
Don't touch me. (m)	atnkañ	አትንካኝ
Go away (m/f)	hidlñ / hijlñ	ሂድልኝ / ሂጅልኝ
I would like to be by myself.	b'chayon mehon ïfelgalehu.	ብቻዬን መሆን አፈልጋለሁ።
Leave me alone (m)	teweñ.	ተወኝ።
No. (I don't want.)	alfelgm.	አልፈልግም።
Shut up (m).	zm bey.	ዝም በይ።
Stop it.	aqum.	አቁም።
That is not fair.	tegebi aydelem.	ተገቢ አይደለም።
What are you looking at? (f)	mn ïyayesh new	ምን እያየሽ ነው?
You are lying. (m)	ïyewasheh new.	እየዋሸህ ነው።
You are lying. (f)	ïyewashesh new.	እየዋሸሽ ነው።
You are rude. (m)	balegie neh.	ባለጌ ነህ።
You are disturbing me. (m)	ïyerebesh'keñ new.	እየረበሽከኝ ነው።

146

(male)	yrdah.	ይርዳህ።
(female)	yrdash.	ይርዳሽ።
(plural)	yrdachhu.	ይርዳችሁ
(older male/female)	yrdawot.	ይርዳዎት።

COMMANDS / IMPERATIVE PHRASES

Note that in Amharic, imperative phrases have a unique suffix depending on if the command is spoken to a male, a female, or a plural. For the male form, the suffix depends on the verb. But for a command to a female, the suffix is an *i* (ee) sound. For a command to more than one person, the suffix is an *u* sound. If there is a direct object in the verb (*to me, to her* etc) or the suffix for the direct object will follow the verb suffix. In the following table, examine the example *Give / Give me* etc, to compare the order of the suffixes.

Be careful.	(m)	te*t*enqeq.	ተጠንቀቅ።
	(f)	te*t*enqeqi.	ተጠንቀቂ።
Be happy.	(m)	des ybelh.	ደስ ይበልህ።
	(f)	des ybelsh.	ደስ ይበልሽ።
Be quiet. (shut up.)	(m)	*t*set bel.	ፀጥ በል።
	(f)	*t*set bey.	ፀጥ በይ።
Bring it to me.	(m)	am*t*alñ.	አምጣልኝ።
	(f)	am*chi*lñ.	አምጪልኝ።
Call me.	(m)	dew'l'lñ.	ደውልልኝ።
	(f)	dewy'lñ.	ደውይልኝ።
	(pl)	dewlulñ.	ደውሉልኝ።
Calm down.	(m)	atnaded / qes bel / teregaga.	አትናደድ / ቀስ በል / ተረጋጋ
	(f)	atnadej / qes bey / teregagi.	አትናደጅ / ቀስ በይ / ተረጋጊ
Cancel it.	(m)	serzew.	ሰርዘው።
	(f)	serzhiw.	ሰርዢው።
Catch / hold.	(m)	yaz.	ያዝ።
	(f)	yazhi.	ያዢ።
Choose	(m)	m'ret	ምረጥ
	(f)	m're*chi*	ምረጪ
Close the door.	(m)	berun zgaw.	በሩን ዝጋው።
	(f)	berun zgiw.	በሩን ዝጊው።
Come.	(m)	na.	ና።

147

	(f)	ney.	ነይ።
	(pl)	nu.	ኑ።
Come in. / get in. (young male)	(m)	gba.	ግባ።
Come in / get in (young female)	(f)	gbi.	ግቢ።
Come in. / get in. (older person)	(m/f)	ygbu.	ይግቡ።
Drink.	(m)	*teta.*	ጠጣ።
	(f)	*techi.*	ጠጪ።
Do it.	(m)	adrg.	አድርግ።
	(f)	adrgi.	አድርጊ።
Don't disturb.	(m)	at'rebsh.	አትረብሽ።
	(f)	at'rebshi.	አተረብሺ።
Don't ask me.	(m)	at'*te*yqeñ.	አትጠይቀኝ።
	(f)	at'*te*yqiñ.	አትጠዪቂኝ።
Don't be late.	(m)	ïn'datzegey.	እንዳትዘገይ።
	(f)	ïndatzegeyi.	እንዳትዘገዪ።
Don't cry.	(m)	atalqs.	አታልቅስ።
	(f)	atalqshi.	አታልቅሺ።
Don't forget.	(m)	at'rsa.	አትርሳ።
	(f)	atr'shi.	አትርሺ።
Don't give up.	(m)	tesfa atqure*t.*	ተስፋ አትቋረጥ።
	(f)	tesfa atqure*chi.*	ተስፋ አትቋረጪ።
Don't lose it.	(m)	ata*t*faw.	አታጥፋው።
	(f)	ata*t*fiw.	አታጥፊው።
Eat.	(m)	b'la.	ብላ።
	(f)	b'yi.	ብዪ።
	(pl)	b'lu	ብሉ።
Follow me.	(m)	teketeleñ.	ተከተለኝ።
	(f)	teketeyiñ.	ተከተዪኝ።
Get it.	(m)	agñew.	አግኘው።
	(f)	agñiw.	አግኚው።
Get out.	(m)	w*ta.*	ውጣ።
	(f)	w*chi.*	ውጪ።
Get up.	(m)	tenes.	ተነስ።
	(f)	teneshi.	ተነሺ።
Give	(m)	s*t.*	ስጥ

148

	(f)	s'chi.	ስቺ
Give her.	(f)	s'tat.	ስጣት።
Give him.	(m)	s'tew.	ስጠው።
Give me.	(m/f)	s'teñ / s'chiñ.	ስጠኝ / ስቺኝ።
Go. / leave.	(m)	hid / lqeq.	ሂድ / ልቀቅ።
	(f)	hiji / lqeqi.	ሂጂ / ልቀቂ።
Guess.	(m)	gem't.	ገምት።
o	(f)	gemchi.	ገምቺ።
Help me.	(m)	ïrdañ.	እርዳኝ።
	(f)	ïrjiñ.	እርጂኝ።
	(pl)	ïrduñ.	እርዱኝ።
Hurry up.	(m)	tolo bel.	ቶሎ በል።
	(f)	tolo bey.	ቶሎ በይ።
Knock on the door.	(m)	berun ankuakua.	በሩን አንኳኳ።
	(f)	berun ankuakui.	በሩን አንኳኪ።
Lay down.	(m)	gadem bel.	ጋደም በል።
	(f)	gadem bey.	ጋደም በይ።
Leave it alone.	(m)	tewew.	ተወው።
	(f)	teyiw.	ተዪው።
Let's go.	(m/f)	ïnhid.	እንሂድ።
Let's stay.	(m/f)	ïnqoy.	እንቆይ።
Listen to me.	(m)	s'mañ.	ስማኝ።
	(f)	s'miñ.	ስሚኝ።
Listen.	(m)	s'ma.	ስማ።
	(f)	s'mi.	ስሚ።
Lock the door.	(m)	berun qolfew.	በሩን ቆልፈው።
	(f)	berun qolfiw.	በሩን ቆልፈው።
Look.	(m)	temelket.	ተመልከት።
	(f)	temelkechi.	ተመልከቺ።
Move.	(m)	tenqesaqes.	ተንቀሳቀስ።
	(f)	tenqesaqeshi.	ተንቀሳቀሺ።
Open the door.	(m)	berun kfetew.	በሩን ክፈተው።
	(f)	berun kfechiw.	በሩን ክፈቺው።
Pay attention.	(m)	astewl.	አስተውል።
	(f)	astewyi.	አስተውዪ።
	(pl)	astewlu.	አስተውሉ።

Pick it up.	(m)	ansaw.	አንሳው።
	(f)	anshiw.	አንሺው።
Please leave.	(m)	ïbakh hid.	እባክህ ሂድ።
	(f)	ïbaksh hiji.	እባክሽ ሂጂ።
Proceed / go ahead.	(m)	qetl.	ቀጥል።
	(f)	qetyi.	ቀጥዪ።
Put it there.	(m)	ïza asqmtew.	እዛ አስቀምጠው።
	(f)	ïza asqemchiw.	እዛ አስቀምጪው።
Put on____ .	(m)	____ lbes.	____ ልበስ።
	(f)	____ lbeshi.	____ ልበሺ።
Read it.	(m)	anb'bew.	አንብበው።
	(f)	anb'biw.	አንብቢው።
Repeat after me.	(m)	kenie behuala dgem.	ከኔ በኋላ ድገም።
	(f)	kenie behuala dgemi.	ከኔ በኋላ ድገሚ።
Run.	(m)	rut.	ሩጥ።
	(f)	ruchi.	ሩጪ።
	(pl)	rutu.	ሩጡ።
Send me a text.	(m)	yetshuf melïkt lakl' ñ.	የጽሁፍ መልዕክት ላክልኝ።
	(f)	yetshuf melïkt lakil'ñ.	የጽሁፍ መልዕክት ላኪልኝ።
Shut it off.	(m)	zgaw.	ዝጋው።
	(f)	zgiw.	ዝጊው።
Sit down.	(m)	quch bel.	ቁጭ በል።
	(f)	quch bey.	ቁጭ በይ።
Sleep.	(m)	teña.	ተኛ።
	(f)	teñi.	ተኚ።
Stop	(m)	aqum.	አቁም።
	(f)	aqumi.	አቁሚ።
Study	(m)	at'na.	አጥና።
	(f)	at'ñi.	አጥኚ።
Take off.(remove)____ .	(m)	____ awlqew.	____ አውልቀው።
	(f)	____ awlqiw.	____ አውልቂው።
Taste it.	(m)	____qmesew.	____ ቅመሰው።
	(f)	____qmeshiw.	____ ቅመሺው።
Tell me.	(m)	ngereñ.	ንገረኝ።
	(f)	ngeriñ.	ንገሪኝ።
Think about it.	(m)	asb'bet.	አስብበት።

	(f)	asbibet.	አስቢቤት፡፡
Trust. / believe me.	(m)	ïmeneñ.	እመነኝ፡፡
	(f)	ïmeñiñ.	እመኚኝ፡፡
Try it.	(m)	mokrew.	ሞክረው፡፡
	(f)	mokriw.	ሞክሪው፡፡
Turn on. (the lights.)	(m)	(mebratun) abraw.	(መብራቱን) አብራው፡፡
	(f)	(mebratun) abriw.	(መብራቱን) አብሪው፡፡
Wait.	(m)	qoy.	ቆይ፡፡
	(f)	qoyi.	ቆዪ፡፡
Wake up.	(m)	tenes.	ተነስ፡፡
	(f)	teneshi.	ተነሺ፡፡
Write it.	(m)	*ts*afew.	ፃፈው፡፡
	(f)	*ts*afiw.	ፃፊው፡፡

by Eldon Katter

NON-CATEGORIZED WORDS

about	s'le	ስለ
about / nearly / almost	letnsh	ለትንሽ
absent	yeliele / yegodele	የሌለ / የጎደለ
accomplishment	f*ts*amie / dl	ፍፃሜ / ድል
action	tegbar	ተግባር
activity	ïnqsqasie	እንቅስቃሴ
additional / supplementary	te*ch*emari	ተጨማሪ
advertisement / notice	mastaweqiya	ማስታወቂያ

151

advice / consultancy	mkr	ምክር
affair / issue	guday	ጉዳይ
aggressive	qu*tu*	ቁጡ
alien	ïngda / yaltaweqe	እንግዳ / ያልታወቀ
alone	bcheña	ብቻኛ
also	degmo	ደግሞ
alternative	amara*ch*	አማራጭ
although	yhun ïnji	ይሁን እንጂ
anything	man'ñawum	ማንኛውም
applicant	amelkach	አመልካች
appointment	qe*t*ero	ቀጠሮ
appreciation / admiration	adnaqot	አድናቆት
art	sïl / *t*beb	ስእል / ጥበብ
at random	ïndaga*t*eme / be'ïdl	እንዳጋጠመ / በእድል
basket	meyazha	መያዣ
because / reason	mknyat	ምክንያት
benefit	*t*qm	ጥቅም
breast feeding	*tu*t ma*t*bat	ጡት ማጥባት
bundle	*t*ql	ጥቅል
busy	mulu / be s'ra me*t*emed	ሙሉ / በስራ መጠመድ
by the way	benegera*ch*n lay	በነገራችን ላይ
ceremony	s'nes'r*at* / akebaber	ስነስርዓት / አከባበር
certificate	y'mskr wereqet	የምስክር ወረቀት
chance / luck	ïdl	እድል
change / transformation	lew'*t*	ለውጥ
characteristic	tse*bay	ፀባይ
chart / figure/ diagram	sen*t*erezh / sïl	ሰንጠረዥ / ስእል
cheating	matalel	ማታለል
collection	sbsb	ስብስብ
combination	*t*mret	ጥምረት
common	yegara	የጋራ
comparison	n'*ts* '*ts*r / w'd'dr	ንፅፅር / ውድድር
complicated / complex	w'sb'sb	ውስብስብ
compliment	msgana	ምስጋና
compromise	megbabat / mesmamat	መግባባት / መስማማት
concept	hasab	ሃሳብ
concert	z'gjt	ዝግጅት

152

concern	asabinet	አሳቢነት
conclusion	mateqaleya	ማጠቃለያ
connection	g'n'ñunet	ግንኙነት
consequence	wutiet	ውጤት
constant	quami	ቋሚ
contribution	astewats'o	አስተዋፅኦ
conversation	n'g'gr / hasab melewawet	ንግግር / ሃሳብ መለዋወጥ
copy	qj	ቅጅ
correction	mastekakeya / ïrmat	ማስተካከያ / እርማት
creation / innovation	fetera	ፈጠራ
criteria	wesañ hunieta / mes'fert	ወሳኝ ሁኔታ / መስፈርት
criticism	weqesa	ወቀሳ
data	chbt / yetemezegebe / qutr	ጭብጥ / የተመዘገበ / ቁጥር
deadline	yegizie gedeb	የጊዜ ገደብ
deal	sm'm'net	ስምምነት
decision	wusanie	ውሳኔ
demonstration	masaya	ማሳያ
dependent	tgeña	ጥገኛ
design	ïqd / plan	እቅድ / ፕላን
desire	flagot	ፍላጎት
destiny	ïdl / mechitesfa	እድል / መጪ ተስፋ
detail / explanation	zrzr / mabrariya	ዝርዝር / ማብራሪያ
development	ïdget / chmari / meshashal	እድገት / ጭማሪ / መሻሻል
discovery	gñt	ግኝት
distribution	makefafeya	ማከፋፈያ
division	k'f'fl	ክፍፍል
document	sened	ሰነድ
doll	ashangulit	አሻንጉሊት
doubt	trtarie	ጥርጣሬ
drawing	ms'l / s'ï'l	ምስል / ስዕል
each	ïyandandu	እያንዳንዱ
encouragement	maberetacha	ማበረታቻ
entrance	megbiya	መግቢያ
equipment	mesariya	መሳሪያ
error	sh'tet	ስህተት
established	mequaquam	መቋቋም
estimate / guess	g'mt	ግምት

153

evaluation	gmgema	ግምገማ
event	k's'tet	ክስተት
everybody	hulum sew	ሁሉም ሰው
everything	hulum neger	ሁሉም ነገር
example	msalie	ምሳሌ
exit	me'wcha	መውጫ
expectation	tesfa / ïmnet	ተስፋ / እምነት
experience	lmd / ïwqet / chlota	ልምድ / እውቀት / ችሎታ
expert	bale moya	ባለ ሞያ
fair / fairness (just)	dehna	ደህና
famous / known / popular	tawaqi	ታዋቂ
fault	s'htet / tfat	ስህተት / ጥፋት
favor	wuleta	ውለታ
file	mez'geb	መዝገብ
final	ye'mecheresha	የመጨረሻ
for the future	lewedefit	ለወደፊት
forever	lezelalem	ለዘልአለም
forgetfulness	mersat	መርሳት
former / prior	yeqedmo / yefiteña	የቀድሞ / የፊተኛ
fragile	ye'miseber	የሚሰበር
funding	yegenzeb dgaf	የገንዘብ ድጋፍ
gigantic / huge	gzuf	ግዙፍ
glory	kbr	ክብር
goal / objective	gb	ግብ
greed	s'gb'gbnet	ስግብግብነት
guest / visitor	ïngda	እንግዳ
hard work	kebad s'ra	ከባድ ስራ
headquarters	wana mes'riya biet	ዋና መስሪያ ቤት
hero	jegna	ጀግና
hidden	d'bq	ድብቅ
high quality	kefteña t'rat	ከፍተኛ ጥራት
historic	tarikawi	ታሪካዊ
hobby	gizie masalefiya	ጊዜ ማሳለፊያ
hole / gap	kftet	ክፍተት
illogical	meserete - bis	መሰረተ - ቢስ
influence	gfit / chana	ግፊት / ጫና
information	mereja / meglecha	መረጃ / መግለጫ

English	Transliteration	Amharic
inheritence	wers	ውርስ
interest	f'lagot / s'miet / weled	ፍላጎት / ስሜት / ወለድ
intersection	g'nuññet	ግንኙነት
item (thing)	ïqa / neger	እቃ / ነገር
joke	qeld	ቀልድ
junk	wagabis / qoshasha	ዋጋቢስ / ቆሻሻ
layer	medeb	መደብ
liar	w'shetam	ውሸታም
lie	megadem	መጋደም
light weight	qelal kbdet	ቀላል ክብደት
livelihood	ye'gebi mnch	የገቢ ምንጭ
logical	mknyatawi / asamañ yehone	ምክንያታዊ / አሳማኝ የሆነ
lost	ye'tefa	የጠፋ
luxury	ye'mchot	የምቾት
machine	mesriya / moter	መስሪያ / ሞተር
match stick	ye'kbrit ïnchet	የክብሪት እንጨት
maybe	m'nalbat	ምናልባት
meeting	sb'seba	ስብሰባ
member	abal	አባል
memory	t'wsta	ትውስታ
method	zedie	ዘዴ
mistake	s'htet / tfat	ስህተት / ጥፋት
mixture	ql'ql	ቅልቅል
model	msalie / qj	ምሳሌ / ቅጅ
more than enough	kebeqi belay	ከበቂ በላይ
mutual	yegara	የጋራ
not much	ïmbzam	እምብዛም
nowhere	yetm	የትም
nudity	raqut mehon	ራቁት መሆን
obedient	tazazh	ታዛዥ
of course	be'rgteñ'net	በርግጠኛነት
only	bcha	ብቻ
opinion / idea	hasab	ሃሳብ
opportunity / luck	tqm / ïdl	ጥቅም / እድል
original	meseretawi / lyu	መሰረታዊ / ልዩ
other	leila	ሌላ
outward	wchawi	ውጫዊ

155

overall	beteqlala	በጠቅላላ
paint / ink	qelem	ቀለም
painter	qelem qebi	ቀለም ቀቢ
pair / couple	tnd	ጥንድ
participation	tesat'fo	ተሳትፎ
partner	shrk / mahberteña	ሸርክ / ማህበርተኛ
patience	t'ïgst	ትእግስት
perception	t'zbt	ትዝብት
performance	bqat	ብቃት
permission / permit	fqad	ፍቃድ
perspective	amelekaket	አመለካከት
possible	ye'michal	የሚቻል
possibly	mnalbat	ምናልባት
potential	aqm	አቅም
precaution / warning	tnqaqie	ጥንቃቄ
predication	tnbit	ትንቢት
preference	yeqdmiya mrcha	የቅድሚያ ምርጫ
presentation	ye'mitay / ye'miqerb	የሚታይ / የሚቀርብ
print	ïtm	እትም
private	ye'gl	የግል
process	hidet	ሂደት
probably	mnalbat	ምናልባት
product	mrt	ምርት
progress	ïdget	እድገት
project	ïqd	እቅድ
proposal	hasab / mamelkecha	ሀሳብ / ማመልከቻ
purpose	alama / mkn'yat	አላማ / ምክንያት
rare	lyu / ye'maygeñ	ልዩ / የማይገኝ
ready	zgju	ዝግጁ
reality	chbt / ïwnet	ጭብጥ / እውነት
record (file) (v)	mezgeb	መዝገብ
reflection	netsebraq	ነፀብራቅ
regular / common	yetelemede	የተለመደ
relief	netsa mehon	ነፃ መሆን
remainder	t'rafi / qeri	ትራፊ / ቀሪ
report	meg'lecha	መግለጫ
reputation	sm / tebay / qumena	ስም / ጠባይ / ቁመና

156

research	mr'mr	ምርምር
reward	shlmat / maberetacha	ሽልማት / ማበረታቻ
revival	magegem	ማገገም
ripe / matured	yebesele / yederese	የበሰለ / የደረሰ
row (horizontal line)	agdami	አግዳሚ
scarcity	ïtret	እጥረት
schedule	ajenda / yegizie selieda	አጄንዳ / የጊዜ ሰሌዳ
sculpture	qrts / hawlt	ቅርፃ / ሃውልት
secret / mystery	mstir	ምስጢር
serious	kostara / kelb / betena	ኮስታራ / ከልብ / በጠና
several (two, three)	yetewesene	የተወሰነ
shadow / shade	t'la	ጥላ
shame	hafret	ሃፍረት
sharp	s'letam / fetan / mlach	ስለታም / ፈጣን / ምላጭ
shift / movement	melewet / menqesaqes	መለወጥ / መንቀሳቀስ
shiny	antsebaraqi	አንፀባራቂ
shy	ayne afar	አይነ አፋር
situation / condition	hunieta	ሁኔታ
skill	ch'lota	ችሎታ
slippery	amualach	አሟላጭ
something	yehon neger	የሆነ ነገር
stability	meregagat	መረጋጋት
stack	m'kr	ክምር
standard	dereja	ደረጃ
stationary	ye'maynqesaqes	የማይንቀሳቀስ
stick	btr	ብትር
sting	mendef	መንደፍ
storage	makemacha	ማከማቻ
stripes	zngurgur	ዝንጉርጉር
stuff	neger / ïqa	ነገር / እቃ
success	dl	ድል
suffering	meseqayet	መሰቃየት
sufficient	beqi / amerqi	በቂ / አመርቂ
support	dgaf	ድጋፍ
surroundings / environs	akababi	አካባቢ
system	zedie / denb /sr'at	ዘዴ / ደንብ / ስርዓት
talent	ch'lota / bqat	ችሎታ / ብቃት

therefore	s'lezih	ስለዚህ
things	negeroch	ነገሮች
thorough	be*t*nqaqie / bezrzr	በጥንቃቄ / በዝርዝር
tolerable	ye'michal / teqebaynet yalew	የሚቻል / ተቀባይነት ያለው
tolerance	metages	መታገስ
toy	ashangulit	አሻንጉሊት
training	s'ltena	ስልጠና
type	aynet	አይነት
typical	ye'telemede	የተለመደ
unavailable	ye'maygeñ	የማይገኝ
unavoidable	ye'mayqer	የማይቀር
undeniable	ye'maykad	የማይካድ
universal	alemaqef / *te*qlala	አለምአቀፍ / ጠቅላላ
unless	kalhone	ካልሆነ
until now	ïskahun	እስካሁን
varieties	lyu lyu aynet	ልዩ ልዩ አይነት
various	lyu lyu	ልዩ ልዩ
very	be*t*am	በጣም
viewpoint	amelekaket	አመለካከት
visit	gubñt	ጉብኝት
waste	qoshasha / yebakene	ቆሻሻ / የባከነ
wax	sm	ሰም
wealth / treasure	habt	ሃብት
whatever	mnm yhun mn	ምንም ይሁን ምን
whistle	fuchet	ፉጨት
widespread	be'sfat	በስፋት

COGNATES

There are words that are the same – or similar to English. These are called **cognates**. Many of these are related to science, technology, or culture that was developed long after the Amharic language was established. Following are an abbreviated list that mean the same thing in both languages, and are pronounced very similarly.

- actor
- airplane
- ambulance
- bank
- battery
- bomb
- camera
- chemical
- cinema
- college
- computer
- credit card
- embassy
- fax
- democracy
- garage

- grocery
- helmet
- hip hop
- hospital
- hotel
- industry
- internet
- jacket
- laptop
- lighter
- memory (phone)
- mobile
- motor
- network
- pharmacy

- photo
- radio
- report
- taxi
- technology
- television
- theater
- thermos
- ticket
- tourist
- traffic
- university
- video
- virus
- visa
- x-ray

Following are examples of Amharic slang, or informal language. Like slang anywhere, it varies by region and may be more or less relevant depeneding on the location.

Exclamation said when you are tired of some thing.	ie*ch*	ኤጭ
When you are surprised by what someone is telling you.	arebakh! / arebak'sh !	አረባከህ! / አረባከሽ!
Similar to *cool* in English.	arif	አሪፍ
Informal way to say *please*.	benat'h/benat'sh	በናትህ / በናትሽ
Really! Seriously! Honestly!	be'ïw'net	በእውነት
Really! Seriously! Honestly!	ïndie!	እንዴ!
Bye	chaw (ciao)	ቻው
Good / great	shega	ሽጋ
Used to describe a profitable job	shqela	ሽቀላ
sorry (pardon me)	yqrta	ይቅርታ
Said when something bad happens to someone and you wish it had happened to you instead.	ïnien	እኔን
You use it to express when you are surprised, scare (with facial expression.)	wey'nie	ወይኔ!
Said when taking rest after a hard work or journey. The word comes with long exhale.	ïfoy	አፎይ
A very smart person according to his/her social living environment. Example: She became 'arada' after they tried to fool her	arada	አራዳ
A person who has performed a heroic activity.	jebeded	ጀበደደ
Informal way to say "I don't know"	ïnanja	እኔንጃ
Informal way to say "Suit your self"	ïndefelegh / ïndefelegsh	እንደ ፈልህ / እንደ ፈለግሽ

by Meron Bekele

ANTONYMS

Following are antonyms, or words that are opposite eachother. Learning the following can be quite useful for speaking Amharic. Note that (v) indicates verb infinitives.

very	be*t*am	በጣም
not very	ïmbizam	እምብዛም
above	belay	በላይ
below	betach	በታች
ahead	wede fit	ወደ ፊት
behind	ke____huala	ከ____ኋላ
already	derese	ደረሰ
not yet	gena	ገና
before	befit	በፊት
after	behuala	በኋላ
first	qdmiya	ቅድሚያ
last	me*ch*eresha	መጨረሻ
forward	wede fit	ወደ ፊት
backward	qe*t*ay	ቀጣይ
high	lay	ላይ
low	tach	ታች
in front	fit-le-fit	ፊትለፊት
in back	kejerba	ከጀርባ
inside	ws*t*	ውስጥ
outside	w*ch*	ውጭ

near	qrb	ቅርብ
far	ruq	ሩቅ
the next time	beqeṭayu gizie	በቀጣዩ ጊዜ
the last time	balefew gizie	ባለፈው ጊዜ
to (person / place)	le / wede	ለ / ወደ
from	ke	ከ
up	lay	ላይ
down	tach	ታች
with	ke ___ gar	ከ ___ ጋር
without	kale	ካለ___
awake	menqat	መንቃት
asleep	meteñat	መተኛት
brave	jegna	ጀግና
coward	feri	ፈሪ
educated	yetemare	የተማረ
uneducated	mehaym	መሃይም
fat	wefram	ወፍራም
thin	qechn	ቀጭን
friendly (m/f)	techawach	ተግባቢ
unfriendly	gtr	ግትር
funny (m)	asqiñ	አስቂኝ
serious	kostara	ኮስታራ
happy	desta	ደስታ
sad	hazen	ሀዘን
male	wend	ወንድ
female	siet	ሴት
married	yageba	ያገባ
single	yalageba	ያላገባ
modest	t'hut	ትሁት
arrogant	kurateña	ኩራተኛ
polite	chewa	ጨዋ
rude	balegie	ባለጌ
rich	habtam	ሀብታም
poor	deha	ደሃ
shy	aynafar	አይናፋር
sociable	tgbabi	ተግባቢ

162

sick	hmemteña	ህመምተኛ
healthy	tieneña	ጤነኛ
similar	temesasay	ተመሳሳይ
opposite	teqarani	ተቃራኒ
smart	gobez / qeltafa	ቀልጣፋ
stupid	senef	ሰነፍ
strong	tenkara	ጠንካራ
weak	dekama	ደካማ
success	s'kiet	ስኬት
failure	wd'qet	ውድቀት
tall	rezhm	ረዥም
short	achr	አጭር
thin	kechn	ቀጭን
thick	dendana	ደንዳና
wise	lbam	ልባም
foolish	moñ	ሞኝ
safe	astemamañ	አስተማማኝ
dangerous	adegeña	አደገኛ
easy	qelal	ቀላል
difficult	kebad	ከባድ
organized	ye'tesedere	የተሰደረ
disorganized	bkun	ብኩን
interesting	maraki	ማራኪ
boring	aselchi	አሰልቺ
true	ïwnet	እውነት
false	wshet	ውሸት
right	qeñ	ቀኝ
left	gra	ግራ
correct / right	t'k'kl	ትክክል
incorrect / wrong	s'htet	ስህተት
I'm satisfied	rekchalehu	ረክቻለሁ
I'm unsatisfied	alrekahum	አልረካሁም
I understand	gebtoñal	ገብቶኛል
I don't understand	algebañ'm	አልገባኝም
famous (known)	tawaqi	ታዋቂ
unknown	ye'maytaweq	የማይታወቅ

simple	qelal	ቀላል
complicated	wsbsb	ውስብስብ
positive	awentawi	አወንታዊ
negative	alutawi	አሉታዊ
tight	*t*bq	ጥብቅ
loose	l'l	ልል
smooth	lmu*t*	ልሙጥ
rough	shakara	ሻካራ
straight	qe*t*'ta	ቀጥታ
crooked	*ch*nqnq	ጭንቅንቅ
loud	*chu*kht	ጩኸት
quiet	*tse't*'ta	ፀጥታ
flat	mieda	ሜዳ
hilly / mountainous	kefta / korebtama	ከፍታ / ኮረብታማ
hot	moqat	ሞቃት
cold	qezqaza	ቀዝቃዛ
ordinary	yetelemede	የተለመደ
rare	yaltelemede	ያልተለመደ
reasonable	mknyatawi	ምክንያታዊ
unreasonable	imizanawi	ኢሚዛናዊ
full	mulu	ሙሉ
empty	bado	ባዶ
normal	yetelemede	የተለመደ
abnormal	yaltelemede	ያልተለመደ
exact	be't'k'kl	በትክክል
inexact	yaltemuala	ያልተሟላ
beautiful (m/f)	qonjo	ቆንጆ
ugly	asqeyami	አስቀያሚ
early	qedem b'lo	ቀደም ብሎ
late	qes b'lo	ቀስ ብሎ
dry	derek	ደረቅ
wet	ïrtb	እርጥብ
busy	s'ra yebezabet	ሥራ የበዛበት
not busy	s'ra yalbezabet	ሥራ ያልበዛበት
on	bertual	በርቱል
off	*te*ftual	ጠፍቱል

164

finished / completed	yaleqe	ያለቀ
unfinished / incomplete	yalaleqe	ያላለቀ
still	yerega	የረጋ
moving	ye'minqesaqes	የሚንቀሳቀስ
permanent	quami	ቋሚ
temporary	gizieyawi	ጊዜያዊ
expected	yetasebe / yete*t*ebeqe	የታሰበ / የተጠበቀ
unexpected	yaltasebe / yalte*t*ebeqe	ያልታሰበ / ያልተጠበቀ
better	yeteshale	የተሻለ
worse	asqeyami	አስቀያሚ
large / big	tlq	ትልቅ
small / little	tnsh	ትንሽ
natural	tefe*t*'roawi	ተፈጥሮአዊ
man-made	sew serash	ሰው ሰራሽ
edible	ye'mibela	የሚበላ
non-edible	ye'maybela	የማይበላ
modern	zemenawi	ዘመናዊ
traditional	bahlawi	ባህላዊ
important	*t*eqami	ጠቃሚ
unimportant	ye'may*t*eqm	የማይጠቅም
clean	n*ts*uh	ንፁህ
dirty	qoshasha	ቆሻሻ
foreign	yewch	የውጭ
domestic	yehager ws*t*	የሀገር ውስጥ
efficient	bqu	ብቁ
inefficient	bqat yelielew	ብቃት የሌለው
comfortable	mchu	ምቹ
uncomfortable	ye'maymech	የማይመች
young (person)	we*t*a*t*	ወጣት
old (person)	arogit / shmaglie	አሮጊት / ሽማግሌ
fast	fe*t*an	ፈጣን
slow	zegemtegna	ዘገምተኛ
working	ye'misera	የሚሰራ
not working	ye'maysera	የማይሰራ
complete	yetemuala	የተሟላ
incomplete	yaltemuala	ያልተሟላ

cheap	rkash	ርካሽ
expensive	wd	ውድ
dead	mut	ሙት
alive	behy'wet menor	በህይወት መኖር
sure	ïrgteña	እርግጠኛ
unsure	ïrgteña yalhone	እርግጠኛ ያልሆነ
public	yehzb	የህዝብ
private	yegil	የግል
deep	tlq	ጥልቅ
shallow	qrb	ቅርብ
relaxing	ye'miyaz'nana	የሚያዝናና
stressful	ye'miyachenan'q	የሚያጨናንቅ
similar	temesasay	ተመሳሳይ
different	yeteleyaye	የተለያየ
legal	hgaw	ህጋዊ
illegal	hge-wet	ህገ-ወጥ
lucky	ïdleña	እድለኛ
unlucky	ïdlebis	እድለቢስ
major	wana	ዋና
minor	teqetay	ተቀጣይ
functional	ye'miyagelegl	የሚያገለግል
dysfunctional	ye'mayagelegl	የማያገለግል
convenient	ye'mimech	የሚመች
inconvenient	ye'maymech	የማይመች
basic	meseretawi	መሰረታዊ
complex	w'sb'sb	ውስብስብ
possible	ye'michal	የሚቻል
impossible	ye'maychal	የማይቻል
responsible	ye'mimeleketew	የሚመለከተው
irresponsible	halafinet ye'maywesd	ሃላፊነት የማይወስድ
real	t'k'kl	ትክከል
fake	wshet	ውሸት
vertical	quami	ቋሚ
horizontal	agdami	አግዳሚ
visible	ye'mitay	የሚታይ
invisible	ye'maytay	የማይታይ

balanced	mizanawi	ሚዛናዊ
imbalanced	ïmizanawi	ኢሚዛናዊ
useful	tekame	ጠቃሚ
useless	ye'mayteqm	የማይጠቅም
sharp	s'letam	ስለታም
blunt	duldum	ዱልዱም
timid	debzaza	ደብዛዛ
bold	demaq	ደማቅ
new (thing)	adis	አዲስ
old (thing)	arogie	አሮጌ
young / younger (person)	tn'sh / tanash	ትንሽ / ታናሽ
old / older (person)	tl'q / talaq	ትልቅ / ታላቅ
exterior	wchawi	ውጫዊ
interior	wstawi	ውስጣዊ
hard	tenkara	ጠንካራ
soft	leslasa	ለስላሳ
tolerant	tagash	ታጋሽ
intolerant	ye'maytages / glf teña	የማይታገስ / ግልፍተኛ
truthful	haqeña	ሀቀኛ
dishonest	achberbari	አጭበርባሪ
entrance	mgbiya	መግቢያ
exit	mewcha	መውጫ
start	mejemeriya	መጀመሪያ
finish	mecheresha	መጨረሻ
problem	chgr	ችግር
solution	mefthie	መፍትሄ
minimum	zqteña	ዝቅተኛ
maximum	kefteña	ከፍተኛ
first name	ye'mejemeriya sm	የመጀመሪያ ስም
last name (sur name)	ye'abat sm	የአባት ስም
night	mata	ማታ
day	qen	ቀን
sun rise	yetsehay mewcha	የፀሀይ መውጫ
sun set	yetsehay megbiya	የፀሀይ መግቢያ
love	fqr	ፍቅር
hate	tlacha	ጥላቻ

war	tornet	ጦርነት
peace	selam	ሰላም
developing countries	tadagi hagerat	ታዳጊ ሀገራት
developed country	yadegu hagerat	ያደጉ ሀገራት
adult	golmasa	ጎልማሳ
child	htsan	ህፃን
open (v)	mekfet	መክፈት
close (v)	mezgat	መዝጋት
increase (v)	mechemer	መጨመር
decrease (v)	meqenes	መቀነስ
find (v)	magñet	ማግኘት
lose (v)	matat	ማጣት
win (m/f)	ashenefe / ashenefech	አሸነፈ / አሸነፈች
lose (m/f)	teshenefe / teshenefech	ተሸነፈ / ተሸነፈች
give (v)	mestet	መስጠት
take (v)	meqebel / mewsed	መቀበል / መውሰድ
catch (v)	meyaz	መያዝ
throw (v)	mewerer	መወርወር
build (v)	megenbat	መገንባት
destroy (v)	mafres	ማፍረስ
send (v)	melak	መላክ
receive (v)	meqebel	መቀበል
join (v)	meqelaqel	መቀላቀል
separate (v)	meleyayet	መለያየት
push (v)	megfast	መግፋት
pull (v)	mesab	መሳብ
Sit down (m/f).	teqemet /teqemechi	ተቀመጥ / ተቀመጪ
Stand up (m/f).	qum / qumi	ቁም / ቁሚ
Pick it up (m/f).	ansaw / anshiw	አንሳው / አንሺው
Put it down (m/f).	asqemtew / askemchw	አስቀምጠው / አስቀምጭው
come (v)	memtat	መምጣት
go (v)	mehied	መሄድ
combine / mix (v)	matamer	ማጣመር
separate (v)	meleyayet	መለያየት
remember (v)	mastawes	ማስታወስ
forget (v)	mersat	መርሳት

VERB LIST

Following are verbs listed in their **infinitive** form, as well as **first person**, and the **first person past tense**. By studying these, one can memorize the conjugation or make assumptions based on patterns. See the grammar section on verb conjugation to understand how to conjugate for other tenses (2nd, 3rd, male, female, plural, etc). Note that each verb infinitve starts with **me** or **ma**.

There are actually two ways to conjugate verbs in the past tense. These, generally speaking, represent *short term(ST) past*, and *long term (LT) past*. In the following table, the verbs ending with **ku** or *hu* or short-term past. The verbs ending with **alehu**, are for more long term past. The alternatives to these conjugations are provided after the forward slash. Either one can be used in the Amharic grammar use.

English verb	Amharic infinitive	Present tense – 1st person	Past tense – (ST / LT) 1st person
absorb	መምጠጥ	እመጣለሁ	መጠጥኩ / መጥጫለሁ
	mem'*tet*	ïme*ta*lehu	me*tet*'ku / me*t'cha*lehu
accept / receive	መቀበል	እቀበላለሁ	ተቀበልኩ / ተቀብያለሁ
	meqebel	ïqebelalehu	teqebelku / teqeb'yalehu
accompany	ማጀብ	አጅባለሁ	አጀብኩ / አጅቤአለሁ
	majeb	aj'balehu	ajeb'ku / ajbie'alehu
accomplish	መፈፀም	እፈፅማለሁ	ፈፀምኩ / ፈፅሚያለሁ
	mefe*tse*m	ïfe*ts*malehu	fetsemku / fe*ts*mie'alehu
accuse	መክሰስ	እክሳለሁ	ከሰስኩ / ከስሻለሁ
	mekses	ïkesalehu	kesesku / kes'shalehu
acquire	ማግኘት	አገኛለሁ	አገኘሁ / አግኝቻለሁ
	mañet	ageñalehu	ageñehu / agñ'chalehu

169

adapt	መልመድ	እለምዳለሁ	ለመድኩ / ለምጃለሁ
	melmed	ïlemdalehu	lemedku / lemjalehu
add / increase	መጨመር	እጨምራለሁ	ጨመርኩ / ጨምሬአለሁ
	mechemer	ïchemralehu	chemerku / chemrie'alehu
adjust	ማስተካከል	አስተካክላለሁ	አስተካከልኩ / አስተካክያለሁ
	mastekakel	astekaklalehu	astekakelku / astekak'yalehu
admire	ማድነቅ	አደንቃለሁ	አደነቅሁ / አድንቄአለሁ
	mad'neq	adenqalehu	adeneqhu / adnqie'alehu
advise / consult	መምከር	እመክራለሁ	መከርኩ / መከሬያለሁ
	memker	ïmekralehu	mekerku / mekrie'alehu
affirm / prove	ማረጋገጥ	አረጋግጣለሁ	አረጋገጥኩ / አረጋግጫለሁ
	maregaget	aregagtalehu	aregaget'ku / aregag'chalehu
agree	መስማማት	እስማማለሁ	ተስማማሁ / ተስማምቻለሁ
	mesmamat	ïsmamalehu	tesmamahu / tesmamchalehu
aim	ማለም	አልማለሁ	አለምኩ / አልሜአለሁ
	malem	almalehu	alemku / almie'alehu
allow/permit	መፍቀድ	እፈቅዳለሁ	ፈቀድኩ / ፈቅጃለሁ
	mefqed	ïfeqdalehu	feqed'ku / feqjalehu
alter	መለወጥ	አለውጣለሁ	ለወጥኩ / ለውጫለሁ
	melewet	ïlewtalehu	lewet'ku / lewchalehu
amaze	መገረም	እገረማለሁ	ተገረምኩ / ተገርሜአለሁ
	megerem	ïgeremalehu	tegeremku / tegermie'alehu
amputate	መቆረጥ	አቆረጣለሁ	ተቆረጥኩ / ተቆርጫለሁ
	meqoret	ïqoretalehu	teqoret'ku / teqorchalehu
amuse	ማስደሰት	አስደስታለሁ	አስደሰትኩ / አስደስቻለሁ
	madeset	asdestalehu	asdesetku / asdes'chalehu
analyze	መተንተን	እተነትናለሁ	ተነተንኩ / ተንትኛለሁ
	metenten	ïtenet'nalehu	tenetenku / tentñalehu
annoy	ማናደድ	አናድዳለሁ	አናደድኩ / አናድጃለሁ
	manaded	anad'dalehu	anaded'ku / anad'jalehu
applause/clap	ማጨብጨብ	አጨበጭባለሁ	አጨበጨብኩ / አጨበጭቤአለሁ
			achebechebku /
	macheb'cheb	achebech'balehu	achebech'bie'alehu
approach / be near	መቅረብ	እቀርባለሁ	ቀረብኩ / ቀርቤአለሁ
	meqreb	ïqerbalehu	qerebku / qerbie'alehu
appreciate	ማመስገን	አመስግናለሁ	አመሰገንኩ / አመስግኛለሁ
	mamesgen	amesegnalehu	amesegenku / amesgñalehu
approve / permit	መፍቀድ	እፈቅዳለሁ	ፈቀድኩ / ፈቅጃለሁ

170

	mefqed	ïfeqdalehu	feqedku / feqjalehu
argue	መከራከር	እከራከራለሁ	ተከራከርኩ / ተከራከርኣለሁ
	mekeraker	ïkerakeralehu	tekerakerku / tekerakrie'alehu
arrange	ማዘጋጀት	አዘጋጃለሁ	አዘጋጀሁ / አዘጋጅቻለሁ
	mazegajet	azegajalehu	azegajehu / azegaj'chalehu
arrest	ማሰር	አሰራለሁ	አሰርኩ / አስሬአለሁ
	maser	asralehu	aserku / asrie'alehu
arrive	መድረስ	እደርሳለሁ	ደረስኩ / ደርሻለሁ
	medres	ïdersalehu	deres'ku / dershalehu
ask	መጠየቅ	እጠይቃለሁ	ጠየቅኩ / ጠይቄያለሁ
	meteyeq	ïteyqalehu	teyeqku / teyqie'alehu
assemble	መገጣጠም	እገጣጥማለሁ	ገጣጠምኩ / ገጣጥሜአለሁ
	megetatem	ïgetat'malehu	getatemku / getat'mie'alehu
assess	መገምገም	እገመግማለሁ	ገመገምኩ / ገምግሜአለሁ
	megem'gem	ïgemegmalehu	gemegemku / gemg'mie'alehu
assign	መመደብ	እመድባለሁ	መደብኩ / መድቤአለሁ
	memedeb	ïmed'balehu	medeb'ku / medbie'alehu
assist	ማገዝ	አግዛለሁ	አገዝኩ / አግዜአለሁ
	magez	agzalehu	agezku / agzie'alehu
attach	ማያያዝ	አያይዛለሁ	አያያዝኩ / አያይዜአለሁ
	mayayaz	ayay'zalehu	ayayazku / ayay'zie'alehu
attack	ማጥቃት	አጠቃለሁ	አጥቅቼአለሁ / አጠቃሁ
	matqat	ateqalehu	ateqahu / atqchie'alehu
attempt (try)	መሞከር	እሞክራለሁ	ሞከርኩ / ሞክሬአለሁ
	memoker	ïmokralehu	mokerku / mokrie'alehu
avoid	ማስወገድ	አስወግዳለሁ	አስወገድኩ / አስወግጃለሁ
	masweged	aswegdalehu	aswegedku / aswegjalehu
bake	መጋገር	እጋግራለሁ	ጋገርኩ / ጋግሬአለሁ
	megager	ïgagralehu	gagerku / gagrie'alehu
bathe	መታጠብ	እታጠባለሁ	ታጠብኩ / ታጥቤአለሁ
	metateb	ïtatebalehu	tatebku / tat'bie'alehu
be (become)	መሆን	እሆናለሁ	ሆንኩ / ሆኛለሁ
	mehon	ïhonalehu	honku / hoñalehu
be able	መቻል	እችላለሁ	ቻልኩ / ችያለሁ
	mechal	ïchlalehu	chalku / chiyalehu
be better	መሻል	እሻላለሁ	ተሻልኩ / ተሽያለሁ
	meshal	ïshalalehu	teshalku / teshyalehu

171

be born	መወለድ	እወለዳለሁ	ተወለድኩ / ተወልጃለሁ
	meweld	ïweledalehu	teweledku / teweljalehu
be busy	መባከን	እባክናለሁ	ባከንኩ / ባከኛለሁ
	mebaken	ïbaknalehu	bakenku / bakñalehu
be called	መጠራት	እጠራለሁ	ተጠሩ / ተጠርቻለሁ
	meterat	ïteralehu	teterahu / teterchalehu
be found	መገኘት	እገኛለሁ	ተገኙ / ተገኝቻለሁ
	megeñet	ïgeñalehu	tegeñehu / tegeñ'chalehu
be full	መሙላት	እሞላለሁ	ሞላሁ / ሞልቻለሁ
	memulat	ïmolalehu	molahu / molchalehu
be happy	መደሰት	እደሰታለሁ	ተደሰትኩ / ተደስቻለሁ
	medeset	ïdesetalehu	tedesetku / tedeschalehu
be healthy	ጤናማ መሆን	ጤናማ እሆናለሁ	ጤናማ ሆንኩ / ጤናማ ሆኛለሁ
	tenama	tenama	tenama honku / tenama
	mehon	ïhonalehu	hoñalehu
be hungry	መራብ	እራባለሁ	ተራብኩ / ተርቤአለሁ
	merab	ïrabalehu	terabku / terbie'alehu
be ill	መታመም	እታመማለሁ	ታመምኩ / ታምሜአለሁ
	metamem	ïtamemalehu	tamemku / tamammie'alehu
be jealous	መቅናት	እቀናለሁ	ቀናሁ / ቀንቻለሁ
	meqnat	ïqenalehu	qenahu / qenchalehu
be known	መታወቅ	እታወቃለሁ	ታወቁ / ታወቄአለሁ
	metawq	ïtaweqalehu	taweqhu / tawqie'alehu
be located	መገኘት	እገኛለሁ	ተገኙ / ተገኝቻለሁ
	megeñet	ïgeñalehu	tegeñehu / tegeñchalehu
be moving /shaking	መንቀጥቀጥ	እንቀጠቀጣለሁ	ተንቀጠቀጥኩ / ተንቀጥቀጭለሁ
			tenqeteqer'ku /
	menqet'qet	ïn'qeteqetalehu	tenqet'qchalehu
be next	መቀጠል	እቀጥላለሁ	ቀጠልኩ / ቀጥያለሁ
	meqetel	ïqet'lalehu	qetel'ku / qet'yalehu
be present	መገኘት	እገኛለሁ	ተገኙ / ተገኝቻለሁ
	megeñet	ïgeñalehu	tegeñehu / tegeñchalehu
be sick	metamem	እታመማለሁ	ታመምኩ / ታምሜአለሁ
	መታመም	ïtamemalehu	tamemku / tam'mie'alehu
be sorry / sad	ማዘን	አዝናለሁ	አዘንኩ / አዝኛለሁ
	mazen	aznalehu	azenku / azñalehu
be stressed	መጨነቅ	እጨነቃዘለሁ	ተጨነቅሁ / ተጨንቄአልሁ
	mecheneq	ïchenqalehu	techeneq'hu / techenqie'alehu
be suitable	መመቸት	እመቻለሁ	ተመቹ / ተመችቻለሁ

172

	memechet	ïmechalehu	temechehu / temech'chalehu
be taller / extend	መርዘም	እረዝማለሁ	ረዘምኩ / ረዝሜአለሁ
	merzem	ïrezmalehu	rezemku / rezmie'alehu
be thirsty	መጠማት	እጠማለሁ	ተጠማሁ / ተጠምቻለሁ
	me*t*emat	ï*t*emalehu	te*t*emahu / te*t*emchalehu
be tired	መድከም	እደከማለሁ	ደከምኩ / ደከሜአለሁ
	medkem	ïdekmalehu	dekemku / dekmie'alehu
be unable to find	ማጣት	አጣለሁ	አጣሁ / አጥቻለሁ
	ma*t*at	a*t*alehu	a*t*ahu / a*t*'chalehu
be useful	መጥቀም	እጠቅማለሁ	ጠቀምኩ / ጠቅሜአለሁ
	me*t*'qem	ï*t*eqmalehu	*t*eqemku / *t*eqmie'alehu
be / become / happen	መሆን	እሆናለሁ	ሆንኩ / ሆኛለሁ
	mehon	ïhonalehu	honku / hoñalehu
be amazed / surprised	መገረም	እገረማለሁ	ተገረምኩ / ተገርሜአለሁ
	megerem	ïgeremalehu	tegeremku / tegermie'alehu
be angry	መናደድ	እናደዳለሁ	ተናደድኩ / ተናድጃለሁ
	menaded	ïnadedalehu	tenadedku / tenad'jalehu
beat / hit	መምታት	እመታለሁ	መታሁ / መትቻለሁ
	memtat	ïmetalehu	metahu / metchalehu
be younger / be less	ማነስ	አነሳለሁ	አነስኩ / አንሻለሁ
	manes	ansalehu	anesku / anshalehu
beautify / decorate	ማስዋብ	አስውባለሁ	አስዋብኩ / አስውቤአለሁ
	maswab	aswbalehu	aswabku / aswbie'alehu
beg	መለመን	እለምናለሁ	ለመንኩ/ ለምኛለሁ
	melemen	ïlemnalehu	lemenku / lemñalehu
become good / successful	ውጤታማ መሆን	ውጤታማ እሆናለሁ	ውጤታማ ሆንኩ / ውጤታማ ሆኛለሁ
	w*t*ietama mehon	w*t*ietama ïhonalehu	w*t*ietama honku / w*t*ietama hoñalehu
believe	ማመን	አምናለሁ	አመንኩ / አምኛለሁ
	mamen	amnalehu	amenku / amñalehu
bite	መንከስ	እነክሳለሁ	ነከስኩ / ነከሼአለሁ
	menkes	ïneksalehu	nekesku / nekshie'alehu
blame	መወቀስ	እወቅሳለሁ	ወቀስኩ / ወቅሻለሁ
	mew'qes	ïweqsalehu	weqesku / weq'shalehu
bleed	መድማት	እደማለሁ	ደማሁ / ደም'ቻለሁ
	med'mat	ïdemalehu	demahu / dem'chalehu
bless	መባረክ	እባርካለሁ	ባረኩ / ባርኬአለሁ

173

		mebarek	ïbarkalehu	bareku / bar'kie'alehu
blow / pump	መንፈስ		እነፍሳለሁ	አነፈስኩ / አንፍሻለሁ
		menfes	anef'salehu	anefesku / anfshalehu
boil	ማፍላት		አፈላለሁ	አፈላሁ / አፍልቻለሁ
		maflat	afelalehu	afelahu / aflchalehu
borrow (and return)	መዋስ		እዋሳለሁ	ተዋስኩ / ተውሻለሁ
		mewas	ïwasalehu	tewasku / tewshalehu
borrow (consumable)	መበደር		እበደራለሁ	ተበደርኩ / ተበድሬአለሁ
		mebeder	ïbederalehu	tebederku / tebed'rie'alehu
bother	ማስቸገር		አስቸግራለሁ	አስቸገርኩ / አስቸግሬአለሁ
		mascheger	aschegralehu	aschegerku / aschegrie'alehu
break	መስበር		እሰብራለሁ	ሰበርኩ / ሰብሬአለሁ
		mesber	ïsebralehu	seberku / sebrie'alehu
bring	ማምጣት		አመጣለሁ	አመጣሁ / አምጥቻለሁ
		mam*t*at	ame*t*alehu	ame*t*ahu / amtchalehu
brush	መቦረሽ		እቦርሻለሁ	ቦረሽኩ / ቦርሻለሁ
		meboresh	ïbor'shalehu	boresh'ku / borshalehu
build / construct	መገንባት		እገነባለሁ	ገነባሁ / ገንብቻለሁ
		megenbat	ïgenebalehu	genebahu / genbchie'alehu
burn	ማቃጠል		አቃጥላለሁ	አቃጠልኩ / አቃጥያለሁ
		maqa*t*el	aqa*t*lalehu	aqa*t*elku / aqa*t*yalehu
buy	መግዛት		እገዛለሁ	ገዛሁ / ገዝቻለሁ
		megzat	ïgezalehu	gezahu / gezchalehu
calculate	ማስላት		አሰላለሁ	አሰላሁ / አስልቻለሁ
		maslat	aselalehu	aselahu / aslchalehu
call	መደወል		እደውላለሁ	ደወልኩ / ደውያለሁ
		medewel	ïdewlalehu	dewelku / dewyalehu
cancel	መሰረዝ		እሰርዛለሁ	ሰረዝኩ / ሰርዣለሁ
		meserez	iserzalehu	serezku / serzhalehu
capture	መማረክ		አማርካለሁ	ማረኩ / ማርኪአለሁ
		memarek	ïmarkalehu	mareku / markie'alehu
carry	መሸከም		እሸክማለሁ	ተሸከምኩ / ተሸክሜአለሁ
		meshkem	ïshekemalehu	teshekemku / teshekmie'alehu
catch	መያዝ		አይዛለሁ	ያዝኩ / ይዣለሁ
		meyaz	ïyzalehu	yazku / yzhalehu
cease / stop	ማስቆም		አስቆማለሁ	አስቆምኩ / አስቁሜአለሁ
		masqom	asqomalehu	asqom'ku / asqumie'alehu

174

celebrate	ማክበር	አከብራለሁ	አከበርኩ / አከብሬአለሁ
	makber	akebralehu	akeberku / akbrie'alehu
change	መቀየር	እቀይራለሁ	ቀየርኩ / ቀይሬአለሁ
	meqeyer	ïqeyralehu	qeyerku / qeyrie'alehu
change money	መዘርዘር	እዘረዝራለሁ	ዘረዘርኩ / ዘርዝሬአለሁ
	mezerzer	ïzerezralehu	zerezerku / zerzrie'alehu
chase	ማሳደድ	አሳድዳለሁ	አሳደድኩ / አሳድጃለሁ
	masaded	asad'dalehu	asaded'ku / asad'jalehu
chat	መወያየት	እወያያለሁ	ተወያየሁ / ተወያይቻለሁ
	meweyayet	ïweyayalehu	teweyayehu / teweyay'chalehu
cheat / trick	ማታለል	አታልላለሁ	አታለልኩ / አታልያለሁ
	matalel	atal'lalehu	atalelku / atalyalehu
chew	ማኘክ	አኝካለሁ	አኘኩ / አኝኬአለሁ
	mañek	añkalehu	añeku / añkie'alehu
choose	መምረጥ	እመርጣለሁ	መረጥኩ / መርጫለሁ
	memret	ïmertalehu	mererku / merchalehu
chop / cut	መቁረጥ	እቆርጣለሁ	ቆረጥኩ / ቆርጫለሁ
	mequret	ïqortalehu	qoretku / qorchalehu
circle / orbit	ማክበብ	አከባለሁ	አከበብኩ / አከብቤአለሁ
	makbeb	akebalehu	akebeb'ku / akb'bie'alehu
clap	ማጨብጨብ	አጨበጭባለሁ	አጨበጨብኩ / አጨብጭቤአለሁ
	machebcheb	achebechbalehu	achebechebku / achebchbie'alehu
clarify	መግለፅ	እገልፃለሁ	ገለፅኩ / ገልጫለሁ
	meglets	ïgeltsalehu	geletsku / gelchalehu
clean	ማፅዳት	አፀዳለሁ	አፀዳሁ / አፅድቻለሁ
	matsdat	atsedalehu	atsedahu / atsdchalehu
close / shut	መዝጋት	እዘጋለሁ	ዘጋሁ / ዘግቻለሁ
	mz'gat	ïzegalehu	zegahu / zgchalehu
collect	መሰብሰብ	እሰበስባለሁ	ሰበሰብኩ / ሰብስቤአለሁ
	mesebseb	ïsebes'balehu	sebeseb'ku / sebs'bie'alehu
combine / mix	ማዋሀድ	አዋህዳለሁ	አዋሀድኩ / አዋህጃለሁ
	mawahad	awahdalehu	awahadku / awahjalehu
come	መምጣት	እመጣለሁ	መጣሁ / መጥቻለሁ
	mem'tat	ïmetalehu	metahu / met'chalehu
come back / return	መመለስ	እመለሳለሁ	ተመለስኩ / ተመልሻለሁ
	memeles	ïmelesalehu	temelesku / temel'shalehu
complain	መቃወም	እቃወማለሁ	ተቃወምኩ / ተቃውሜአለሁ

175

	meqawem	ïqawemalehu	teqawemku / teqaw'mie'alehu
comply	መተግበር	እተገብራለሁ	ተገበርኩ / ተግብሬአለሁ
	metegber	ïtegebralehu	tegeberku / tegbrie'alehu
conceal / hide	መደበቅ	እደብቃለሁ	ደበቅኩ / ደብቄአለሁ
	medebeq	ïdebqalehu	debeqku / debqie'alehu
conceive (think)	ማሰብ	አስባለሁ	አሰብኩ / አስቤአለሁ
	maseb	asbalehu	asebku / asbie'alehu
conceive (pregnant)	መፀጠር	እፅጥራለሁ	ፀጠርኩ / ፅጥሬአለሁ
	mequater	ïquat'ralehu	quaterku / quat'rie'alehu
connect	ማገናኘት	አገናኛለሁ	አገናኙ / አገናኝቻለሁ
	magenañet	agenañalehu	agenañehu / agenañ'chalehu
conserve	መቆጠብ	እቆጥባለሁ	ቆጠብኩ / ቆጥቤአለሁ
	meqoteb	ïqot'balehu	qoteb'ku / qotebie'alehu
console	ማባበል	አባብላለሁ	አባበልኩ / አባብያለሁ
	mababel	abab'lalehu	ababel'ku / abab'yalehu
contact / touch	መነካካት	እነካካለሁ	ተነካሁ / ተነካክቻለሁ
	menekakat	ïnekakalehu	tenekakahu / tenekak'chalehu
continue	መቀጠል	እቀጥላለሁ	ቀጠልኩ / ቀጥያለሁ
	meqetel	ïqet'lalehu	qetelku / qet'yalehu
control	መቆጣጠር	እቆጣጠራለሁ	ተቆጣጠርኩ / ተቆጣጥሬአለሁ
	meqotater	ïqotateralehu	teqotaterku / teqotat'rie'alehu
cook	ማብሰል	አበስላለሁ	አበሰልኩ / አብስያለሁ
	mabsel	abeslalehu	abeselku / absyalehu
cough	ማሳል	አስላለሁ	አሳልኩ / አስያለሁ
	masal	as'lalehu	asalku / asyalehu
count	መቆጠር	እቆጥራለሁ	ቆጠርኩ / ቆጥሬአለሁ
	mequter	ïqot'ralehu	qoterku / qot'rie'alehu
correct	ማረም	አርማለሁ	አረምኩ / አርሜአለሁ
	marem	armalehu	aremku / armie'alehu
cover / cap / wear	መከደን	አከድናለሁ	ከደንኩ / ከድኛለሁ
	mekden	ïkednalehu	kedenku / kedñalehu
cover / conceal	መሸፈን	እሸፍናለሁ	ሸፈንኩ / ሸፍኛለሁ
	meshefen	ïshefnalehu	shefenku / shefñalehu
create / invent	መፍጠር	እፈጥራለሁ	ፈጠርኩ / ፈጥሬአለሁ
	mefter	ïfetralehu	feterku / fetrie'alehu
cross	መሻገር	እሻገራለሁ	ተሻገርኩ / ተሻግሬአለሁ
	meshager	ïshageralehu	teshagerku / teshagrie'alehu

cry / weep	ማልቀስ	አለቅሳለሁ	አለቀስኩ / አልቅሻለሁ
	malqes	aleqsalehu	aleqesku / alqshalehu
cure	ማዳን	አድናለሁ	አዳንኩ / አድኛለሁ
	madan	ad'nalehu	adanku / ad'ñalehu
cut	መቁረጥ	እቆጣለሁ	ቆረጥኩ / ቆርጫለሁ
	mequret	ïqortalehu	qoretku / qorchalehu
dance	መደነስ	እደንሳለሁ	ደነስኩ / ደንሻለሁ
	medens	ïdensalehu	denesku / denshalehu
decide / determine	መወሰን	እወስናለሁ	ወሰንኩ / ወስኛለሁ
	mewesen	ïwesnalehu	wesenku / wesñalehu
deforest	መጨፍጨፍ	እጨፈጭፋለሁ	ጨፈጭፍኩ / ጨፍጭፌአለሁ chefechef'ku /
	mechef'chef	ïchefechfalehu	chefch'fie'alehu
delete	መሰረዝ	እሰርዛለሁ	ሰረዝኩ / ሰርዣለሁ
	meserez	ïserzalehu	serezku / serzhalehu
deny	መካልከል	እከለከላለሁ	ከለከልኩ / ከልክያለሁ
	mekelkel	ïkelek'lalehu	kelekelku / kelk'yalehu
depend	መመርኮዝ	እመረኮዛለሁ	ተመረኮዝኩ / ተመርኮግለሁ
	memerkoz	ïmerekozalehu	temerekozku
describe	መግለጽ	እገልጻለሁ	ገለጽኩ / ገልጫለሁ
	meglets	ïgel'tsalehu	gelets'ku / gelchalehu
destroy	ማውደም	አወድማለሁ	አወደምኩ / አው-ድሚአለሁ
	mawdem	awedmalehu	awedemku / awdmie'alehu
die	መሞት	እሞታለሁ	ሞትኩ / ሞቻለሁ
	memot	ïmotalehu	motku / mochalehu
dig	መቆፈር	እቆፍራለሁ	ቆፈርኩ / ቆፍሬአለሁ
	meqofer	ïqofralehu	qoferku / qofrie'alehu
disagree	አለመስማማት	አልስማማ ም	አልተስማማሁም
	alemesmamat	alsmamam	altes'mamahum
disappear	መጥፋት	እጠፋለሁ	ጠፋሁ / ጠፍቻለሁ
	metfat	ïtefalehu	tefahu / tefchalehu
distribute	ማደል	አድላለሁ	አደልኩ / አድያለሁ
	madel	adlalehu	adelku / adyalehu
disapoint	ማሳዘን	አሳዝናለሁ	አሳዘንኩ / አሳዝኛለሁ
	masazen	asaznalehu	asazenku / asazñalehu
dislike	አለመውደድ	አልወድም	አልወደርኩም
	alemewded	alwedm	alwededkum
dismiss (employee)	መሰናበት	እሰናታለሁ	ተሰናበትኩ / ተሰናብቻለሁ

177

	mesenabet	ïsenabetalehu	tesenabetku / tesenab'chalehu
disobey / refuse	መቃወም	እቃወማለሁ	ተቃወምኩ / ተቃወሜአለሁ
	meqawem	ïqawemalehu	teqawemku / teqaw'mie'alehu
dispose	መጣል	እጥላለሁ	ጣልኩ / ጥያለሁ
	metal	ït'lalehu	talku / t'yalehu
distribute	ማከፋፈል	አከፋፍላለሁ	አከፋፈልኩ / አከፋፍያለሁ
	makefafel	akefaf'lalehu	akefafelku / akefaf'yalehu
divide	ማካፈል	አካፍላለሁ	አካፈልኩ / አካፍያለሁ
	makafel	akaf'lalehu	akafelku / akafyalehu
do	መስራት	እሰራለሁ	ሰራሁ / ሰርቻለሁ
	mesrat	ïseralehu	serahu / ser'chalehu
drain	ማድረቅ	አደርቃለሁ	አደረቅሁ / አድርቄአለሁ
	madreq	aderqalehu	adereq'hu / adrqie'alehu
draw	መሳል	እስላለሁ	ሳልኩ / ስያለሁ
	mesal	ïslalehu	salku / syalehu
dream	ማለም	አልማለሁ	አለምኩ / አልሜአለሁ
	malem	almalehu	alemku / almie'alehu
dress	መልበስ	እለብሳለሁ	ለበስኩ / ለብሻለሁ
	mel'bes	ïlebsalehu	lebesku / leb'shalehu
drink	መጠጣት	እጠጣለሁ	ጠጣሁ / ጠጥቻለሁ
	metetat	ïtetalehu	tetahu / tetchalehu
drive	መንዳት	እነዳለሁ	ነዳሁ / ነድቻለሁ
	mendat	ïnedalehu	nedahu / ned'chalehu
drown	መስመጥ	እሰምጣለሁ	ሰመጥኩ / ሰምጫለሁ
	mesmet	ïsemtalehu	semerku / semchalehu
dry	ማድረቅ	አደርቃለሁ	አደረቅሁ / አድርቄአለሁ
	madreq	aderqalehu	adereq'hu / adrqie'alehu
earn	መከፈል	እከፈላለሁ	ተከፈልኩ / ተከፍያለሁ
	mekefel	ïkefelalehu	tekefel'ku / tekef'yalehu
eat	መብላት	እበላለሁ	በላሁ / በልቻለሁ
	meblat	ïbelalehu	belahu / belchalehu
edit	ማረም	አርማለሁ	አረምኩ / አርሜአለሁ
	marem	armalehu	aremku / armie'alehu
elect	መምረጥ	እመርጣለሁ	መረጥኩ / መርጫለሁ
	memret	ïmertalehu	mererku / merchalehu
embarrass	ማፈር	አፍራለሁ	አፈርኩ / አፍሬአለሁ
	mafer	afralehu	aferku / afrie'alehu

178

embrace	ማቀፍ	አቀፋለሁ	አቀፍኩ / አቅፌአለሁ
	maqef	aqfalehu	aqefku / aqfie'alehu
encourage	ማበረታታት	አበረታታለሁ	አበረታታሁ / አበረታትቻለሁ
	maberetatat	aberetatalehu	aberetatahu / aberetat'chalehu
endure	መጽናት	እጸናለሁ	ጸናሁ / ጸንቻለሁ
	me*ts*'nat	ï*ts*enalehu	*ts*enahu / *ts*en'chalehu
enjoy	መዝናና	እዝናናለሁ	ተዝናናሁ / ተዝናንቻለሁ
	meznanat	ïznanalehu	teznanahu / teznanchalehu
enter	መግባት	እገባለሁ	ገባሁ / ገብቻለሁ
	megbat	ïgebalehu	gebahu / gebchalehu
erase	ማጥፋት	አጠፋለሁ	አጠፋሁ / አጥፍቻለሁ
	ma*t*'fat	a*t*efalehu	a*t*efahu / a*t*'fchalehu
err / to be wrong	መሳሳት	እሳሳታለሁ	ተሳሳትኩ / ተሳስቻለሁ
	mesasat	ïsasatalehu	tesasatku / tesaschalehu
escape / runaway	ማምለጥ	አመልጣለሁ	አመለጥኩ / አምልጫለሁ
	mamle*t*	amel*t*alehu	amele*t*ku / aml*cha*lehu
establish / found	ማግኘት	አገኛለሁ	አገኙ / አግኝቻለሁ
	magñet	ageñalehu	ageñehu / agñ'chalehu
evaluate	መገምገም	እገመግማለሁ	ገመገምኩ / ገምግሜአለሁ
	megemgem	ïgemegmalehu	gemegemku / gemgmie'alehu
examine	መመርመር	እመረምራለሁ	መረመርኩ / መርምሬአለሁ
	memermer	ïmeremralehu	meremerku / mermrie'alehu
exceed / surpass	ማለፍ	አልፋለሁ	አለፍኩ / አልፌአለሁ
	malef	alfalehu	alefku / alfie'alehu
exchange	መቀያየር	እቀያየራለሁ	ተቀያየርኩ /
	meqeyayer	ïqeyayeralehu	teqeyayerku / teqeyay'rie'alehu
exit	መውጣት	እወጣለሁ	ወጣሁ / ወጥቻለሁ
	mew'ta*t*	ïwe*t*alehu	we*t*ahu / we*t*'chalehu
explain	መግለፅ	እገልፃለሁ	ገለፅኩ / ገልጫለሁ
	megle*ts*	ïgel*ts*alehu	gele*ts*ku / gel*cha*lehu
explode	ማፈንዳት	አፈነዳለሁ	አፈነዳሁ / አፈንድቻለሁ
	mafendat	afenedalehu	afenedahu / afendchalehu
explore	ማድረስ	አደርሳለሁ	አደረስኩ / አድርሻለሁ
	madres	adersalehu	aderesku / adr'shalehu
fail / fall down	መውደቅ	እወድቃለሁ	ወደቅኩ / ወድቄአለሁ
	mewdeq	ïwedqalehu	wedeqku / wedqie'alehu
farm / plough	ማረስ	አርሳለሁ	አረስኩ / አርሻለሁ

	mares	arsalehu	aresku / arshalehu
fear	መፍራት	እፈራለሁ	ፈራሁ / ፈርቻለሁ
	mefrat	ïferalehu	ferahu / ferchie'alehu
feed	መመገብ	እመግባለሁ	ተመገብኩ / ተመግቤአለሁ
	memegeb	ïmegebalehu	temegebku / temegbie'alehu
feel	መሰማት	ይሰማኛል	ተሰማኝ / ተሰምቶኛል
	mesemat	ysemañal	tesemañ / tesemtoñal
fight	መጣላት	እጣላለሁ	ተጣላሁ / ተጣልቻለሁ
	metalat	ïtalalehu	tetalahu / tetalchalehu
fill	መሙላት	እሞላለሁ	ሞላሁ / ሞልቻለሁ
	memulat	ïmolalehu	molahu / mol'chalehu
find / get	ማግኘት	አገኛለሁ	አገኘሁ / አግኝቻለሁ
	magñet	ageñalehu	ageñehu / agñchalehu
finish	መጨረስ	እጨርሳለሁ	ጨረስኩ / ጨርሻለሁ
	mecheres	ïchersalehu	cheresku / chershalehu
fix / repair	መጠገን	እጠግናለሁ	ጠገንኩ / ጠግኛለሁ
	metegen	ïtegnalehu	tegenku / tegñalehu
flee (run away)	መሸሽ	እሸሻለሁ	ሸሹ / ሸሽቻለሁ
	meshesh	ïsheshalehu	sheshehu / shesh'chalehu
flow	ማፍሰስ	አፈሳለሁ	አፈሰስኩ / አፍስሻለሁ
	mafses	afesalehu	afesesku / afs'shalehu
fly	መብረር	እበራለሁ	በረርኩ / በርሬአለሁ
	mebrer	ïberalehu	bererku / berrie'alehu
follow up / chase / track down	መከታተል	እከታተላለሁ	ተከታተልኩ / ተከታትያለሁ
	meketatel	ïketatelalehu	teketatelku / teketatyalehu
force / compel	ማስገደድ	አስገድዳለሁ	አስገደድኩ / አስገድጃለሁ
	masgded	asgeddalehu	asgededku / asgedjalehu
forget / neglect	መርሳት	እረሳለሁ	ረሳሁ / ረስቻለሁ
	mersat	ïresalehu	resahu / reschalehu
forgive	መማር	እምራለሁ	ማርኩ / ምሬአለሁ
	memar	ïm'ralehu	marku / mrie'alehu
fry	መጥበስ	እጠብሳለሁ	ጠበስኩ / ጠብሻለሁ
	metbes	ïtebsalehu	tebesku / tebshalehu
gain / increase	መጨመር	እጨምራለሁ	ጨመርኩ / ጨምሬአለሁ
	mechemer	ïchemralehu	chemerku / chemrie'alehu
get	ማግኘት	አገኛለሁ	አገኘሁ / አግኝቻለሁ
	magñet	ageñalehu	ageñehu / agñchalehu

get on	መወጣት	እወጣለሁ	ወጣሁ / ወጥቻለሁ
	mewtat	ïwetalehu	wetahu / wet'chalehu
get off	መውረድ	እወርዳለሁ	ወረድኩ / ወርጃለሁ
	mew'red	ïwerdalehu	weredku / wer'jalehu
give	መስጠት	እሰጣለሁ	ሰጠሁ / ሰጥቻለሁ
	mestet	ïsetalehu	setehu / setchalehu
give back (return a thing)	መመለስ	እመልሳለሁ	መለስኩ / መልሻለሁ
	memeles	ïmelsalehu	melesku / melshalehu
give birth	መውለድ	እወልዳለሁ	ወለድኩ / ወልጃለሁ
	mewled	ïweldalehu	weledku / weljalehu
go (depart)	መሄድ	እሄዳለሁ	ሄድኩ / ሄጃለሁ
	mehied	ïhiedalehu	hiedku / hiejalehu
go out	መውጣት	እወጣለሁ	ወጣሁ / ወጥቻለሁ
	mewtat	ïwetalehu	wetahu / wtchalehu
gossip	ማማት	አማለሁ	አማሁ / አምቻለሁ
	mamat	amalehu	amahu / amchalehu
govern	ማስተዳደር	አስተዳድራለሁ	አስተዳደርኩ / አስተዳድሬአለሁ
	mastedader	astedad'ralehu	astedaderku / astedad'rie'alehu
graze	መጋጥ	እግጣለሁ	ጋጥኩ / ግጫለሁ
	megat	ïg'talehu	gat'ku / gchalehu
greet	መተዋወቅ	እተዋወቃለሁ	ተዋወቁሁ / ተዋውቄአለሁ
	metewaweq	ïtewaweqalehu	tewaweq'hu / tewawqie'alehu
grieve	ማዘን	አዝናለሁ	አዘንኩ / አዝኛለሁ
	mazen	aznalehu	azenku / azñalehu
grin / smile	ማሾፍ	አሾፋለሁ	አሾፍኩ / አሹፌአለሁ
	mashof	ashofalehu	ashofku / ashufie'alehu
grind	መፍጨት	እፈጫለሁ	ፈጨሁ / ፈጭቻለሁ
	mefchet	ïfechalehu	fechehu / fechchalehu
grow	ማብቀል	አበቅላለሁ	አበቀልኩ / አበቅያለሁ
	mabqel	abeqlalehu	abeqelku / abqyalehu
grow up / raise	መጨመር	እጨምራለሁ	ጨመርኩ / ጨምሬአለሁ
	mechemer	ïchemralehu	chemerku / chemrie'alehu
grow old	ማርጀት	አረጃለሁ	አረጀሁ / አርጅቻለሁ
	marjet	arejalehu	arejehu / arj'chalehu
growl	መጮህ	እጮሃለሁ	ጮህኩ / ጮኪአለሁ
	mechoh	ïchohalehu	choh'ku / chokie'alehu
guard / protect	መጠበቅ	እጠብቃለሁ	ጠበቁሁ / ጠብቄአለሁ

	metebeq	ïteb'qalehu	tebeqhu / teb'qie'alehu
guess	መገመት	እገምታለሁ	ገመትኩ / ገምቻለሁ
	megemet	ïgemtalehu	gemetku / gem'chalehu
haggle / negotiate	መደራደር	እዳራደራለሁ	ተደራደርኩ / ተደራድሬአለሁ
	mederader	ïderaderalehu	tederaderku / tederad'rie'alehu
hang	መስቀል	እሰቅላለሁ	ሰቀልኩ / ሰቅያለሁ
	mesqel	ïseqlalehu	seqel'ku / seq'yalehu
hangout	ጊዜ ማጥፋት	ጊዜ እጠፋለሁ	ጊዜ አጠፋሁ / ጊዜ አጥፍቻለሁ
	gizie marfat	gizie atefalehu	gizie atefahu / gizie arfchie'alehu
harass	ማስፈራራት	እስፈራራለሁ	አስፈራራሁ / አስፈራርቻለሁ
	masferarat	asferaralehu	asferarahu / asferar'chalehu
harm / injure	መጎዳት	እጎዳለሁ	ተጎዳሁ / ተጎድቻለሁ
	megodat	ïgodalehu	tegodahu / tegod'chalehu
harvest	ማamረት	አመርታለሁ	አመርትኩ / አምርቻለሁ
	mam'ret	amertalehu	ameretku / amrchalehu
hate	መጥላት	እጠላለሁ	ጠላሁ / ጠልቻለሁ
	met'lat	ïtelalehu	telahu / telchalehu
have	መኖር	ይኖረኛል	ኖረኝ / ኖሮኛል
	menor	y'noreñal	noreñ / noroñal
have sex	ወሲብ መፈፀም	ወሲብ እፈፅማለሁ	ወሲብ ፈፀምኩ / ወሲድ ፈጽሜአለሁ
	wesib mefetsem	wesib ïfetsemalehu	wesib fetsemku / wesib fetsmie'alehu
hear	መስማት	እሰማለሁ	ሰማሁ / ሰምቻለሁ
	mesmat	ïsemalehu	semahu / semchalehu
help	መርዳት	እረዳለሁ	ረዳሁ / ረድቻለሁ
	merdat	ïredalehu	redahu / red'chalehu
hide	መደበቅ	እደብቃለሁ	ደበቅኩ / ደብቄአለሁ
	medebeq	ïdebqalehu	debeqku / debqie'alehu
hire	መቅጠር	እቀጥራለሁ	ቀጠርኩ / ቀጥሬአለሁ
	meqter	ïqet'ralehu	qeterku / qet'rie'alehu
hit	መምታት	እመታለሁ	መታሁ / መትቻለሁ
	memtat	ïmetalehu	metahu / met'chalehu
hold	መያዝ	እይዛለሁ	ያዝኩ / ይዣለሁ
	meyaz	ïy'zalehu	yazku / y'zhalehu
hug	ማቀፍ	አቅፋለሁ	አቀፍኩ / አቅፌአለሁ
	maqef	aqfalehu	aqefku / aqfie'alehu
hunt	ማደን	አድናለሁ	አደንኩ / አድ'ኛለሁ
	maden	adnalehu	adenku / ad'ñalehu

English	Amharic		
hurry	ማቀላጠፍ	አቀላጥፋለሁ	አቀላጥፍኩ / አቀላጥፌአለሁ
	maqelatef	aqelatfalehu	aqelatefku / aqelatfie'alehu
hurt	መጉዳት (ሌሎችን)	እንዳለሁ (ሌሎችን)	ጎዳሁ (ሌሎችን) / ጎድቻለሁ
	megudat	ïgodalehu	godahu / godchalehu
ignore	ቸላ ማለት	ቸላ እላለሁ	ቸላ አልኩ / ቸላ ብያለሁ
	ch'la malet	ch'la ï'lalehu	ch'la al'ku / ch'la b'yalehu
imagine	ማሰብ	አስባለሁ	አሰብኩ / አስቤአለሁ
	maseb	asbalehu	aseb'ku / asbie'alehu
immigrate	መሰደድ	እሰደዳለሁ	ተሰደድኩ / ተሰድጃለሁ
	meseded	ïsededalehu	tesededku / tesedjalehu
immunize	መከተብ	እከተባለሁ	ተከተብኩ / ተከትቤአለሁ
	meketeb	ïketebalehu	teketebku / teket'bie'alehu
impale	መስቀል	እሰቅላለሁ	ሰቀልኩ / ስቅያለሁ
	mesqel	iseq'lalehu	seqelku / seq'yalhu
impede / hamper	ማስተጓጎል	አስተጓጉላለሁ	አስተጓጎልኩ / አስተጓጉያለሁ
	masteguagol	asteguagulalehu	asteguagolku / asteguaguyalehu
imply / suggest	መጠቆም	እጠቁማለሁ	ጠቆምኩ / ጠቁሜአለሁ
	meteqom	ïtequmalehu	teqom'ku / tequmie'alehu
improve	ማሻሻል	አሻሽላለሁ	አሻሻልኩ / አሻሽያለሁ
	mashahsal	ashashlalehu	ashashalku / ashashyalehu
include	ማካተት	አካትታለሁ	አካተትኩ / አካትቻለሁ
	makatet	akat'talehu	akatet'ku / akat'chalehu
infect	መቁሰል	እቆስላለሁ	ቆሰልኩ / ቆስያለሁ
	mequsel	ïqos'lalehu	qosel'ku / qos'yalehu
influence	መጫን	እጫናለሁ	ተጫንኩ / ተጭኛለሁ
	mechan	ïchanalehu	techan'ku / tech'ñalehu
ingest	መዋጥ	እውጣለሁ	ዋጥኩ / ውጫለሁ
	mewat	ïwtalehu	wat'ku / w'chalehu
inherit	መውረስ	እወርሳለሁ	ወረስኩ / ወርሻለሁ
	mewres	ïwersalehu	weres'ku / wer'shalehu
inquire / ask	መጠየቅ	እጠይቃለሁ	ጠየቁ / ጠይቄአለሁ
	meteyeq	ïtey'qalehu	teyeqhu / teyqie'alehu
inspect	መመርመር	እመረምራለሁ	መረመርኩ / መርም'ሪአለሁ
	memermer	ïmeremralehu	meremerku / merm'rie'alehu
inspire / motivate	መበረታታት	እበረታታለሁ	ተበረታታሁ / ተበረታትቻለሁ
	meberetatat	ïberetatalehu	teberetatahu / teberetat'chalehu

183

insult	መስደብ	እሰድባለሁ	ሰደብኩ / ሰድቤአለሁ
	mes'ded	ïsedbalehu	sedebku / sed'bie'alehu
intend	ማሰብ	አሰባለሁ	አሰብኩ / አስቤአለሁ
	maseb	as'balehu	asebku / asbie'alehu
interrupt	ማቋረጥ	አቋርጣለሁ	አቋረጥኩ / አቋርቻለሁ
	maquaret	aquar*ta*lehu	aquaret'ku / aquar*cha*lehu
intimidate	ማስፈራራት	አስፈራራለሁ	አስፈራራሁ / አስፈራርቻለሁ
	mas'ferarat	asferaralehu	asferarahu / as'ferarchalehu
introduce (people)	ማስተዋወቅ	አስተዋወቃለሁ	አስተዋወኩ / አስተዋወቄአለሁ
	mastewaweq	astewawqalehu	astewaweku / astewawqie'alehu
invite	መጋበዝ	እጋብዛለሁ	ጋበዝኩ / ጋብዣለሁ
	megabez	ïgabzalehu	gabezku / gabzhalehu
joke	መቀለድ	እቀልዳለሁ	ቀለድኩ / ቀልጃለሁ
	meqeled	ïqeldalehu	qeledku / qel'jalehu
jump	መዝለል	እዘላለሁ	ዘለልኩ / ዘልያለሁ
	mezlel	ïzelalehu	zelelku / zelyalehu
keep	መያዝ	እይዛለሁ	ያዝኩ / ይዤአለሁ
	meyaz	ïyzalehu	yazku / yzhalehu
kick	መምታት	እመታለሁ	መታሁ / መትቻለሁ
	memtat	ïmetalehu	metahu / metchalehu
kill	መግደል	እገድላለሁ	ገደልኩ / ገድያለሁ
	megdel	ïgedlalehu	gedelku / gedyalehu
kiss	መሳም	እስማለሁ	ሳምኩ / ስሜአለሁ
	mesam	ïsmalehu	samku / smie'alehu
knock (on door)	ማንኳኳት	አንኳኳለሁ	አንኳኳሁ / አንኳኩቻለሁ
	mankuakuat	ankuakualehu	ankuakuahu / ankuakuchalehu
know / recognize	ማወቅ / መለየት	አውቃለሁ / አለያለሁ	አወቅሁ / ለየሁ / አውቄአለሁ / ለይቻለሁ
	maweq / meleyet	aw'qalehu / ïleyalehu	aweq'hu / leyehu / aw'qie'alehu / leychalehu
laugh	መሳቅ	እስቃለሁ	ሳቅሁ / ስቄአለሁ
	mesaq	ïs'qalehu	saq'hu / s'qie'alehu
launder (wash)	ማጠብ	አጥባለሁ	አጠብኩ / አጥቤአለሁ
	ma*t*eb	a*t*'balehu	a*t*ebku / a*t*'bie'alehu
lay down	መተኛት	እተኛለሁ	ተኛሁ / ተኝቻለሁ
	meteñat	ïteñalehu	teñahu / teñ'chalehu
lead	መምራት	እመራለሁ	መራሁ / መርቻለሁ
	memrat	ïmeralehu	merahu / merchalehu
leak	ማፍሰስ	አፈሳለሁ	አፈሰስኩ / አፍስሻለሁ

184

	mefses	afesalehu	afesesku / afs'shalehu
learn	መማር	እማራለሁ	ተማርኩ / ተምሬአለሁ
	memar	ïmaralehu	temarku / temrie'alehu
leave	መተው	እተዋለሁ	ተውኩ / ትቻለሁ
	metew	ïtewalehu	tewku / tchalehu
lend / loan	መበደር	እበደራለሁ	ተበደርኩ / ተበድሬአለሁ
(a consumable)	mebeder	ï'bederalehu	tebederku / tebedrie'alehu
lend (short term)	መዋስ	እዋሳለሁ	ተዋስኩ / ተውሻለሁ
	mewas	ïwasalehu	tewasku / tewshalehu
lessen	ማሳነስ	አሳንሳለሁ	አሳነስኩ / አሳንሻለሁ
	masanes	asansalehu	asanes'ku / asanshalehu
lick	መላስ	እልሳለሁ	ላስኩ / ልሻለሁ
	melas	ïlsalehu	lasku / lshalehu
lie (liar)	መዋሸት	እዋሻለሁ	ዋሸሁ / ዋሽቻለሁ
	mewashet	ïwashalehu	washehu / washchalehu
lift	ማንሳት	አነሳለሁ	አነሳሁ / አንስቻለሁ
	mansat	anesalehu	anesahu / anschalehu
like / love	መውደድ	እወዳለሁ	ወደድኩ / ወድጃለሁ
	mewded	ïwedalehu	wededku / wedjalehu
limp	ማነከስ	አነክሳለሁ	አነከስኩ / አንክሻለሁ
	manekes	anek'salehu	anekesku / ank'shalehu
listen	ማዳመጥ	አዳምጣለሁ	አዳመጥኩ / አዳምጬለሁ
	madamet	adamtalehu	adametku / adamchalehu
live / be available	መገኘት	እገኛለሁ	ተገኘሁ / ተገኝቻለሁ
	megeñet	ïgeñalehu	tegeñehu / tegeñchalehu
lock	መቆለፍ	እቆልፋለሁ	ቆለፍኩ / ቆልፌአለሁ
	meqolef	ïqolfalehu	qolefku / qolfie'alehu
look / see	ማየት	አያለሁ	አየሁ / አይቻለሁ
	mayet	ayalehu	ayehu / aychalehu
lose (game, etc)	መሸነፍ	እሸነፋለሁ	ተሸነፍኩ / ተሸነፌአለሁ
	meshenef	ïshenefalehu	teshenefku / teshenfie'alehu
lose (possession)	ማጥፋት	አጠፋለሁ	አጠፋሁ / አጥፍቼአለሁ
	matfat	atefalehu	atefahu / atfchie'alehu
love	ማፍቀር	አፈቅራለሁ	አፈቀርኩ / አፍቅሬአለሁ
	mafqer	afeqrlehu	afeqerku / afqrie'alehu
lower	መቀነስ	እቀንሳለሁ	ቀነስኩ / ቀንሻለሁ
	meqenes	ïqensalehu	qenesku / qenshalehu

185

magnify / increase	መጨመር	እጨምራለሁ	ጨመርኩ / እጨምራለሁ
	mechemer	ïchem'ralehu	chemerku / ïchem'ralehu
make	መስራት	እሰራለሁ	ሰራሁ / ሰርቻለሁ
	mesrat	ïseralehu	serahu / serchalehu
make fertile	ማልማት	አለማለሁ	አለማሁ / አልምቻለሁ
	malmat	alemalehu	alemahu / almchalehu
manufacture / produce	ማምረት	አመርታለሁ	አመረትኩ / አምርቻለሁ
	mamret	amertalehu	ameretku / amrchalehu
marry	ማግባት	አገባለሁ	አገባሁ / አግብቻለሁ
	magbat	agebalehu	agebahu / agb'chalehu
measure / weigh	መለካት	እለካለሁ	ለካሁ / ለክቻለሁ
	melekat	ïlekalehu	lekahu / lek'chalehu
meet	መገናኘት	እገናኛለሁ	ተገናኘሁ / ተገናኘሁ
	megenañet	ïgenañalehu	tegenañehu / tegenañchalehu
meet / encounter	ማገናኘት	አገናኛለሁ	አገናኘሁ / አገናኝቻለሁ
	magenañet	agenañalehu	agenañehu / agenañchalehu
memorize	ማስታወስ	አስታውሳለሁ	አስታወስኩ / አስታውሻለሁ
	mastawes	astawsalehu	astawesku / astawshalehu
to miss (an item)	ማጣት	አጣለሁ	አጣሁ / አጥቻለሁ
	matat	atalehu	atahu / atchalehu
milk	ማለብ	አልባለሁ	አለብኩ / አልቤአለሁ
	maleb	albalehu	alebk'u / albie'alehu
mimic / imitate	ማስመሰል	አስመስላለሁ	አስመሰልኩ / አስመስያለሁ
	masmesel	asmes'lalehu	asmeselku / asmes'yalehu
to miss (a bus, a class, etc)	ማምለጥ	ያመልጠኛል	አመለጠኝ / አምልጠኛል
	mamlet	yamelteñal	ameleteñ / amltoñal
miss (a person)	መናፈቅ	እናፍቃለሁ	ናፈቁሁ / ናፍቄአለሁ
	menafeq	ïnafqalehu	nafeq'hu / nafqie'alehu
mix	መቀላቀል	እቀላቅላለሁ	ቀላቀልኩ / ቀላቅያለሁ
	meqelaqel	ïqelaq'lalehu	qelaqelku / qelaqyalehu
moan / groan	ማቃሰት	እቃስታለሁ	እቃስትኩ / እቃስቻለሁ
	maqaset	aqastalehu	aqasetku / aqaschalehu
mourn	ማልቀስ	አለቅሳለሁ	አለቀስኩ / አልቅሻለሁ
	malqes	aleqsalehu	aleqesku / alqshalehu
move	መንቀሳቀስ	እንቀሳቀሳለሁ	ተንቀሳቀስኩ / ተንቀሳቅሻለሁ
	menqesaqes	ïnqesaqesalehu	tenqesaqesku
multiply	ማባዛት	አባዛለሁ	አባዛሁ / አባዝቻለሁ

186

	mabazat	abazalehu	abazahu / abazchalehu
need	መፈለግ	እፈልጋለሁ	ፈለግሁ / ፈልጌአለሁ
	mefeleg	ïfelgalehu	feleghu / felgie'alehu
nominate	መሰየም	እሰይማለሁ	ሰየምኩ / ሰይሜአለሁ
	meseyem	ïseymalehu	seyemku / seymie'alehu
notice	ማስታወቅ	አስታውቃለሁ	አስታወቅሁ / አስታወቄአለሁ
	mastaweq	astawqalehu	astawq'hu / astaw'qie'alehu
notify	ማሳወቅ	አሳውቃለሁ	አሳወቅሁ / አሳወቄአለሁ
	masaweq	asawqalehu	asaweqhu / asawqie'alehu
obey	መታዘዝ	እታዘዛለሁ	ታዘዝኩ / ታዝጌአለሁ
	metazez	ïtazezalehu	tazezku / taz'zhie'alehu
offend	መሳደብ	እሳደባለሁ	ተሳደብኩ / ተሳድቤአለሁ
	mesadeb	ïsadebalehu	tesadeb'ku / tesad'bie'alehu
open / uncork	መከፈት	እከፍታለሁ	ከፈትኩ / ከፍቻለሁ
	mekfet	ïkeftalehu	kefetku / kefchalehu
organize	ማደራጀት	አደራጃለሁ	አደራጀሁ / አደራጅቻለሁ
	maderajet	aderajalehu	aderajehu / aderajchalehu
oppress	መጨቆን	እጨቁናለሁ	ጨቆንኩ / ጨቁኛለሁ
	mecheqon	ïchequnalehu	cheqonku / chequñalehu
optimize	ማመቻቸት	አመቻቻለሁ	አመቻቸሁ / አመቻችቼአለሁ
	mamechachet	amechachalehu	amechachehu / amechach'chie'alehu
organize	ማደራጀት	አደራጃለሁ	አደራጀሁ / አደራጅቻለሁ
	maderajet	aderajalehu	aderajehu / aderaj'chalehu
own / possess	መኖር	ይኖረኛል	ኖረኝ / ኖሮኛል
	menor	ynoreñal	noreñ / noroñal
paint	መቀባት	እቀባለሁ	ቀባሁ / ቀብቻለሁ
	meqebat	ïqebalehu	qebahu / qebchalehu
pass / pass by	ማለፍ	አልፋለሁ	አለፍኩ / አልፌአለሁ
	malef	alfalehu	alefku / alfie'alehu
pay	መክፈል	እከፍላለሁ	ከፈልኩ / ከፍያለሁ
	mekfel	ïkeflalehu	kefelku / kefyalehu
pee / urinate	መሽናት	እሽናለሁ	ሽናሁ / ሽንቻለሁ
	meshnat	ïshenalehu	shenahu / shenchalehu
peel	መላጥ	እልጣለሁ	ላጥኩ / ልጬአለሁ
	melaṭ	ïlṭalehu	laṭku / lchalehu
pierce / perforate	መብሳት	እበሳለሁ	በሳሁ / በስቻለሁ
	meb'sat	ïbesalehu	besahu / beschalehu

187

pile	መስቀል	እሰቅላለሁ	ሰቀልኩ / ስቀያለሁ
	mesqel	ïseqlalehu	seqelku / seq'yalehu
plan / devise	ማቀድ	እቀዳለሁ	አቀድኩ / አቅጃለሁ
	maqed	aqdalehu	aqedku / aqjalehu
plant	መትከል	እተክላለሁ	ተከልኩ / ተከያለሁ
	me'tkel	ïteklalehu	tekelku / tekyalehu
play	መጫወት	እጫወታለሁ	ተጫወትኩ / ተጫው·ቻለሁ
	mechawet	ïchawetalehu	techawetku / techawchalehu
plow	ማረስ	አርሳለሁ	አረስኩ / አርሻለሁ
	mares	arsalehu	aresku / arshalehu
pollute	መበከል	እበክላለሁ	በከልኩ / በከያለሁ
	mebekel	ïbeklalehu	bekelku / bek'yalehu
point	መጠቆም	እጠቁማለሁ	ጠቆምኩ / ጠቁሜአለሁ
	meteqom	ïtequmalehu	teqom'ku / tequmie'alehu
poop (defecate)	ማራት	አራለሁ	አራሁ / አርቻለሁ
	marat	aralehu	arahu / archalehu
pour	ማፍሰስ	አፈሳለሁ	አፈሰስኩ / አፍስሻለሁ
	mafses	afesalehu	afesesku / afs'shalehu
practice	መለማመድ	እለማመዳለሁ	ተለማመድኩ / ተለማምጃለሁ telemamedku /
	melemamed	ïlemamedalehu	telemam'jalehu
preach	መስበክ	እሰብካለሁ	ሰበኩ / ሰብኬአለሁ
	mesbek	ïseb'kalehu	sebeku / seb'kie'alehu
predict	መተንበይ	እተነብያለሁ	ተነበይኩ / ተንብያለሁ
	metenbey	ïteneb'yalehu	tenebey'ku / tenb'yalehu
prefer	መምረጥ	እመርጣለሁ	መረጥኩ / መርጫለሁ
	memret	ïmertalehu	meretku / merchalehu
prepare	ማዘጋጀት	አዘጋጃለሁ	አዘጋጀሁ / አዘጋጅቻለሁ
	mazegajet	azegajalehu	azegajehu / azegaj'chalehu
pretend	ማስመሰል	አስመስላለሁ	አስመሰልኩ / አስመስያለሁ
	masmesel	asmeslalehu	asmeselku / asmesyalehu
prevent	መከላከል	እከላከላለሁ	ተከላከልኩ / ተከላከያለሁ
	mekelakel	ïkelakelalehu	tekelakelku / tekelak'yalehu
print	ማተም	አትማለሁ	አተምኩ / አትሜአለሁ
	matem	atmalehu	atemku / atmie'alehu
profit	ማትረፍ	አተርፋለሁ	አተረፍኩ / አትርፌአለሁ
	matref	aterfalehu	aterefku / atrfie'alehu
prohibit	ማሳገድ	አሳግዳለሁ	አሳገድኩ / አስግጃለሁ

188

	masaged	asag'dalehu	asagedku / asag'jalehu
protest	መቃወም	እቃወማለሁ	ተቃወምኩ / ተቃወሜአለሁ
	meqawem	ïqawemalehu	teqawemku / teqawmie'alehu
pull	መጎተት	እጎታለሁ	ጎተትኩ / ጎትቻለሁ
	megotet	ïgotalehu	gotetku / gotchalehu
punch	መምታት	እምታለሁ	መታሁ / መትቻለሁ
	memtat	ïmetalehu	metahu / metchalehu
punish	መቅጣት	እቀጣለሁ	ቀጣሁ / ቀጥቻለሁ
	meqṭat	ïqeṭalehu	qeṭahu / qeṭ'chalehu
push	መግፋት	እገፋለሁ	ገፋሁ / ገፍቻለሁ
	megfat	ïgefalehu	gefah / gefchalehu
put	ማስቀመጥ	አስቀምጣለሁ	አስቀመጥኩ / አስቀምጫለሁ
	masqemet	asqemtalehu	asqemeṭku / asqemchalehu
quit	መተው	እተዋለሁ	ተውኩ / ትቻለሁ
	metew	ïtewalehu	tewku / tchalehu
rain	ማዝነብ	አዘንባለሁ	አዘነብኩ / አዝንቤአለሁ
	mazneb	azenbalehu	azenebku / aznbie'alehu
read	ማንበብ	አነባለሁ	አነበብኩ / አንብቤአለሁ
	manbeb	anebalehu	anebebku / anb'bie'alehu
record	መቅረጽ	እቀርጻለሁ	ቀረጽኩ / ቀርጫለሁ
	meq'rets	ïqertsalehu	qeretsku / qerchalehu
realize	መገንዘብ	እገነዘባለሁ	ተገነዘብኩ / ተገነዘቤአለሁ
	megenzeb	ïgenezebalehu	tegenezebku / tegenzbie'alehu
receive	መቀበል	እቀበላለሁ	ተቀበልኩ / ተቀብያለሁ
	meqebel	ïqebelalehu	teqebelku/teqebyalehu
reduce / decrease	መቀነስ	እቀንሳለሁ	ቀነስኩ / ቀንሻለሁ
	meqenes	ïqensalehu	qenesku / qenshalehu
regret	መጸጸት	እጸጸታለሁ	ተጸጸትኩ / ተጸጸቻለሁ
	metsetset	ïtsetsetalehu	tetsetsetku / tetsetschalehu
relax	መዝናናት	እዝናናለሁ	ተዝናናሁ / ተዝናንቻለሁ
	mez'nanat	ïznanalehu	teznanahu / teznanchalehu
remain	መቅረት	እቀራለሁ	ቀረሁ / ቀርቻለሁ
	meqret	ïqeralehu	qerehu / qerchalehu
remember	ማስታወስ	አስታውሳለሁ	አስታወስኩ / አስታውሻለሁ
	mastawes	astawsalehu	astawesku / astawshalehu
remind	ማስታወስ	ያስታውሰኛል	አስታወሰኝ / አስታውሶኛል
	mastawes	yastaw'señal	astaweseña / astawsoñal

189

rent	መከራየት	እከራያለሁ	ተከራየሁ / ተከራይቻለሁ
	mekerayet	ïkerayalehu	tekerayehu / tekeray'chalehu
repair	መጠገን	እጠግናለሁ	ጠገንኩ / ጠግኛለሁ
	me*t*egen	ï*t*egnalehu	*t*egenku / *t*egñalehu
repeat	መድገም	አደግማለሁ	ደገምኩ / ደግሜአለሁ
	medgem	ïdegmalehu	degemku / degmie'alehu
replace	መቀየር	እቀይራለሁ	ቀየርኩ / ቀይሬአለሁ
	meqeyer	ïqeyralehu	qeyerku / qeyrie'alehu
report	መግለፅ	እገልፃለሁ	ገለፅኩ / ገልጫለሁ
	megle*ts*	ïgel*ts*alehu	gele*ts*ku / gel*ch*alehu
respect	ማክበር	አከብራለሁ	አከበርኩ / አከብሬአለሁ
	makber	akebralehu	akeberku / akbrie'alehu
restrain	መቆጣጠር	እቆጣጠራለሁ	ተቆጣጠርኩ / ተቆጣጥሬአለሁ
	meqo*t*a*t*er	ïqo*t*a*t*eralehu	teqo*t*a*t*erku / teqo*t*a*t*rie'alehu
ride	መንዳት	እነዳለሁ	ነዳሁ / ነድቻለሁ
	mendat	ïnedalehu	nedahu / ned'chalehu
ripen /mature	ማብሰል	አበስላለሁ	አበሰልኩ / አብስያለሁ
	mabsel	abeslalehu	abeselku / absyalehu
roast	መጥበስ	እጠብሳለሁ	ጠበስኩ / ጠብሻለሁ
	me*t*'bes	ï*t*ebsalehu	*t*ebesku / *t*eb'shalehu
rob	መዘረፍ	እዘርፋለሁ	ዘረፍኩ / ዘርፌአለሁ
	mezref	ïzerfalehu	zerefku / zerfie'alehu
rot	መበስበስ	እበሰብሳለሁ	በሰበስኩ / በስብሻለሁ
	mebesbes	ïbesebsalehu	besebesku / besb'shalehu
rotate	ማሽከርከር	አሽከረከራለሁ	አሽከረከርኩ / አሽከርከሬአለሁ
			ashkerekerku /
	mash'kerker	ashkerek'ralehu	ashkerkrie'alehu
run	መሮጥ	እሮጣለሁ	ሮጥኩ / ሮጫለሁ
	mero*t*	ïro*t*alehu	ro*t*ku / ro*ch*alehu
satisfy	መርካት	እረካለሁ	እረካሁ / እረክቻለሁ
	merkat	ïrekalehu	ïrekahu / ïrekchalehu
save / keep	መቆጠብ	እቆጥባለሁ	ቆጠብኩ / ቆጥቤአለሁ
	meqo*t*eb	ïqo*t*'balehu	qo*t*ebku / qo*t*'bie'alehu
saw	መቁረጥ	እቆርጣለሁ	ቆረጥኩ / ቆርጫለሁ
	mequre*t*	ïqor*t*alehu	qore*t*ku / qor*ch*alehu
say	መናገር	እናገራለሁ	ተናገርኩ / ተናግሬአለሁ
	menager	ïnageralehu	tenagerku / tenagrie'alehu
scoop	መዛቅ	እዝቃለሁ	ዛቅሁ / ዝቄአለሁ

190

	mezaq	ïzqalehu	zaqhu / zqie'alehu
scream / shriek	መጮህ	እጮሃለሁ	ጮህኩ / ጮኪአለሁ
	mechoh	ïchohalehu	chohku / chokie'alehu
search / seek	መፈለግ	እፈልጋለሁ	ፈለግኩ / ፈልጌአለሁ
	mefeleg	ïfelgalehu	felegku / felgie'alehu
see	ማየት	አያለሁ	አየሁ / አይቻለሁ
	mayet	ayalehu	ayehu / aychalehu
seem / appears	መምሰል	ይመስለኛል	መሰለኝ / መስሎኛል
	memsel	ymes'leñal	meseleñ / mesloñal
sell	መሸጥ	እሸጣለሁ	ሸጥኩ / ሸጫለሁ
	meshet	ïshetalehu	sherku / shechalehu
send / mail	መላክ	እልካለሁ	ላኩ / ልኬአለሁ
	melak	ïlkalehu	lakhu/lkie'alehu
separate	መለያየት	እለያያለሁ	ለያየሁ / ለያይቻለሁ
	meleyayet	ïleyayalehu	leyayehu / leyaychalehu
serve	ማገልገል	አገለግላለሁ	አገለገልኩ / አገልግያለሁ
	magelgel	ageleglalehu	agelegelku / agelgyalehu
sew / knit	መስፋት	እሰፋለሁ	ሰፋሁ / ሰፍቻለሁ
	mesfat	ïsefalehu	sefahu / sefchalehu
share	ማካፈል	አካፍላለሁ	አካፈልኩ / አካፍያለሁ
	makafel	akaflalehu	akafelku / akafyalehu
sharpen	መቅረጽ	እቀርጻለሁ	ቀረጽኩ / ቀርጫለሁ
	meqrets	ïqertsalehu	qeretsku / qerchalehu
shave	መላጨት	እላጫለሁ	ላጨሁ / ላጭቻለሁ
	melachet	ïlachalehu	lachehu / lachchalehu
shoot	መተኮስ	እተኩሳለሁ	ተኮስኩ / ተኩሻለሁ
	metekos	ïtekusalehu	tekosku / tekushalehu
shop	መገብየት	እገበያለሁ	ገበየሁ / ገብዪቻለሁ
	megebyet	ïgebeyalehu	gebeyehu / gebyichalehu
show / indicate	ማሳየት	አሳያለሁ	አሳየሁ / አሳይቻለሁ
	masayet	asayalehu	asayehu / asay'chalehu
shut	መዝጋት	እዘጋለሁ	ዘጋሁ / ዘግቻለሁ
	mezgat	ïzegalehu	zegahu / zegchie'alehu
shift	መተካት	እተካለሁ	ተካሁ / ተክቻለሁ
	metekat	ïtekalehu	tekahu / tek'chalehu
shock	መደንገጥ	አደነግጣለሁ	ደነገጥኩ / ደንግጫለሁ
	medenget	ïdeneg'talehu	deneget'ku / deng'chalehu

sign	መፈረም	አፈርማለሁ	ፈረምኩ / ፈርሜአለሁ
	meferem	ïfermalehu	feremku / fermie'alehu
signify / mean	ማመልከት	አመለክታለሁ	አመለከትኩ / አመልከቻለሁ
	mamelket	amelktalehu	ameleket'ku / amelkchalehu
sing	መዘፈን	እዘፍናለሁ	ዘፈንኩ / ዘፍኛለሁ
	mezfen	ïzefnalehu	zefenku / zefñalehu
sit	መቀመጥ	አቀመጣለሁ	ተቀመጥኩ / ተቀምጫለሁ
	meqemet	ïqemetalehu	teqemetku / teqemchalehu
slaughter	ማረድ	አርዳለሁ	አረድኩ / አርጃለሁ
	mared	ardalehu	ared'ku / arjalehu
sleep	መተኛት	እተኛለሁ	ተኛሁ / ተኝቻለሁ
	meteñat	ïteñalehu	teñahu / teñchalehu
slip	ማንሸራተት	ያንሸራትተኛል	አንሸራተተኝ / አንሸራቶኛል
	mansheratet	yansherat'teñal	anşherateteñ / anşheratoñal
smash / crush	መጨፍለቅ	እጨፈልቃለሁ	ጨፈለቅሁ / ጨፍልቄአለሁ
	mechefleq	ïchefel'qalehu	chefeleqhu / cheflqie'alehu
smell	ማሽተት	አሽታለሁ	አሸተትኩ / አሽትቻለሁ
	mashtet	ashetalehu	ashetetku / ashtchalehu
snatch	መንጠቅ	እነጥቃለሁ	ነጠቅኩ / ነጥቄአለሁ
	menteq	ïnetqalehu	neteqku / netqie'alehu
soak	መዘፍዘፍ	እዘፈዝፋለሁ	ዘፈዘፍኩ / ዘፍዝፌአለሁ
	mezefzef	ïzefezfalehu	zefezefku / zefzfie'alehu
sow / plant	መዝራት	እዘራለሁ	ዘራሁ / ዘርቻለሁ
	mezrat	ïzeralehu	zerahu / zerchalehu
speak	መናገር	እናገራለሁ	ተናገርኩ / ተናግሬአለሁ
	menager	ïnageralehu	tenagerku / tenagrie'alehu
spend the day	መዋል	እውላለሁ	ዋልኩ / ውያለሁ
	mewal	ïwulalehu	walku / wyalehu
spend the evening	ማምሸት	አመሻለሁ	አመሸሁ / አምሽቻለሁ
	mamshet	ameshalehu	ameshehu / amshchalehu
spend the night	ማደር	አድራለሁ	አደርኩ / አድሬአለሁ
	mader	adralehu	aderku / adrie'alehu
to spend and stay a week or more	መከረም	እከርማለሁ	ከረምኩ / ከርሜአለሁ
	mekrem	ïkermalehu	keremku / kermie'alehu
spit	መትፋት	እተፋለሁ	ተፋሁ / ተፍቻለሁ
	met'fat	ïtefalehu	tefahu / tefchalehu
squeeze	መጭምቅ	እጨምቃለሁ	ጨመቅሁ / ጨምቄአለሁ

	mech'meq	ïchem'qalehu	chemeqhu / chemqie'alehu
stand	መቆም	እቆማለሁ	ቆምኩ / ቆሜአለሁ
	meqom	ïqomalehu	qomku / qomie'alehu
startle	መገረም	እገረማለሁ	ተገረምኩ / ተገርሜአለሁ
	megerem	ïgeremalehu	tegeremku / tegrmie'alehu
stay	መቆየት	እቆያለሁ	ቆየሁ / ቆይቻለሁ
	meqoyet	ïqoyalehu	qoyehu / qoy'chalehu
steal	መስረቅ	እሰርቃለሁ	ሰረቅኩ / ሰርቄአለሁ
	mesreq	ïserqalehu	sereqku / serqie'alehu
steer	መንዳት	እነዳለሁ	ነዳሁ / ነድቻለሁ
	mendat	ïnedalehu	nedahu / nedchalehu
step down	መውረድ	እወርዳለሁ	ወረድኩ / ወርጃለሁ
	mewred	ïwerdalehu	weredku / werjalehu
step on / tread on	መርገጥ	እረግጣለሁ	ረገጥኩ / ረግጫለሁ
	merget	ïregtalehu	regetku / regchalehu
sting	መንደፍ	እነደፋለሁ	ተነደፍኩ / ተነድፌአለሁ
	mendef	ïnedefalehu	tenedefku / tenedfie'alehu
stir	መነቃቀት	እነቃቃለሁ	ተነቃቃሁ / ተነቃቅቻለሁ
	meneqaqat	ïneqaqalehu	teneqaqahu / teneqaq'cha'ehu
study	ማጥናት	አጠናለሁ	አጠናሁ / አጥንቻለሁ
	matnat	atenalehu	atenahu / atnchalehu
stumble	መደናቀፍ	ያደናቀፈኛል	ተደናቀፍኩ / ተደናቅፌአለሁ
	medenaqef	yadenaq'feñal	tedenaqef'ku / tedenaq'fie'alehu
subtract / discount	መቀነስ	እቀንሳለሁ	ቀነስኩ / ቀንሻለሁ
	meqenes	ïqensalehu	qenesku / qenshalehu
succeed	ማሳካት	አሳካለሁ	አሳካሁ / አሳክቻለሁ
	masakat	asakalehu	askahu / asak'chalehu
suffer	መሰቃየት	እሰቃያለሁ	ተሰቃየሁ / ተሰቃይቻለሁ
	meseqayet	ïseqayalehu	teseqayehu / teseqaychalehu
suffice (be enough)	መብቃት	ይበቃኛል	በቃኝ / በቅቶኛል
	mebqat	ybeqañal	bqañ / beqtoñal
supply	ማቅረብ	አቀርባለሁ	አቀረብኩ / አቅርቢአለሁ
	maqreb	aqerbalehu	aqereb'ku / aq'rbie'alehu
support	ማገዝ	አግዛለሁ	አገዝኩ / አግዣለሁ
	magez	agzalehu	agezku / agzhalehu
surprise	ማስደመም	አስደምማለሁ	አስደመምኩ / አስደምሜአለሁ

			asdemem'ku / asdem'mie'alehu
	masdemem	asdemmalehu	
surround	መከበብ	እከባለሁ	ከበብኩ / ከብቤአለሁ
	mekbeb	ïkebalehu	kebeb'ku / keb'bie'alehu
suspect	መጠርጠር	እጠረጥራለሁ	ጠረጠርኩ / ጠርጥሬአለሁ
	meterter	ïteret'ralehu	tereterku / tert'rie'alehu
swallow	መዋጥ	እውጣለሁ	ዋጥኩ / ውጫለሁ
	mewat	ïwtalehu	wat'ku / wchalehu
sweat	ማላብ	ያልበኛል	አላበኝ / አልበኛል
	malab	yalbeñal	alabeñ / alboñal
sweep	መጥረግ	እጠርጋለሁ	ጠረግኩ / ጠርጌአለሁ
	metreg	ïtergalehu	teregku / tergie'alehu
sweeten	ማጣፈጥ	አጣፍጣለሁ	አጣፈጥኩ / አጣፍጬአለሁ
	matafet	ataftalehu	atafet'ku / ataf'chalehu
swim	መዋኘት	እዋኛለሁ	ዋኘሁ / ዋኝቻለሁ
	mewañet	ïwañalehu	wañehu / wañchalehu
take	መውሰድ	እወስዳለሁ	ወሰድኩ / ወስጃለሁ
	mewsed	ïwesdalehu	wesedku / wesjalehu
take a picture	ፎቶ ማንሳት	ፎቶ አነሳለሁ	ፎቶ አነሳሁ / ፎቶ አንስቻለሁ
	foto mansat	foto anesalehu	foto anesahu / foto ans'chalehu
take care	መጠንቀቅ	እጠነቀቃለሁ	ተጠነቀቅሁ / ተጠንቀቄአለሁ
	meten'qeq	ïteneqeqalehu	teteneqeqhu / tetenq'qie'alehu
talk	ማውራት	አወራለሁ	አወራሁ / አውርቻለሁ
	mawrat	aweralehu	awerahu / awrchalehu
taste	መቅመስ	እቀምሳለሁ	ቀመስኩ / ቀምሻለሁ
	meqmes	ïqemsalehu	qemesku / qemshalehu
teach	ማስተማር	አስተምራለሁ	አስተማርኩ / አስተምሬአለሁ
	mastemar	astemralehu	astemarku / astemrie'alehu
tear	ማልቀስ	አለቅሳለሁ	አለቀስኩ / አልቅሻለሁ
	mal'qes	aleqsalehu	aleqesku / alq'shalehu
tell	መንገር	እነግራለሁ	ነገርኩ / ነግሬአለሁ
	menger	ïnegralehu	negerku / negrie'alehu
thank / praise	ማመስገን	አመሰግናለሁ	አመሰገንኩ / አመስግኛለሁ
	mames'gen	amesegnalehu	amesegenku / amesgñalehu
think	ማሰብ	አስባለሁ	አሰብኩ / አስቤአለሁ
	maseb	asbalehu	asebku / asbie'alehu
threaten	ማስፈራራት	አስፈራራለሁ	አስፈራራሁ / አስፈራርቻለሁ
	mas'ferarat	as'feraralehu	as'ferarahu / as'ferar'chalehu

throw	መወርወር	እወረወራለሁ	ወረወርኩ / ወርውሬአለሁ
	mewerwer	iwerewralehu	werewerku / werwrie'alehu
tie / bind	ማሰር	አስራለሁ	አሰርኩ / አስሬአለሁ
	maser	asralehu	aserku / asrie'alehu
touch	መንካት	እነካለሁ	ነካሁ / ነክቻለሁ
	menkat	inekalehu	nekahu / nekchalehu
trade	መነገድ	እነግዳለሁ	ነገድኩ / ነግጃለሁ
	meneged	ineg'dalehu	negedku / neg'jalehu
translate	መተርጎም	እተረጉማለሁ	ተረጎምኩ / ተርጉሜአለሁ
	metergom	iteregumalehu	teregomku / tergumie'alehu
travel	መጓዝ	እጓዛለሁ	ተጓዝኩ / ተጉዛለሁ
	meguaz	iguazalehu	teguazku / teguzhalehu
treat (a patient)	ማከም	አከማለሁ	አከምኩ / አከሜአለሁ
	makem	akmalehu	akemku / akmie'alehu
trust	ማመን	አምናለሁ	አመንኩ / አምኛለሁ
	mamen	amnalehu	amenku / am'ñalehu
try	መሞከር	እሞክራለሁ	ሞከርኩ / ሞክሬአለሁ
	memoker	imokralehu	mokerku / mokrie'alehu
try on	መለካት	እለካለሁ	ለካሁ / ለክቻለሁ
	melekat	ilekalehu	lekahu / lekchalehu
turn (direction)	መታጠፍ	እታጠፋለሁ	ታጠፍኩ / ታጥፌአለሁ
	metatef	itatefalehu	tatefku / tat'fie'alehu
turn (page)	መግለጥ	እገልጣለሁ	ገለጥኩ / ገልጫለሁ
	meglet	igel'talehu	geletku / gel'chalehu
turnover	መገልበጥ	እገለብጣለሁ	ገለበጥኩ / ገልብጫለሁ
	megel'bet	igeleb'talehu	gelebet'ku / gelbchalehu
understand	መረዳት	እረዳለሁ	ተረዳሁ / ተረድቻለሁ
	meredat	iredalehu	teredahu / tered'chalehu
unite	መሰብሰብ	እሰበሳለሁ	ተሰበስብኩ / ተሰብስቤአለሁ
	mesebseb	isebesebalehu	tesebesbku / tesebs'bie'alehu
untie	መፍታት	እፈታለሁ	ፈታሁ / ፈትቻለሁ
	meftat	ifetalehu	fetahu / fetchalehu
update	ማደስ	አድሳለሁ	አደስኩ / አድሻለሁ
	mades	adsalehu	adesku / adshalehu
vote	መምረጥ	እመርጣለሁ	መረጥኩ / መርጫለሁ
	memret	imertalehu	meretku / merchalehu
use	መጠቀም	እጠቀማለሁ	ተጠቀምኩ / ተጠቅሜአለሁ

195

	meteqem	ïteqemalehu	teteqemku / teteqmie'alehu
visit	መጎብኘት	እጎበኛለሁ	ጎበኘሁ / ጎብኛቻለሁ
	megobñet	ïgobeñalehu	gobeñehu / gobñchalehu
vomit	ማስታወክ	አስታወካለሁ	አስታወኩ / አስታወኬአለሁ
	mastawek	astawkalehu	astaweku / astawkie'alehu
vote	መምረጥ	እመርጣለሁ	መረጥኩ / መርጫለሁ
	memret	ïmertalehu	meret 'ku / merchalehu
wait	መጠበቅ	እጠብቃለሁ	ጠበቅኩ / ጠብቄአለሁ
	metebeq	ïtebqalehu	tebeqku / tebqie'alehu
wake (someone)	መቀስቀስ	እቀስቅሳለሁ	ቀስቀስኩ / ቀስቅሻለሁ
	meqesqes	ïqeseqsalehu	qeseqesku / aesq'shalehu
wake (awaken)	መንቃት	እነቃለሁ	ነቃሁ / ነቅቻለሁ
	menqat	ïneqalehu	neqahu / neqcalehu
walk	መራመድ	እራመዳለሁ	ተራመድኩ / ተራምጃለሁ
	meramed	ïramedalehu	teramedku / teramjalehu
want	መፈለግ	እፈልጋለሁ	ፈለግኩ / ፈልጌአለሁ
	mefeleg	ïfelgalehu	felegku / felgie'alehu
warn	ማስጠንቀቅ	አስጠነቅቃለሁ	አስጠነቀቅሁ / አስተንቅቄአለሁ
	mastenqeq	asteneq'qalehu	asteneqeq'hu / astenq'qie'alehu
wash	ማጠብ	አጥባለሁ	አጠብኩ / አጥቤአለሁ
	mateb	at 'balehu	ateb'ku / at 'bie'alehu
waste	ማባከን	አባክናለሁ	አባከንኩ / አባክ'ኛለሁ
	mabaken	abak'nalehu	abakenku / abak'ñalehu
wear	መልበስ	እለብሳለሁ	ለበስኩ / ለብሻለሁ
	melbes	ïlebsalehu	lebesku / lebshalehu
weed	መዘራት	እዘራለሁ	ዘራሁ / ዘርቻለሁ
	mezrat	ïzeralehu	zerahu / zerchalehu
welcome	መቀበል	እቀበላለሁ	ተቀበልኩ / ተቀብዬአለሁ
	meqebel	ïqebelalehu	teqebelku / teqebie'alehu
win (defeat)	ማሸነፍ	አሸንፋለሁ	አሸነፍኩ / አሸነፌአለሁ
	mashenef	ashenfalehu	ashenefku / ashenfie'alehu
whistle	ማፉጨት	አፉጫለሁ	አፉጨሁ / አፉጭቻለሁ
	mafuachet	afuachalehu	afuachehu / afuach'chalehu
win / defeat	ማሸነፍ	አሸንፋለሁ	አሸነፍኩ / አሸነፌአለሁ
	mashenef	ashenfalehu	ashenefku / ashenfie'alehu
wip	መግረፍ	እገርፋለሁ	ገረፍኩ / ገርፌአለሁ
	megref	ïgerfalehu	gerefku / gerfie'alehu

wipe / rub clean	መጥረግ	አጠርጋለሁ	ጠረግሁ / ጠርጌአለሁ
	met'reg	ïtergalehu	tereg'hu / tergie'alehu
wonder	መገረም	እገረማለሁ	ተገረምኩ / ተገርሜአለሁ
	megerem	ïgeremalehu	tegeremku / tegermie'alehu
work	መስራት	እሰራለሁ	ሰራሁ / ሰርቻለሁ
	mesrat	ïseralehu	serahu / serchalehu
worry	መጨነቅ	እጨነቃለሁ	ተጨነቅሁ / ተጨንቄአለሁ
	mecheneq	ïcheneqalehu	techeneqhu / techen'qie'alehu
write	መጻፍ	እጸፋለሁ	ጸፍኩ / ጸፊአለሁ
	metsaf	ïtsfalehu	tsafku / tsfiealehu
yawn	ማዛጋት	አዛጋለሁ	አዛጉ / አዛግቻለሁ
	mazagat	azagalehu	azagahu / azag'chalehu

About the Authors:

Andrew Tadross served two years as a Peace Corps Volunteer and has taught landscape architecture at the University of Mekele and the University of Addis Ababa. He is the co-author/editor of *The Essential Guide to Tigrinya* and *Afan Oromo*.

Abraham Teklu was born, raised and completed high school in Adwa, Tigray, Ethiopia. He attended Addis Ababa University before completing his Bachelor of Science at the University of North Carolina. Abraham earned Masters Degree in Education at Western Governors University. He has worked as a designer for an engineering company, as a manager for a development organization, as a volunteer trainer for an endowment institution. Currently, he manages a nonprofit organization, which supports impoverished elderly and children.

In addition to *The Essential Guide to Amharic,* Abraham has written children's books, magazines and two volumes of English-Tigrigna Dictionary, as well as "The Essential Guide to Tigrinya, the Language of Eritrea and Northern Ethiopia"

Printed in Great Britain
by Amazon